Skills and Inequality

Skills and Inequality studies the political economy of education and training reforms from the perspective of comparative welfare state research. Highlighting the striking similarities between established worlds of welfare capitalism and educational regimes, Marius R. Busemeyer argues that both have similar political origins in the postwar period. He identifies partisan politics and different varieties of capitalism as crucial factors shaping choices about the institutional design of post-secondary education. The political and institutional survival of vocational education and training as an alternative to academic higher education is then found to play an important role in the later development of skill regimes. Busemeyer also studies the effects of educational institutions on social inequality and patterns of public opinion on the welfare state and education. Adopting a multi-method approach, this book combines historical case studies of Sweden, Germany, and the United Kingdom with quantitative analyses of macro-level aggregate data and micro-level survey data.

MARIUS R. BUSEMEYER is Professor of Political Science in the Department of Politics and Public Administration at the University of Konstanz, Germany. His research focuses on comparative political economy and welfare state research, education and social policy, public spending, theories of institutional change, and, more recently, public opinion on the welfare state. He has published a large number of journal articles and edited *The Political Economy of Collective Skill Formation* (with Christine Trampusch, 2011) and a special issue of the *Socio-Economic Review* on *The Political Economy of Skills and Inequality* (with Torben Iversen).

Skills and Inequality

Partisan Politics and the Political Economy of Education Reforms in Western Welfare States

MARIUS R. BUSEMEYER

CAMBRIDGE
UNIVERSITY PRESS

University Printing House, Cambridge CB2 8BS, United Kingdom

Cambridge University Press is part of the University of Cambridge.

It furthers the University's mission by disseminating knowledge in the pursuit of education, learning and research at the highest international levels of excellence.

www.cambridge.org
Information on this title: www.cambridge.org/9781107062931

© Marius R. Busemeyer 2015

This publication is in copyright. Subject to statutory exception and to the provisions of relevant collective licensing agreements, no reproduction of any part may take place without the written permission of Cambridge University Press.

First published 2015

A catalogue record for this publication is available from the British Library

ISBN 978-1-107-06293-1 Hardback

Cambridge University Press has no responsibility for the persistence or accuracy of URLs for external or third-party internet websites referred to in this publication, and does not guarantee that any content on such websites is, or will remain, accurate or appropriate.

Contents

List of figures	*page* vi
List of tables	viii
Preface and acknowledgments	xi
List of abbreviations	xiv
Introduction	1
Part I The political and institutional determinants of education policy	
1 Theoretical framework: partisan politics in context	29
2 The politics of education and training reform: case studies	58
3 Worlds of skill formation: cross-national quantitative analysis	123
Part II The impact of educational institutions on outcomes and popular attitudes	
4 Educational institutions and socioeconomic inequality	177
5 The impact of educational institutions on popular attitudes and preferences	215
6 Conclusion	253
Appendix: Data sources for quantitative analyses (all chapters)	266
Bibliography	269
Index	298

Figures

1.1	De-commodification and stratification in education systems	page 32
3.1	De-commodification and stratification in education systems	124
3.2	Results of a hierarchical cluster analysis of countries	133
3.3	Public spending on educational institutions and social policies as percentage of GDP, average values 1997–2008	135
3.4	Private share of education funding and public social spending, 1997–2008	138
3.5	Partisan politics (1945–2000) and private share of education spending (1997–2008)	139
3.6	Educational stratification and the ratio of VET enrollment to the entry rate into higher education	146
3.7	Importance of VET relative to higher education and combined cabinet share of Christian and social democrats	148
3.8	Share of upper-secondary students in VET (average 1997–2008) and cabinet share of Christian democrats (1945–2000)	151
3.9	Economic coordination and the apprenticeship training share	155
4.1	Wage dispersion and educational inequality	182
4.2	VET share and inequality	191
4.3	Apprenticeship training and inequality	193
4.4	Higher education and inequality	194
4.5	VET and educational inequality	196
4.6	VET and youth unemployment	198
4.7	Predicted effect on inequality of an increase in the respective independent variable by one standard deviation	205
5.1	Percentage share of respondents in favor of "more" or "much more" government spending on education, ISSP Role of Government IV, 2006	220

List of figures

5.2 Share of respondents recommending general and academic studies rather than VET to school-leavers, Eurobarometer 62.1, 2004   223
5.3 Comparison of the impact of income and educational background on spending preferences   230
5.4 Levels of socioeconomic inequality and public support for more government spending on education   239
5.5 Interaction between income and VET share   240
5.6 Interaction between income and private share of education spending   242
5.7 Popular support for redistribution and private share of tertiary education spending   251

Tables

3.1 The diversity of education and training systems in
OECD countries *page* 125
3.2 Selected quantitative indicators, cross-national averages,
1997–2008 126
3.3 Partisan politics, social spending and the private share of
education spending, cross-sectional regression analyses 140
3.4 Partisan politics and the determinants of different types of
education spending, cross-sectional regression analyses 142
3.5 Educational stratification and enrollment patterns in
upper- and post-secondary education, average values
1997–2008 144
3.6 Partisan politics and enrollment patterns in upper- and
post-secondary education (I) 147
3.7 Partisan politics and enrollment patterns in upper- and
post-secondary education (II) 149
3.8 Determinants of private share of education spending,
1993–2008, panel-corrected standard errors and
panel-specific AR(1) error correction 160
3.9 Determinants of gross level of enrollment, 1971–2008,
error-correction model with country fixed effects 162
3.10 Regression analysis: left-wing government and gross
enrollment levels in tertiary education, 1993–2008,
panel-corrected standard errors with lagged
dependent variable 167
3.11 Determinants of levels of enrollment in VET, 1993–2008,
panel-corrected standard errors and panel-specific AR(1)
error correction 170
3.12 Determinants of levels of enrollment in apprenticeship
training, 1993–2008, panel-corrected standard errors and
panel-specific AR(1) error correction 172

List of tables

4.1	Educational institutions as determinants of socioeconomic inequality, cross-sectional regressions	200
4.2	Socioeconomic inequality and VET share, 1997–2008	202
4.3	Socioeconomic inequality and the public/private division of labor in education financing, 1997–2008	204
4.4	Education spending and socioeconomic inequality (Gini index), 1997–2008	206
4.5	Interactions between private involvement and enrollment patterns	208
4.6	Educational institutions and wage inequality, 1997–2008	210
4.7	Determinants of youth unemployment, 1997–2008	212
5.1	Individual-level determinants of preferences on education spending	225
5.2	The individual level determinants of preferences for social spending, ISSP Role of Government IV, 2006	226
5.3	Multilevel regression of individual support for government spending on education, ISSP 2006	234
5.4	Multilevel regression (cross-level interactions) of individual support for government spending on education, ISSP 2006	236
5.5	Multilevel regression of preferences for different kinds of education, Eurobarometer 62.1, 2004	243
5.6	Multilevel regressions of preferences for redistribution, ISSP 2006	246

Preface and acknowledgments

This book represents the culmination and summary of my research on education politics and policies over a period of approximately the last five years. I started working on this topic during my doctoral dissertation at the University of Heidelberg in a project directed by Manfred G. Schmidt, who got me interested not only in education, but also in the role of partisan politics as a crucial factor explaining differences in policy output. I continued doing research on education during my postdoc years at the Max Planck Institute for the Study of Societies in Cologne. Working with Wolfgang Streeck and Kathleen Thelen broadened my perspective and prompted me to give more serious consideration to the role of vocational education and training and the impact of socioeconomic institutions. Much of the theoretical perspective of this book is motivated by the attempt to bring together these two different theoretical perspectives of partisan theory and historical institutionalism. Moving beyond these more conventional approaches to comparative public policy, however, this book also looks at the impact of educational institutions on inequality and individual attitudes, two topics that have dominated my research agenda in the past two years and will continue to do so in the coming ones.

There are many, many people who have contributed directly and indirectly to making this project possible. First and foremost, I would like to thank my mentors, advisors, and employers – Manfred G. Schmidt, Wolfgang Streeck, and Kathleen Thelen – who played a crucial role in guiding me towards the study of education from different perspectives during the various stages of my academic career. I have also benefited enormously from the thoughts, comments, and ideas of a large group of colleagues, co-authors, and collaborators. I feel at once extremely privileged and humbled to be part of this academic community of scholars, who are not only colleagues but also personal friends. There were several "critical junctures" in the last couple of years when the "positive feedback" I received from my peers was crucial in motivating me to write this book. I am deeply grateful for this support through the years and for the numerous invitations to present parts of the book (or in exceptional circumstances of extreme bravery, the entire thing) at research workshops, conferences, and invited talks. It would take several pages to highlight the critical input of each member of this group of scholars, which lies beyond the scope of the present foreword. For this reason, I will ask preemptively for your forgiveness (and for the understanding of any who were inadvertently overlooked) before I present the following list of colleagues in alphabetical order. Each of them contributed in their own way to the success of the project, whether by commenting on a paper or chapter, inviting me for a talk or a workshop, co-authoring a paper, or simply sharing a meal: Klaus Armingeon, Frank Castles, Maria A. Cattaneo, Ute Clement, Pepper Culpepper, Johan Bo Davidsson, Thomas Deißinger, Bernhard Ebbinghaus, Werner Eichhorst, Patrick Emmenegger, Simon Franzmann, Achim Goerres, Peter Hall, Silja Häusermann, Thomas Hinz, Martin Höpner, Evelyne Huber, Torben Iversen, Carsten Jensen, André Kaiser, Desmond King, Herbert Kitschelt, Bernhard Kittel, Stephan Leibfried, Johannes Lindvall, Philip Manow, Cathie Jo Martin, Paul Marx, Dick Moraal, Renate Neubäumer, Rita Nikolai, Herbert Obinger, Harald Pfeifer, Matthias Pilz, David Rueda, Paul Ryan, Armin Schäfer, Josef Schmid, Manfred G. Schmidt, Carsten Q. Schneider, Heike Solga, David Soskice, John D. Stephens, Markus Tepe, Kathleen Thelen, Christine Trampusch, Pieter Vanhuysse, Stefanie Walter, Felix Wenzelmann, Frieder Wolf, Stefan Wolter, Nick Ziegler, Reimut Zohlnhöfer, and many others that I cannot possibly mention here. I would also like to especially thank my colleagues at the Department of Politics and Public Administration at the University of Konstanz for their continued support and intellectual stimulation, in particular Christian Breunig, Katharina Holzinger, Sven Jochem, Christoph Knill, Gerald Schneider, Volker Schneider, Wolfgang Seibel, Peter Selb, Susumu Shikano, and Nils Weidmann. Last, but certainly not least, I want to thank my team of postdocs and doctoral researchers, with whom I have worked most closely over the last couple of years. They all provided important and critical input during various stages of the project and "volunteered" to read the manuscript (several times, actually). In particular, I am grateful to Aurélien Abrassart, Michael Dobbins, Julian Garritzmann, Ulrich Glassmann, Susanne Münn, Erik Neimanns, Roula Nezi,

Raphaela Schlicht-Schmälzle, and Janis Vossiek. Margot Beier provided excellent secretarial support. I am also grateful to Dana Behrens, Anne Sophie Fendrich, Aline Grünewald, Adrian Rinscheid, Tobias Tober, and Marie Zeller for excellent research assistance. Thanks also to John Haslam and Carrie Parkinson at Cambridge University Press for their editorial support (as well as the anonymous reviewers of the book manuscript for extremely helpful comments and suggestions) and Casey Butterfield for language editing.

I would also like to thank the various institutions and organizations that supported me in various ways for the duration of this project. First of all, I thank the University of Konstanz, in particular Rector Ulrich Rüdiger, for providing crucial institutional and financial support. The Center for European Studies at Harvard University hosted me during a long research stay in 2009/10 (sponsored by the MPI for the Study of Societies) and a shorter one in 2012. In both cases, the project benefited enormously from the input of the CES community (in particular Kathleen Thelen, Torben Iversen, Cathie Jo Martin, and Peter Hall). I am also grateful to Nuffield College at Oxford (and David Soskice and David Rueda in particular), which hosted me during a short research stay in January 2012. A generous fellowship from the Institute for Advanced Study Konstanz in the academic year 2013/14 provided me with the opportunity to finish the book project in a congenial, interdisciplinary environment with a gorgeous view of Lake Constance. Most importantly, I am grateful to the Deutsche Forschungsgemeinschaft (DFG) for providing financial support for the project "The Politics of Education and Training Reforms in Western Welfare States" (Grant No. BU 1852/4–1).

Finally, I would like to thank my friends and family for supporting me during the challenges of these past few years.

Abbreviations

ABB	Arbeitsstelle für Betriebliche Berufsausbildung
ABF	Workers' Educational Association
AMB	Area Manpower Board
BAFöG	Bundesausbildungsförderungsgesetz
BBiG	Berufsbildungsgesetz
BDI	Bundesverband der Deutschen Industrie
BerBiFG	Berufsbildungsförderungsgesetz
BGJ	Berufsgrundbildungsjahr
BIBB	Bundesinstitut für Berufsbildung
BLK	Bund-Länder Kommission für Bildungsplanung und Forschungsförderung
CBI	Confederation of British Industry
CDU	Christlich Demokratische Union Deutschlands
CME	Coordinated market economy
DATSCH	Deutscher Ausschuß für Technisches Schulwesen
DGB	Deutscher Gewerkschaftsbund
DIHT	Deutscher Industrie- und Handelstag
ERA	Education Reform Act
GNVQ	General National Vocational Qualification
ILA	Individual Learning Account
ISCED	International Standard Classification of Education
ITB	Industrial Training Board
ITO	Industrial training organization
KMK	Kultusministerkonferenz; short for Ständige Konferenz der Kultusminister der Länder in der Bundesrepublik Deutschland
LEA	Local Education Authority
LLSC	Local Learning and Skills Council
LME	Liberal market economy
LO	Landsorganisationen i Sverige
LSC	Learning and Skills Council

List of abbreviations

MA	Modern Apprenticeship
MSC	Manpower Services Commission
NCVQ	National Council for Vocational Qualifications
NTI	New Training Initiative
NVQ	National Vocational Qualification
OECD	Organisation for Economic Co-operation and Development
PISA	Programme for International Student Assessment
POS	Polytechnische Oberschule
QCA	Qualifications and Curriculum Authority
SAF	Svenska Arbetsgivareföreningen
SAP	Swedish Social Democrats
SPD	Sozialdemokratische Partei Deutschlands
TCO	Tjänstemännens Centralorganisation
TEC	Training and Enterprise Council
TUC	Trades Union Congress
TVEI	Technical and Vocational Education Initiative
VET	Vocational education and training
VoC	Varieties of capitalism
YOP	Youth Opportunities Programme
YT	Youth Training
YTS	Youth Training Scheme

Introduction

In a seminal contribution to the fledgling comparative literature on welfare state policies, Harold Wilensky once made the fateful claim that "education is special" (Wilensky 1975: 3). More specifically, he argued that:

> A nation's health and welfare effort is clearly and directly a contribution to absolute equality, the reduction of differences between rich and poor, young and old, minority groups and majorities; it is only a secondary contribution to equality of opportunity. In contrast, a nation's educational effort, especially at the higher levels, is chiefly a contribution to equality of opportunity – enhanced mobility for those judged to be potentially able or skilled; it is only a peripheral contribution to absolute equality. (Wilensky 1975: 6)

In other words, Wilensky posited that education needs to be assessed and analyzed separately from other kinds of social policies, because its primary purpose is not necessarily to mitigate socioeconomic inequalities in terms of outcomes. Wilensky's claim is not entirely unjustified: the promotion of educational opportunities, being a meritocratic good, entails both private benefits, in the form of wage increases for the better-educated, and public benefits. Nevertheless, his position has contributed to (or at least symbolizes) the neglect of the study of education in comparative welfare state research and in comparative political science in general (Busemeyer & Nikolai 2010; Busemeyer & Trampusch 2011; Iversen & Stephens 2008; Jakobi *et al.* 2010).

This book seeks to help reintegrate the analysis of education and training systems into comparative welfare state research (see Iversen & Stephens 2008: 602 for a similar argument). It does this not by comparing policy developments in education with other social policies, but primarily by identifying multiple linkages and connections between education and other parts of the welfare state. In brief, the book traces the political and institutional connections between education and the welfare state at large in three domains. The first is *politics*: I argue and show that the politico-economic coalitions that supported the expansion of the welfare state in the postwar decades have also been influential in shaping the institutional design of education and training systems. The second is *outcomes*: the distribution of income and wealth in the political economy is affected by variations in the institutional setup of the education and training system, in particular the importance of vocational education and training (VET) relative to academic education, as well as the division of labor between public and private sources of financing. The third is *citizens' attitudes and preferences vis-à-vis the welfare state*: I document the effects of educational institutions on such attitudes and preferences, which provides the essential micro-foundation upon which to explain the durability and sustainability of welfare state arrangements.

As for Wilensky's claim, I find that although education may be different from other social policies in certain aspects, it is deeply interconnected to other parts of the welfare state via politics, outcomes, and popular attitudes. Neglecting these connections has prevented us from developing a deeper understanding of the driving forces of welfare state and education reforms, socioeconomic inequality, and citizens' attitudes towards the welfare state. The three domains of politics and policy output, socioeconomic outcomes, and public attitudes should be analyzed jointly, because they represent different stages of the policy-making cycle as it unfolds over time: political struggles and decisions during the critical decades of the postwar period shaped the policy-development paths of education regimes while access to higher levels of education was being expanded, and the educational institutions established during that time are now influencing contemporary patterns of socioeconomic inequality. These institutions have also shaped popular expectations of government's role in the provision of social services such as education, contributing to the stabilization of these development paths in the latter twentieth and early twenty-first centuries. To paraphrase Wilensky, education may be different from other kinds of social policies, but variations in the institutional setup of the education and training systems *do* have enormous consequences for the distribution of skills, income, and wealth in the political economy at large.

Common origins, different development paths: the variety of education and training systems in advanced industrial democracies

The starting point and motivation for this book is the observation that in the immediate postwar period, advanced industrial democracies and particularly Western European countries shared a similar institutional setup of education and training systems, but that they started to develop along very different paths quite soon thereafter (Ansell 2010: 164). Because the analytical perspective of this book is rooted in comparative political economy, the focus is on those types of education that are most relevant for labor-market actors (upper-secondary education, VET, and higher education), although I fully recognize that other educational sectors such as early childhood education are also important with regard to welfare state policies (Esping-Andersen 2002), and increasingly so.

Leaving aside the case of the United States for now (which was ahead of European countries in expanding higher education), we can see large historical similarities between the Swedish, German, and British education systems (Heidenheimer 1981: 296, 298): all had an elitist higher education sector and a segregated secondary school system, enforcing a strict distinction and hierarchy between academic and nonacademic types of secondary schooling. With regard to VET, the institutional legacy of firm-based, mostly voluntarist or self-governed apprenticeship training was strong in Germany and the United Kingdom, but less so in Sweden, although even there, firm-based apprenticeships remained rather popular in the 1950s and 1960s (Lundahl 1997: 93; Nilsson 2011: 27).

Today, however, the education systems of the three countries look very different. The British education system is characterized by a bias in favor of academic higher education, much like the US system with its focus on college education. VET is considered to be more important in Britain than it is in the United States, but the UK system is largely voluntarist and employer-dominated in character, which contributes to its perception as an unpopular choice for low-skilled youths who did not make it into higher education (Ryan & Unwin 2001). In Germany, by contrast, VET remains a popular alternative to universities. There is a well-developed dual-apprenticeship system that combines practical education on the job with theoretical learning in vocational schools, whereas academic higher education remains underdeveloped in terms of levels of enrollment, and spending in this area is below the Organisation for Economic Co-operation and Development (OECD) average (Powell & Solga 2011; Schmidt 2007). Higher education in Sweden has expanded rapidly in recent decades and is open to a large share of the younger population. Vocational education remains important, but attempts to expand the involvement of employers in training have mostly failed, so VET is usually provided only in secondary schools. Thus, despite the fact that all three countries started from a very similar position in the immediate postwar period, they have developed in very different directions.

There are also obvious similarities between education systems and other welfare state institutions (Hega & Hokenmaier 2002). The Swedish education system, for example, epitomizes the notion of education as a social citizenship right (Marshall 1964), promoting educational mobility from vocational to academic education by integrating VET into the general secondary school system and offering generous educational subsidies to students. This is strongly reminiscent of the universal or social democratic model of welfare capitalism (Esping-Andersen 1990) and its intent to eliminate market-generated inequalities through the generous provision of welfare state benefits and services, including education. The German education system has characteristics similar to the conservative welfare state model. For one, it is far more tolerant of educational inequalities, as it is one of the very few countries to maintain a segregated secondary school system with early tracking of pupils onto academic and vocational tracks. The distinction between different kinds of education is clearly related to the stratification of welfare state institutions into different types of social insurance based on occupational status (Esping-Andersen 1990: 27). Finally, the liberal character of the British welfare state is mirrored in its voluntarist training regime (King 1997) and its competitive and market-based higher education system, in which the role of the state is increasingly reduced.

In addition to institutional similarities, one can identify regime-specific characterizations of the relationship between education and the welfare state. A pioneer in this respect, Heidenheimer (1973, 1981), pointed to the difference between European welfare states and the United States in their promotion of education as a functional equivalent to social insurance (Heidenheimer 1981: 269). More generally, the relationship between education and the welfare state in different regimes has been characterized as follows (cf. Allmendinger & Leibfried 2003; Allmendinger & Nikolai 2010). In liberal welfare state regimes, the promotion of educational opportunities serves as a functional equivalent to more redistributive social insurance policies. For example, governments in the United Kingdom deliberately supported the promotion of VET as a social policy: a means to fight youth unemployment. In the social democratic or universal welfare state model, education is regarded as an integral part of the welfare state. This is widely acknowledged in Sweden, where the "Nordic model of education" is very much an integral part of the "Nordic model of the welfare state" (Arnesen & Lundahl 2006), both in terms of public perceptions and institutionally (e.g., via active labor-market policies). In the continental welfare states, the occupational stratification evident in the social insurance system is mirrored in a strict separation between education and other social policies in terms of both politics and institutions. The lack of coordination between different kinds of social policy may be a general weakness of the conservative welfare state model, but it is particularly pronounced with regard to education, because of the missing link between the social insurances at the core of the welfare state and education as a distinct policy field. Interestingly, however, when a training system has been used less for specific social policy purposes, as in Britain, a high level of employer commitment to the training of young people has been maintained, which in the end might actually have contributed to low levels of youth unemployment and moderate levels of social inequality.

The core argument

The book has two main goals: first, I want to understand how countries have ended up with different education and training regimes; and second, I want to study the contemporary effects of these educational institutions, which are the reflections of policy choices of the past.

Despite the complexity of the topic, the book's core argument can be summarized in a straightforward way: existing scholarship in comparative welfare state research has underestimated the importance of education as an integral part of welfare state regimes. Furthermore, despite relatively similar starting points in the postwar decades, education systems in Western welfare states developed along distinct historical pathways, displaying obvious institutional similarities to well-known worlds of welfare capitalism (Esping-Andersen 1990). Crucial dimensions of variation are the role of VET relative to higher education and the division of labor between public and private sources in education funding. Partisan politics help explain the political dynamics of education reforms that put countries on different development paths. Institutional choices of the past, in turn, shape contemporary patterns of social inequality and popular attitudes towards education policy and the welfare state.

To elaborate further, the cross-country differences in the balance of power between social democrats, Christian democrats, and conservatives help to explain the different choices in the institutional design of education and training systems in the postwar period. In Western Europe, this period was marked by the strong expansion of educational opportunities at the post-secondary level; that is, after the completion of compulsory schooling. Because this sector of education systems was institutionally underdeveloped, there was a lot of room for different paths of development. The main feasible policy options were to expand either academic higher education or nontertiary post-secondary education (VET). Partisan politics influenced both the speed and the intensity of educational expansion, as well as its direction. In contrast to traditional partisan theory, however, I emphasize in this book that the partisan struggle over policy choices needs to be put in context, in particular by taking into account the importance of socioeconomic institutions and organized labor-market interests. In coordinated market economies (CMEs) (Hall & Soskice 2001), nonmarket forms of coordination among economic actors via strong associations and corporatist institutions facilitate the formation of cross-class coalitions that support the maintenance of VET. Departing from the traditional varieties-of-capitalism (VoC) perspective (Hall & Soskice 2001), I argue that these cross-class coalitions still have a partisan nature, depending on which partisan force dominates the political arena. This is why leftist coalitions of social democrats and unions in Scandinavian countries have pushed for VET to be integrated into the general secondary school system, marginalizing the role of employers in the provision of vocational education. By contrast, the dominance of Christian democratic parties in some continental European CMEs, such as Germany, has contributed to keeping employers in the system by establishing a corporatist framework built around apprenticeship training. In liberal market economies (LMEs) such as the United Kingdom, cross-class compromise between unions and employers, as well as between different parties in the electoral arena, has remained elusive. The absence of cross-class cooperation has led to the eventual decline of VET as a viable educational pathway, channeling the forces of educational expansion into academic higher education. This rapid expansion of higher education cannot be financed by public investment alone, so the private share of education financing has increased over time.

Whether and in what form VET has survived as a viable alternative to academic education and the ensuing division of labor between public and private sources of education funding has strong implications for patterns of socioeconomic inequality. The reason VET is so important with regard to inequality is that it opens up access routes to high-quality training and well-paid employment for individuals in the lower half of the academic skills distribution, who have little chance of being admitted to tertiary academic education. The decline of VET in liberal skill regimes, often accompanied by an increase in private education spending, has contributed to a polarization of skills and income on the labor market in the contemporary period. In contrast, countries with well-established VET systems and a predominance of public financing have significantly lower levels of socioeconomic inequality.

The survival of VET has not only shaped redistributive outcomes but has also influenced popular perceptions of educational alternatives, as well as attitudes towards the welfare state. Understanding these policy feedback effects reveals yet another linkage between education and the welfare state, as well as the causal mechanisms behind how past choices contribute to the consolidation of development paths. For example, in countries where VET has survived, popular support for maintaining and supporting this educational alternative is much higher, which explains why the expansion of academic higher education proceeded much more slowly in countries with well-developed apprenticeship systems. Furthermore, cross-national differences in the division of labor between public and private sources in education financing and institutional stratification shape patterns of public support for education spending and redistribution more generally.

The next section provides a more detailed summary and preview of the individual chapters. The book is divided into two parts. The first (Chapters 1, 2, and 3) approaches the subject from the classical perspective of comparative public policy and welfare state research. Education policy is the dependent variable, and I explain how and why partisan politics and institutions are related to different choices in the institutional design of education and training systems. Chapter 1 develops the theoretical framework for this part, while Chapter 2 applies it to three case studies of historical development paths in Sweden, the United Kingdom (England), and Germany, and Chapter 3 extends it to a larger sample of OECD countries in a quantitative analysis of aggregate data. The second part of the book (Chapters 4, 5, and 6) aims to expand the analytical perspective of comparative public policy. As I argue in more detail below, in order to fully understand the complex dynamic of policy and institutional change, it is not enough to study the determinants of policy output alone; it is also crucial to understand how policies affect socioeconomic outcomes and patterns of popular support, because these feedback effects – between the level of policy-making on the one hand and the level of individuals on the other – are important driving forces of policy and institutional change. This is why in Chapter 4 I study the association between educational institutions and socioeconomic inequality (primarily wage and income inequality, but also youth unemployment), and in Chapter 5 I look at the impact of educational institutions on individual preferences and attitudes. In Chapter 6, I highlight the contribution of the book to current debates about skill-biased technological change and the social investment state.

Explaining variation: partisan politics in context

As stated above, the first part of the book (Chapters 1, 2, and 3) is devoted to explaining the observed variety of education and training institutions. There are two large strands in the literature that are commonly used to explain the differences in skill-formation (education and training) regimes. The first is the VoC school of thought (among many others, see: Hall & Soskice 2001; Hancké 2009; Iversen 2005), which draws a broad distinction between general skills systems, focusing on academic higher education on the one hand and specific skills systems, in which the provision of vocational skills is more important, on the other. The VoC paradigm also emphasizes institutional complementarities between the institutions of the skill-formation regime and the adjacent spheres of the political economy, such as industrial relations between employers and unions, corporate governance, and labor-market policies (Estévez-Abe *et al.* 2001). While the VoC approach may be useful in highlighting broad differences between Anglo-Saxon and European countries, it is less able to account for variation within the group of CMEs (Busemeyer 2009a).

It is therefore necessary to bring in a second stream of literature, namely partisan theory. The standard model of partisan theory distinguishes between the partisan representatives of the upper and lower income classes (right-wing and left-wing parties, respectively) and explains differences in policy output related to the partisan composition of governments by referring to economic interests of the core electoral constituencies of political parties (Hibbs 1977; Schmidt 1982). The role of partisan politics as an explanatory factor for differences in education policy output is by now well recognized in the pertinent literature (Ansell 2008, 2010; Busemeyer 2007, 2009b; Castles 1989, 1998; Rauh *et al.* 2011; Schmidt 2007; Wolf 2009; Wolf & Zohlnhöfer 2009). Compared to other fields of social policy, the link between partisan politics and policy output is more complex and less straightforward, because the redistributive implications of educational investments are not as clear-cut as in the case of social transfers (Ansell 2010; Jensen 2011). Hence, the historical and institutional context matters enormously, as will be argued in greater detail below, when I assess the impact of partisan politics on policy change.

Both theories have certain weaknesses and blind spots that I address by developing a more comprehensive theoretical framework. The VoC paradigm has often been criticized for underestimating the role of politics in general (Streeck 2010), and partisan politics in particular. The VoC framework is helpful in highlighting the crucial role of cross-class coalitions in supporting VET. These broad coalitions are still partisan coalitions, however, and depend on which partisan actor is in charge of their formation. As a consequence, the policy choices made by such coalitions reflect the interests of unions and employers to differing degrees. One typical blind spot of classical partisan theory is in neglecting the institutional and political context in which the struggle between partisan forces plays out (see Häusermann *et al.* 2013 for a similar argument). Some variants of partisan theory (Hibbs 1977; Schmidt 1982) do not take sufficient account of the role of organized interests and economic institutions. The power resources variant (Stephens 1979; Korpi 1983) is very conscious of the formation of coalitions between organized labor-market interests and political parties, but it also assumes a pervasive class struggle between business and labor, negating the possibility of sustainable cross-class coalitions despite their having become an empirical reality in many CMEs.

Compensating for the various blind spots of existing theories, the theoretical framework developed in Chapter 1 begins with the basic assertion that political parties have different policy priorities and that cross-national differences in the balance of power between partisan families explain variations in policy output and institutional choices. The chapter then proposes several extensions to this standard model of partisan theory. The first is that it is necessary to move beyond the dichotomy between left- and right-wing political parties and to recognize the fact that Christian democratic parties pursue a particular ideology that is different from that of secular conservatives in other countries, both in social policy generally (Van Kersbergen 1995; Wilensky 1981) and in education policy in particular. An important reason behind why these differences emerge is that political parties form preferences with regard not only to policy substance (as implied by the standard partisan model), but also to the political process. Christian democratic parties are different from secular conservatives in that they pursue a "politics of mediation" (Van Kersbergen 1999: 356), meaning that they promote cross-class compromise between unions and employers and delegate public responsibilities to corporatist bodies. Christian democrats are therefore much more supportive of collective forms of VET in education policy, even though these may impose short-term costs on employers. Conservatives, by contrast, are more in favor of promoting academic and elite higher and upper-secondary education.

The second extension is to take into account the socioeconomic institutional context in which partisan politics plays out, taking on board crucial insights from the VoC debate. There is value in the distinction between LMEs and CMEs found in the VoC literature, in the sense that the existing institutional structure of the economy shapes the menu of feasible policy options: less so in the initial stages of path formation, and increasingly more so over time. Repeated attempts by various British governments to introduce and resuscitate apprenticeship training have generally failed, for example, because employers could not be convinced to participate in these collective schemes. Instead of falling into the trap of economic functionalism, however, I emphasize that the effects of economic institutions are always mediated by political factors, in particular the prevailing balance of power between partisan forces.

Third, I argue that the long-term balance of power between different partisan families is more important than the short-term effects of partisan government. The shift in perspective from the short to the long term is one of the crucial insights of historical institutionalism (Pierson 2004; Thelen 1999), because even large-scale institutional change can happen in a gradual manner (Streeck & Thelen 2005). Government parties can and do affect policy output in the short term, of course, but the implementation of educational reforms takes a considerable amount of time, often decades, such that the absence of short-term effects should not lead to us to underestimate partisan ideology as a driving force of policy change.

In Chapter 2, I apply the theoretical framework to the three cases of Sweden, Germany, and the United Kingdom. The case studies show that the educational reforms of the postwar period were promoted by the same politico-economic coalitions that were driving the expansion and development of other parts of the welfare state during that time period, indicating a strong connection between the politics of education reform and welfare state expansion in terms of the underlying coalitions. As a consequence, the "worlds of human capital formation" (Iversen & Stephens 2008) are quite similar to the well-known "worlds of welfare capitalism" (Esping-Andersen 1990; see also Busemeyer & Nikolai 2010).

I first discuss the social democratic model of a *statist skill-formation regime*, looking particularly at Sweden as a concrete example of this variety. A powerful alliance between the Social Democrats and rural interests was formed in this country in the 1930s (Anderson 2009: 216–17), which laid the foundation for the universal welfare state model to be established and then expanded and built up in the postwar period. Labor and business ended a period of intense industrial conflict by agreeing to settle disputes peacefully in the historic Saltsjöbaden Agreement of 1938. These coalitional patterns continued to hold well into the postwar period, and are thus tremendously important with respect to the enactment of educational reforms (Nilsson 2011). According to Manow and Van Kersbergen (2009: 27), the universalist character of the Swedish welfare state can largely be attributed to the pivotal position of the agrarian Center Party in its political system, which compelled the Social Democrats to form various minority governments despite their being the strongest political force. The education reforms of the 1950s and 1960s, in particular the gradual introduction of the comprehensive secondary school, were promoted by a universalist coalition between rural interests and the urban working class (Husén 1965), whose declared goal was the full-scale comprehensivization of the whole education system, from primary to post-secondary and higher education. A crucial step in this process was to fully integrate VET into the general secondary education system, which happened in the early 1970s (Lundahl 1997), setting the system on a path towards a school-based VET system. This integration was pushed by a coalition of Social Democrats and unions, although employers reluctantly supported the reform as well (Lundahl 1997: 95). In a classical "battle of the sexes" game, employers agreed to the promotion of VET via schools: they would have liked a more firm-centered system, but still preferred school-based VET over general, nonvocational types of education. In the long term, the leadership of the Social Democrats and unions in promoting school-based VET led to the marginalization of the role of employers in vocational training. Employers, especially large firms, adjusted their hiring practices to rely on the relatively broad vocational skills provided in the school system and augment these with firm-specific training for internal labor markets. As a result of this adaptation, attempts by the nonsocialist government of the early 1990s to expand apprenticeship training largely failed (Lundahl 1997: 98). Access to higher education was opened up as VET was integrated into the secondary school system, in order to maximize educational mobility: while a distinction between an academic and a vocational track remained at the upper-secondary level, completion of the VET track in principle enabled students to go to university. This kept the more well-developed VET track from depressing the expansion of higher education, as it did in the German-speaking countries.

I focus next on the United Kingdom (more specifically, England) as an example of a *liberal skill-formation regime*. In contrast to other countries of the Anglo-Saxon world, such as the United States, the British education system until the postwar period was on a development path quite similar to that of Germany and Sweden, but its postwar record of partisan government and economic governance is less clear-cut. Although the Conservative Party was in power longer than Labour, significant changes in the welfare state were initiated during the brief time Labour dominated after World War II (note that this was not the case in education, as we will see). Before Thatcher, Britain's economic governance regime resembled an uneasy and conflicting mix of Keynesianism and liberal voluntarism. This state of affairs is reflected in the education and training system: as in Sweden, the primary concern after the war was to reform the segregated and elitist secondary school system by gradually introducing comprehensive secondary schools. Unlike the United States, the United Kingdom had a well-established apprenticeship training system (Gospel 1994). The 1964 Industrial Training Act even established a kind of corporatist institutional framework in the form of Industrial Training Boards (ITBs), albeit with a much lower degree of statutory commitment than in the case of Germany, and the institutional legacy of voluntarism lingered on (King 1997). Even more ambitious attempts at corporatist steering, set up by the Labour governments in the 1970s in the form of the Manpower Services Commission (MSC), likewise failed to shore up employers' commitment to training and to prevent craft unions from abusing the system as an instrument to limit access to skilled labor. Thus, various governments were unable to establish a collective training regime because the institutional setup of the economy effectively prevented nonmarket forms of coordination from becoming institutionalized (Finegold & Soskice 1988; Ryan 2000). The decline of the traditional apprenticeship system, furthered by Thatcher's government policies to use training as an instrument of labor-market policy instead of skill formation, contributed to a polarization of skills on the labor market. The concurrent expansion of higher education opened up new access routes for the children of the middle class, but it cemented the distinction between academically talented youth on the one hand and low-skilled youth in precarious employment and low-quality training on the other. Both the Conservative and New Labour governments tried to resuscitate apprenticeship training in the 1990s, but to no avail. By abolishing the traditional apprenticeship system and replacing it with a voluntarist, employer-dominated "quasi-market" of government-subsidized training, the Thatcher government had effectively and deliberately destroyed any foundation for cross-class compromise. This example shows how partisan politics and policies can tip the balance in favor of particular institutional outcomes during critical junctures of path development and contribute to the gradual phasing-out of institutional alternatives that had remained potentially alive during previous periods.

Lastly, I describe the *collective skill-formation regime*, with Germany as a prime example. Collective skill-formation regimes differ from the other two types of systems because employers, unions, and the state are all highly and jointly committed to the promotion of skill formation at the intermediate skills level (i.e., through apprenticeship training) (Busemeyer & Trampusch 2012: 14). In the other systems, either the market or the state dominates in matters of skill formation, whereas in collective skill regimes, market and state actors, including unions, cooperate with each other in forming cross-class coalitions.

A crucial supporting factor for these cross-class coalitions that has been severely underestimated so far is the role of Christian democratic parties in government. Of course, it is well recognized that the state plays an important role in stabilizing and nurturing corporatist coalitions, such as by delegating quasi-public obligations to associations or by acting to mediate conflict between opposing interests (Streeck & Schmitter 1985). In matters of skill formation, Thelen (2004: 20) has argued, state action or inaction is important in supporting or dismantling coalitions that are formed in the socioeconomic arena. In all these accounts, however, the state remains essentially a bureaucratic or at least a nonpartisan actor (even in Martin & Thelen 2007). My argument here is to emphasize the importance of *political ideology* in shaping governments' attitudes towards cross-class coalitions and corporatist decision-making in general, since different political actors will have different ideas about which economic interests should be granted access to decision-making. I have already hinted at the peculiar position of Christian democratic ideology in this respect: in contrast to both liberalism and conservatism, Christian democratic ideology promotes a "politics of mediation" (Van Kersbergen 1999: 356), or the deliberate promotion of cross-class compromise. Christian democrats also cherish the subsidiarity principle, delegating as much autonomy as possible to societal actors, in particular associations.

Christian Democrats were the dominant political force in German government from 1949 until the advent of the Brandt government in 1969. They maintained a strong influence on the policies of the federal government during the 1970s, despite their opposition status in the Bundestag, because of their majority in the second parliamentary chamber, the Bundesrat. The 1950s were a period of intense industrial conflict, and the Christian Democrats aimed to remedy this by promoting the expansion of the welfare state, for example by passing a generous pension reform in 1957. Because of the countermajoritarian nature of German political institutions, and probably also in order to move the Social Democrats from their position on the radical left towards the political center, the Christian Democrats cooperated with the Social Democrats in informal grand coalitions (Schmidt 2008). In line with this, Manow & Van Kersbergen 2009: 22) have claimed that continental welfare states are "the product of a coalition between Social and Christian Democracy (red-black coalition)." Christian Democrats occupied an effective veto position in education policy, blocking moves away from the traditional, elitist, and segregated education model. Opening up of access to higher education did not happen until the 1970s (later than in other countries), when the Social Democrats were in government. The Christian Democrats *did* support the promotion and expansion of firm-based apprenticeship, however. The dual-apprenticeship training system had a long tradition and history, but it was not yet fully institutionalized in the postwar period and it remained for the most part a system of private-interest governance driven and maintained by employer initiative (Thelen 2004: 249). The critical piece of legislation was the 1969 Federal Law on Vocational Education and Training (Berufsbildungsgesetz, BBiG), which created a statutory framework for apprenticeship training and ensured the participation of unions and other stakeholders. This law was in fact supported and passed by a *formal* grand-coalition government of Social and Christian Democrats in power from 1966 until 1969. The institutionalization of a well-developed firm-based training system had huge implications for the future development of the education and training system. Most importantly, it depressed the demand for academic higher education (see Ansell 2010: 191), both among young people and their parents and among employers, who adjusted their production strategies accordingly. In contrast to liberal Conservatives, however, the Christian Democrats did not adopt a voluntarist approach to training. Subsidiarity implies delegating quasi-public obligations, such as the education and training of young people, to associations, but this delegation of authority has a price: economic actors are expected to deliver their part of the deal, namely to provide a sufficient amount of training places for young people.

In sum, the political origins of collective skill regimes in the postwar period lie in cross-class coalitions dominated by Christian democratic government, in combination with high levels of economic coordination.

Chapter 3 continues along the lines of Chapter 2 and broadens the comparative perspective to the larger sample of advanced industrial democracies in the OECD world. It first presents descriptive statistics on central institutional characteristics of education and training systems, including a hierarchical cluster analysis that confirms the existence of three distinct country clusters. Despite some limitations in the dataset, it then engages in cross-national analyses of the determinants of the central characteristics of education systems, such as levels of enrollment in vocational and academic education and the private share of education financing. These analyses confirm the central role of partisan politics and economic coordination: social democratic government is associated with higher levels of public involvement in education, both in higher education and in VET; Christian democratic government correlates with lower levels of enrollment in higher education, but is positively associated with the expansion of opportunities in VET; conservative parties, on the other hand, promote private financing of education and lower spending on VET. There is also a strong positive association between economic coordination and the importance of VET, especially apprenticeship training.

Before moving on, it is important to briefly highlight the limits of the explanatory framework developed in the first part of the book, or, in other words, to define the scope conditions of the argument. The theoretical argument is very much inspired by the three cases of the United Kingdom, Sweden, and Germany – countries of northwest Europe – and therefore does not necessarily apply equally well in other areas of the world with different economic and political conditions. For example, southern European countries could represent a distinct development path of their own, locked into a low-skills trap (Allmendinger & Leibfried 2003). In Chapter 3, however, I show that southern European countries are not that different from other continental European countries and that the peculiar case of Italy, a country with a long history of Christian democratic government but without strong apprenticeship training, may be explained by its complex and conflictual territorial politics. At first glance, it seems that the countries of eastern Asia (Japan and South Korea) and of North America (the United States and Canada) would be difficult to explain with my theory, since there are no Christian democratic parties there. However, it is the very absence of Christian democracy and the dominance of conservative and liberal parties that may explain why these countries turned away from VET and towards academic higher education and expanded private spending, to a much greater extent than the United Kingdom. My theoretical argument does not necessarily apply to the countries of Eastern Europe either, because they went through the phase of post-secondary educational expansion under very different political conditions, namely authoritarian socialist rule.

From policy output to outcomes and popular attitudes: rethinking the scope of policy analysis

The analytical perspective above (as well as of the first part of the book) represents the classical approach to comparative public policy analysis: "the study of how, why, and to what effect different governments pursue particular courses of action or inaction" (Heidenheimer *et al.*, 1990: 3). This definition of the purpose of comparative public policy analysis is mirrored in Scharpf's (2000: 33) distinction between interaction- and problem-oriented policy analysis. According to Scharpf, political science has a comparative advantage compared to other social sciences in interaction-oriented policy analysis, a term that here refers to how strategic interactions between political actors shape policy output. Other disciplines, such as economics and sociology, are better placed to study how policies affect outcomes, and potentially to contribute to the solution of societal problems such as inequality and unemployment. While I certainly agree with Scharpf's diagnosis of the current state of affairs in the prevailing disciplinary division of labor, I would argue that the traditional scope of comparative public policy analysis can and should be expanded, for two reasons. First, from a purely analytical perspective, we need a better and more comprehensive understanding of how the policy-making cycle unfolds over time. Understanding how past decisions influence today's outcomes and popular attitudes towards policy change will improve our understanding of the sources of institutional stability and change. Second, from a more normative perspective based on the principle of democratic accountability, we should ask not only whether "parties matter" (Schmidt 1996) but also to what extent policy output affects societal outcomes and how much popular opinion responds to changes in policies and shapes patterns of policy-making (Soroka & Wlezien 2010).

For this reason, the second part of the book is devoted to studying the impact of educational institutions and policies on outcomes and popular attitudes. If in the first part education policy was the dependent variable, it now becomes a crucial independent variable, explaining variation in other dependent variables such as wage inequality and individual-level support for education spending. The overarching theoretical framework, which provides the binding glue that holds the two large parts together, is inspired by the heuristic model of the policy cycle (cf. Easton 1965; Sabatier 1991). This ideal-typical model of the policy-making process posits in a stylized fashion that voters/individuals have political demands that are aggregated by intermediary associations (organized interests) and political parties to be fed into the policy-making process proper. Earlier research (most famously Hibbs 1977) assumed that policy-makers and government parties could directly influence economic outcomes such as growth, unemployment, and inflation. More recent scholarship is more critical in asking whether and to what extent government policies actually do influence socioeconomic outcomes such as family patterns and educational choices (Castles 2013; Hacker 2004; Schlicht 2010). It may well be the case that actual outcomes are more influenced by structural changes in the economy than by policies as such. In the case of education, for example, a prominent argument by Goldin & Katz (2008) is that the increasing inequality in countries such as the United States is a consequence of the increasing demand for high-skilled (and therefore better-paid) individuals due to technological change. From their perspective, the mediating influence of policies on inequality is limited, because structural effects dominate.

In order to fully understand the impact of partisan politics on societies and economies, however, it is necessary to understand and show that partisan forces shape policy output *and* that policies have an effect on socioeconomic outcomes such as inequality (Hacker 2004). This distinction between policy output and outcomes is not recognized in most of the literature on the determinants of inequality (e.g., Bradley *et al.* 2003; Kenworthy & Pontusson 2005); one notable exception is Rueda (2008). Regarding education policy, the literature cited above has mostly focused on determining the impact of partisan politics on policy output: usually education spending. So far, however, it remains unclear how educational institutions shape patterns of socioeconomic inequality and which particular characteristics of educational institutions tend to do so.

In addition to their impact on outcomes, policies may also shape popular attitudes and individual preferences. This is generally discussed in the literature as the policy feedback effect (Mettler & Soss 2004). Pierson (1993) was one of the first to highlight the importance of positive feedback effects as factors stabilizing divergent policy development paths: he argued (Pierson 1993: 598, 610) that existing policies have both resource and interpretive effects. Welfare state policies distribute and redistribute resources between social groups (see Esping-Andersen 1990 for a similar argument) in a way that causes those groups privileged by a particular policy to develop an interest in the continued existence of the program. One obvious example of this kind of feedback effect would be that pensioners who are beneficiaries of a generous pension scheme have a strong interest in maintaining this system, and may become more politically active as a consequence (see Campbell 2002 for the case in the United States). Other factors besides self-interest that are involved in shaping the "cognitive processes of social actors" (Pierson 1993: 610) are existing policies and institutions, or, to put it simply, popular expectations of government's role as a provider of social services such as education. Taken together, these two mechanisms generate an expectation of positive feedback effects: the longer that institutions are in place, the less likely they are to radically change, because important social groups will have developed a strong interest in maintaining them, and the corresponding popular perceptions of the legitimate role of government in the welfare state and education system will be deeply entrenched.

The innovative contribution of this book is to combine the study of political conflicts during critical junctures from a historical-institutionalist perspective (Chapters 2 and 3) with an analysis of how these institutions systematically shape socioeconomic outcomes (Chapter 4) and patterns of popular support (Chapter 5). This kind of encompassing analytical perspective is necessary if we are to fully understand the dynamic of the policy-making cycle as it unfolds over time. Critical institutional choices in the past have implications for the distribution of resources in the contemporary period. Once institutions are established, they influence popular expectations with regard to the role of the state in the provision and financing of education and the welfare state more generally. Understanding the complex feedback effects of institutions and policies on popular attitudes is therefore necessary in order to explain the long-term political sustainability of institutional paths. Without taking feedback effects into account, it would be hard to understand why in some countries high tuition fees are an accepted part of life, while in others the state is expected to provide and finance education. Feedback effects also help to explain the political sustainability of segmented secondary school systems, which limit social mobility for those in the lower half of the income and skills distribution.

Educational institutions and socioeconomic inequality

If Chapters 2 and 3 identified partisan politics as one important mechanism linking education policies and the welfare state, Chapter 4 addresses the question of whether educational institutions are also relevant determinants of socioeconomic outcomes such as the distribution of income and labor-market stratification. My motivation for studying the implications of educational institutions for socioeconomic inequality is based on an interesting puzzle: as I show at the beginning of Chapter 4, there is no simple (linear) relationship between educational and socioeconomic inequality; higher levels of educational inequality do not automatically translate into higher levels of socioeconomic inequality in terms of wage and income inequality.

The concept of educational inequality is prominent in the field of educational sociology and captures the degree to which access to higher levels of education is affected by parental or family background. For example, educational inequality is higher in cases where the association between parental background and educational performance or access to education is stronger, but a lower degree of educational stratification can still be accompanied by a high level of socioeconomic inequality (in terms of income, wealth, and wages). In the United States, for instance, high levels of socioeconomic stratification are associated with relatively *low* levels of educational inequality. High schools in the United States are comprehensive, and the higher education system offers a huge variety of educational alternatives for different educational needs, which contributes to high levels of tertiary enrollment, although there is of course a hierarchy of more or less prestigious institutions within the higher education sector (Allmendinger 1989). Nevertheless, the level of socioeconomic inequality there is high. The contrasting cases are, of course, the Scandinavian countries. Here educational inequality is low because secondary schools are comprehensive and access to higher education is open to a large share of the population. Unlike in the United States, however, the level of socioeconomic inequality is also

Introduction 21

low. Finally, both Germany and Switzerland have exceptionally high levels of educational inequality, as has often been documented in the OECD Programme for International Student Assessment (PISA) studies (OECD 2010). Family background has a strong impact on educational attainment and the probability of completing higher education (Pfeffer 2008). Note that the level of socioeconomic inequality remains quite moderate: somewhat higher than in the Scandinavian countries, but much lower than in the Anglo-Saxon world.

This observation is important because it points to a large blind spot in the literature, one that in my view is aggravated by a lack of interdisciplinary exchange. Educational sociology has a huge literature documenting the impact of educational institutions on stratification in terms of educational choices and educational inequality (e.g., see Allmendinger 1989; Blossfeld & Shavit 1993; Breen et al. 2009; Müller & Shavit 1998; Pfeffer 2008). One core finding in this literature is that educational inequalities in terms of class biases in access to education are persistent despite the decades-long trend of educational expansion. A second core finding is that segregated educational institutions (early tracking) exacerbate educational inequalities (Pfeffer 2008). This literature essentially equates "inequality" with educational stratification, however, and does not look at the relationship between educational inequalities and stratification of the labor market.

In the political economy literature on the determinants of socioeconomic inequality, by contrast, educational institutions are rarely included as independent variables. Popular topics in this field of research include the various effects on inequality of the power of the left (Bradley et al. 2003; Rueda 2008), VoC (Pontusson et al. 2002; Rueda & Pontusson 2000), collective wage bargaining (Wallerstein 1999), and electoral institutions (Iversen & Soskice 2006, 2009). There are a couple of exceptions, however. Estévez-Abe et al. (2001) have argued that countries with a well-developed vocational training system exhibit lower levels of inequality because the availability of vocational-training opportunities opens up access to high-skilled and well-paid labor for students with few academic skills, but Bradley et al. (2003), as well as Lupu & Pontusson (2011), tested this hypothesis in a way that was more methodologically rigorous than the initial explorative approach applied in Estévez-Abe et al. (2001) and found no support for this claim. One important shortcoming of this research is that it does not distinguish between different *kinds* of VET (school-based versus workplace-based). Addressing this problem, Busemeyer & Iversen (2012) distinguished between public investment in VET on the one hand and employer involvement on the other. This distinction was important because it allowed them to show that public investment in VET *does* in fact reduce wage inequality, but not youth unemployment. Conversely, the strong involvement of employers in training (i.e., a higher share of students in workplace-based forms of apprenticeship training) reduces youth unemployment but has *no* significant effect on inequality.

This book extends the work of Busemeyer & Iversen (2012) by engaging in an in-depth analysis of the role of educational institutions as determinants of socioeconomic inequality and labor-market stratification. In addition to the distinction between academic education on the one hand and different kinds of vocational education on the other, I introduce the division of labor between public and private sources in funding education as a second important dimension of variation. In combination, these two factors contribute significantly to explaining variation in inequality: higher levels of public involvement in the funding of higher and vocational education are associated with reduced levels of wage inequality. However, a high level of statism in the provision of education has negative side effects. In countries like Sweden and Finland (but not Denmark, whose training system is more similar to the German one), the crowding out of employers in the provision of training has led to high levels of youth unemployment.

Policy feedback: the impact of educational institutions on attitudes and preferences

Finally, in Chapter 5 I look at a third linkage (in addition to politics and outcomes) between education and the welfare state at the micro-level of individual preferences and attitudes. It is important to consider this additional linkage in order to fully understand the development of path dependencies over time, as well as the micro-level foundations and causal mechanisms underlying the macro-level associations found in previous chapters. In an ideal world, it would be possible to trace the feedback effects of institutions upon attitudes throughout the entire postwar period. Unfortunately, large cross-national datasets on surveys of public opinion are only available for the last ten to fifteen years. The goal of this chapter is much more modest: I am interested in tracing the effect of past institutional choices, manifested in crossnational differences, on contemporary patterns of popular attitudes and individual preferences.

Above, I presented hypotheses on factors explaining these institutional choices; this is the focus of the first part of the book. In Chapter 5, I am concerned with their consequences and their feedback effects on the politics of institutional change, in particular citizens' attitudes and preferences. This research question is connected to a broader literature analyzing the effects of welfare state institutions on popular attitudes. A well-established finding in this literature is that welfare state cutbacks are unpopular in general, and politicians are unlikely to move forward with large-scale retrenchment against widespread popular opposition (Boeri et al. 2001; Brooks & Manza 2006, 2007). There has also been debate on whether the institutional setup of the welfare state has consequences for individual-level support. Going back to the influential work of Rothstein (1998), the common expectation is that popular support for the welfare state is higher in universal, Scandinavian welfare states than in the means-tested, residual welfare states of the Anglo-Saxon world, but the empirical evidence remains ambiguous (Andreß & Heien 2001; Arts & Gelissen 2001; Blekesaune & Quadagno 2003; Jaeger 2009). A counterargument is provided by the "public as thermostat" model developed by Wlezien (1995) and expanded in Soroka & Wlezien (2010). This model anticipates that popular support for the expansion of the welfare state will decline after a certain threshold is reached; in other words, citizens do not want to expand the welfare state indefinitely.

As a reminder, the crucial variables are whether vocational training as an alternative to academic higher education "survived" (remained a viable and popular educational pathway next to university education) and which division of labor between public and private sources of education funding emerged. The analyses in Chapter 5 confirm that these institutional macro-level contexts have shaped popular attitudes towards education policy and the welfare state more generally. For example, high levels of educational stratification (i.e., a strong class bias in access to higher levels of education) are associated with higher levels of support for public education spending among the rich and the well-educated, since the children of upper income classes are more likely to benefit from these additional investments. Furthermore, a large share of private financing in education is related to a lower willingness to support redistribution at the micro-level, because individuals who have paid for a significant share of their human capital stock out of their own pocket are less likely to support government measures that would reduce their wage premiums. Finally, this chapter also documents the special status of education in comparison to other social policies: I find that individual income and educational background are significant negative determinants of individual-level support for social policies, in line with the model developed by Meltzer & Richard (1981). Richer and better-educated individuals are less likely to support the expansion of the welfare state, because they will largely be the ones to pay for this, in the form of higher taxes. In the case of education, by contrast, there is no statistically significant association between individual income and support for more public education spending, and I even find a positive effect for individual educational background. This indicates that education may indeed be less redistributive than other social policies and that institutional context is paramount in mediating the impact of micro-level variables.

Concluding outlook and added value

The purpose of this book is to promote the reintegration of the study of education into comparative welfare state research. I will show that there are multiple linkages between education and the welfare state in terms of politics, outcomes, and popular attitudes. Despite this broad scope of analysis, however, open questions are bound to remain. With this in mind, in Chapter 6 I will comment briefly on how the project contributes to contemporary debates about the "race between education and technology" (Goldin & Katz 2008) and the social investment state (Morel *et al.* 2012). I also mention avenues for future research, in particular the study of early childhood education and lifelong learning.

Skills and Inequality moves beyond existing scholarship in three ways. First, it combines the study of politics and policy output with an analysis of how policies affect outcomes and popular attitudes. This kind of encompassing analytical perspective is my attempt to transcend the disciplinary boundaries that separate comparative welfare state research, political economy, and labor-market sociology, as well as to extend the classical analytical perspective of comparative public policy. The book also combines different methods – from historical process

Introduction

tracing via quantitative analysis of macro-level data to analysis of micro-level survey data – in order to develop a deeper understanding of the dynamics of welfare state and education reforms.

Second, the book studies different kinds of upper and post-secondary education at the same time: general secondary education, VET, and higher education. Existing scholarship with a similar analytical perspective (rooted in comparative political economy) tends to focus on any one of these without taking into account the feedback effects of institutional developments in adjacent sectors of the education system. For example, Ansell (2008, 2010) focuses primarily on higher education, while Thelen (2004) studies vocational training.

Third, the book proposes several extensions to the standard model of partisan theory. Again, existing scholarship runs the risk of presenting an overly simplified account of the complex dynamics of partisan conflict. For instance, some applications of the partisan model to education policy (Ansell 2008, 2010; Boix 1997, 1998; Busemeyer 2007; Castles 1989) focus on partisan conflict without taking into account the role of organized labor-market interests and the mediating influence of the institutional context. In addition, the peculiar approach of Christian democratic parties to education policy and their divergence from both social democracy and conservatism has not been sufficiently acknowledged in the literature on skill-formation regimes. As I argue in the first chapter, broadening the analytical perspective of the standard model by placing partisan politics into context has the potential to provide us with a better understanding of the complex dynamics of political conflict.

PART I

The political and institutional determinants of education policy

1 | *Theoretical framework*
Partisan politics in context

This chapter develops a theoretical framework that forms the basis for the qualitative case studies of Chapter 2 and the quantitative analyses of Chapter 3. I start with a short depiction of the core dimensions of variation in contemporary education and training regimes in Western democracies, which will be discussed in detail in the quantitative chapter (Chapter 3). I distinguish between the dimensions of public involvement in education on the one hand and educational stratification on the other, which roughly correspond to Esping-Andersen's (1990) well-known concepts of de-commodification and stratification. This description is followed by a short review of how existing approaches – especially the VoC paradigm, historical institutionalism, and power resources theory – try to explain the observed variation, and where they fall short. The core of the chapter is a theoretical framework, which is essentially a proposal to extend the standard model of partisan theory in three important ways: first, by taking into account that political parties have preferences not only about the content of policy but also about how the political process should be organized; second, by reflecting on the interaction between partisan politics and institutional context; and third, by focusing more on the long-term balance of power between political party families than on the partisan composition of governments in the short term. The chapter closes with some remarks on the empirical strategy of the subsequent chapters.

De-commodification and stratification in education systems

As is well known, Esping-Andersen (1990) has identified two dimensions along which contemporary welfare state regimes vary: de-commodification and stratification. These concepts are also useful for understanding education and training regimes. The concept of de-commodification is related to the Marxian notion of the commodification of labor. For Esping-Andersen (1990: 21–2), "de-commodification occurs when a service is rendered as a matter of right, and when a person can maintain a livelihood without reliance on the market." In other words, welfare states achieve a high degree of de-commodification when citizens who are entitled to receive generous welfare state benefits become less dependent on selling their labor on the market. Education differs somewhat from other social policies because the connection to the labor market is different. Whereas the traditional types of social insurance target people who are already on the labor market and are meant to compensate for income loss related to life risks such as illness, unemployment, and old age, individuals receive education *before* they enter the labor market. The purpose of education is not to compensate *ex post* for income loss, but to invest in human capital in order to insure individuals against the prospect of income loss.

Even so, the concept of de-commodification can be meaningfully applied to education. In this case, the decisive question is whether education itself is considered a tradable commodity and capital investment or a social right and entitlement. T.H. Marshall considered education to be an important part of his catalogue of social rights:

The education of children has a direct bearing on citizenship, and, when the State guarantees that all children shall be educated, it has the requirements and the nature of citizenship definitely in mind. It is trying to stimulate the growth of citizens in the making. The right to education is a genuine social right of citizenship, because the aim of education during childhood is to shape the future adult. Fundamentally it should be regarded, not as the right of the child to go to school, but as the right of the adult citizen to have been educated. (Marshall 1964: 81–2)

Human-capital theory (Becker 1993) takes the opposite perspective: that the amount of individual investment in education is determined by individual costs and benefits in terms of higher wages. Education is not regarded as a social right as such, but as the outcome of an individual choice under constraints such as innate academic abilities and credit market constraints.

On the level of cross-country comparison, differences in the division of labor between public and private sources of funding are likely to reflect cross-national variations in how much the provision of education has been commodified. When a large share of education funding comes from private sources (mostly in the form of tuition fees paid by households and individuals), individual educational choices are more likely to resemble the cost–benefit calculus depicted in human-capital theory. Conversely, when the involvement of the state in financing and providing education is high, the provision of education may be regarded as a social right and entitlement, and as part and parcel of a comprehensive welfare state model.

Esping-Andersen's second dimension of stratification captures the degree to which welfare state institutions themselves contribute to the formation of distinct welfare state clientele groups or classes (Esping-Andersen 1990: 23). This specific approach to stratification does not pick up on the effect of welfare state institutions at the level of outcomes in terms of socioeconomic inequality. Instead, it focuses on the question of how the welfare state itself creates group identities by defining the beneficiaries of social benefits in particular ways. This concept applies very well to education and training systems, since it is possible to draw on a large literature in educational sociology concerned with educational stratification (see Chapter 4). Education systems vary widely in the strength of class-related inequalities of access to higher levels of education and the degree of educational mobility between different tracks (academic and vocational) within the system. Countries where the secondary school system is segmented and students are put onto different tracks early in their educational careers are generally identified as having high levels of educational inequality (Breen *et al.* 2009; Pfeffer 2008). Comprehensive education at the secondary level and open access to tertiary education lower educational stratification.

Figure 1.1 shows the association between de-commodification and educational stratification in education and training systems. The two measures used in this figure are by no means perfect indicators of the underlying complex concepts but serve as decent proxies. The x axis is a measure of educational stratification, provided by the OECD (2007: 87). For this measure, students were asked whether they expected to complete higher education (at ISCED level 5A or 6) at some point in their educational careers. The measure thus captures the difference in the odds ratio of expectations between students from strong socioeconomic backgrounds and students from weak socioeconomic backgrounds. Unlike other measures of educational inequality (see Chapter 4), therefore, this measure does not capture the direct relationship between socioeconomic background and educational attainment; the institutional setup of the education system is more important, especially the relative openness of access to higher academic education as

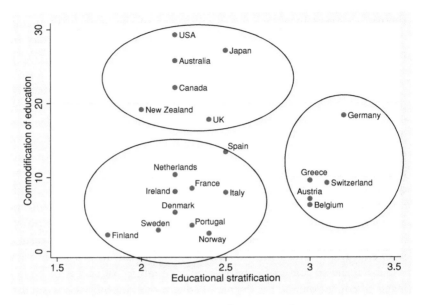

Figure 1.1 De-commodification and stratification in education systems

reflected in student expectations. The y axis is the share of education spending that comes from private sources for all levels of education. Most such private sources are households, but in this case they include contributions from foundations and businesses.[1] Commodification can take different forms depending on the educational sector. In VET, commodification may refer to the role of employers and other private entities in the provision of training. In higher education, it captures the extensiveness of the private sector in the university system, as well as the level of household spending in the form of tuition fees.[2]

As can be seen in Figure 1.1, there is no apparent association between these two dimensions (the bivariate correlation in the cross-sectional sample of OECD countries is −0.04). As in the case of welfare state

[1] Private spending by households is far more important than the other sources. I use the broader measure in the present case because it is available for a larger set of countries. See Appendix for details on sources and definitions. This measure is the average for the time period 1997–2008 (see Chapter 3).
[2] Private household spending that is related to education, but not directed to educational institutions (e.g., parents giving money to their college-bound offspring for food or clothing), is not included here.

regimes more generally, these are two distinct and different dimensions of variation. Nevertheless, it is possible to identify three country groupings or clusters of countries that are reminiscent of the well-known worlds of welfare capitalism (see also Busemeyer & Nikolai 2010). Countries in the liberal cluster combine low levels of de-commodification (expressed as high shares of private education spending) with low levels of stratification. This cluster includes the United States, Canada, Australia, New Zealand, the United Kingdom, and Japan. The second cluster of statist skill regimes, combining low levels of educational stratification with high levels of de-commodification, covers all Scandinavian countries but also includes the Netherlands, France, Ireland, and some southern European countries.[3] Finally, there is a cluster of continental European countries (Germany, Austria, Switzerland, Belgium), as well as Greece, that is characterized by a combination of high levels of educational stratification and medium levels of de-commodification.[4]

It is important to point out that differences in total levels of investment in education are not taken into account in Figure 1.1, since the two dimensions only capture differences in the public/private division of labor in education financing and educational stratification. There are of course many other differences in the institutional setup of education and training systems in advanced democracies besides these two variables, including overall levels of public and private investment in educational institutions; the division of labor between the state, employers, and individuals with regard to the financing and governance of skill formation; the extent of stratification between academic and vocational tracks; and performance in terms of average levels of educational attainment (Allmendinger & Leibfried 2003; Busemeyer & Nikolai 2010; Crouch *et al.* 1999; Hega & Hokenmaier 2002; Iversen & Stephens 2008; Lynch 1994). These other measures will be discussed in greater detail in Chapter 3.

---

[3] The latter may constitute a fourth world of education regimes, as is sometimes argued with regard to their welfare state models (see Chapter 3 for a more extensive discussion of this topic).
[4] The outlier position of Germany is explained by the fact that firms' contributions to the financing of the apprenticeship system are counted as private education spending, which was a more or less arbitrary and politically motivated decision made when the OECD's system of educational statistics was revamped in the 1990s (Heidenheimer 1996).

Explaining variation: the varieties-of-capitalism perspective

How did different countries end up on different development paths constituting different worlds of human capital formation? And which mechanisms explain the sustainability of institutional variation across time? Although there is very little scholarship that deals explicitly with the analysis of the connections between education and the welfare state as it develops over time, we can distinguish two broad perspectives. One is rooted in the VoC debate (Hall & Soskice 2001), which played a crucial role in making mainstream comparative political scientists and welfare state researchers more interested in the study of education (Busemeyer & Trampusch 2011: 424–9). Education and training systems were regarded as one of five institutional spheres of political economies in the original framework developed by Hall & Soskice (2001: 25–6). Inspired by the earlier work of Streeck (1989, 1992), their core argument was that the institutional setup of the education and training system has implications for the availability of different kinds of skills in the political economy, which in turn influences firms' choices of production strategies and patterns of competitiveness. Specific or occupational skills dominate in CMEs such as Germany, which impels firms to specialize in the production of high-end manufacturing products for as long as institutional complementarities between the systems of skill formation and adjacent institutional spheres, such as industrial relations and finance, allow them to adopt a long-term perspective in human-capital management and skill formation (Hall & Soskice 2001: 28). The institutions of LMEs such as the United States encourage investment in more generalized academic skills that can be easily transferred from one job to another. Firms in LMEs hence excel in product markets that value fast-paced innovation and high-level academic skills (IT, biotech, consulting, etc.) (Hall & Soskice 2001: 32).

In the original framework of Hall & Soskice (2001), the welfare state as such was not mentioned as one of the five institutional spheres. The link between skills and the welfare state featured more prominently in related work by Torben Iversen, David Soskice and others (Cusack et al. 2006; Estévez-Abe et al. 2001; Iversen 2005; Iversen & Soskice 2001). In particular, Iversen & Soskice (2001) developed an "asset theory of social policy preferences," which argues that the individual skill portfolios of workers have an impact on their demand for social

Theoretical framework 35

insurance (see also Moene & Wallerstein 2001, 2003 for a related argument). Controlling for other factors such as income or level of education, workers with more specific skills exhibit a higher demand for social insurance, because the risk of their skills becoming obsolete is higher than in the case of general, transferable skills. Estévez-Abe *et al.* (2001) have argued that employers are willing to accommodate this demand for insurance in CMEs because they have an interest in maintaining their competitive advantage in product markets that require specific skills. The counterintuitive prediction that comes out of this line of reasoning is that employers, at least in CMEs, are willing to support the expansion of the welfare state because they would like to maintain workers' willingness to invest in specific skills. Historical work by Mares (2001, 2003) and Swenson (2002) provides additional evidence for employer support of welfare state expansion under certain conditions.

The VoC approach has triggered a huge debate that cannot be adequately summarized here (but see Becker 2007; Hancké 2009; Deeg & Jackson 2006; and Streeck 2009 for critical overviews, as well as Busemeyer 2009a; Emmenegger 2009; and Streeck 2012 for skill formation more specifically). The crucial takeaway for the purpose of this chapter is the stipulation of a functional complementarity between skill formation and welfare state policies. The VoC perspective argues that employers in CMEs support welfare state institutions because they serve an important function: securing an adequate supply of a particular kind of skill. This may help to explain why institutional arrangements that constrain business in the short term still receive considerable support from the business community and thus contribute to the long-term political sustainability of development paths (Hassel 2007; Iversen & Stephens 2008). The original version of the VoC framework is less able to explain the emergence of different varieties of capitalism, however. To be fair, Estévez-Abe *et al.* (2001: 147) have explicitly stated that "our model is *not* intended to explain the origin of specific social policies." Nevertheless, a comprehensive theoretical framework should be able to explain both institutional change and stability.

Recent work in the field has therefore gone back to the late nineteenth and early twentieth centuries with the aim of explaining contemporary varieties of capitalism through the outcomes of political struggles during the critical juncture of industrialization (Iversen &

Soskice 2009; Korpi 2006; Mares 2003; Martin & Swank 2011, 2012; Swenson 2002; Thelen 2004). This is very much in line with the theory of path dependency (Pierson 2000, 2004), which argues that events that happen in the early phase of path formation have a stronger impact on the eventual shape of the development paths than events that happen later. But we must be careful here not to throw the baby out with the bathwater: not everything was preordained by developments during the Industrial Revolution. Political struggles and conflicts in the mid-twentieth century had enormous consequences for the shape of contemporary education and training regimes. The simple reason for this is that education and training systems entered a new phase of development after access to primary education became more or less universal during the first half of the twentieth century. The expansion of post-secondary education, however, took very different forms. Essentially, the force of educational expansion led to the establishment of new educational pathways at the post-secondary level, or at least to a significant transformation of existing institutions (such as the opening up of access to universities). In order to explain this variety of development paths, I now turn to the second broad perspective in the literature: historical institutionalism and partisan theory.

Historical institutionalism, partisan politics, and power resources

How can we explain the different development paths of education and training regimes? Theories in comparative public policy proffer different explanations. One perspective rooted in modernization theory emphasizes the importance of socioeconomic forces over political and institutional determinants (Wilensky 2002). The continued expansion of educational opportunities, particularly at the higher post-secondary level, is regarded as a corollary to societal and economic development. Cross-country differences in policy output are thus attributed to differences in the level of development. A different, but related, perspective is put forward in the theory of the world society (Meyer *et al.* 1992). Here, the massive expansion of educational opportunities during the twentieth century is attributed to the institutionalization of a legitimate model of the nation-state, in which the universal provision of primary and later secondary education is an important element (Meyer *et al.* 1992: 129). In contrast to modernization theory, therefore, the spread of education is not primarily attributed to its functional complementarity to the developing industrial society, but to its appeal as an instrument of legitimation used by societies eager to become part of the fledgling "world society," built upon Western notions of democracy and development. Socioeconomic explanations and world-society approaches are undoubtedly well suited to explain the massive expansion of educational opportunities across the duration of the twentieth century and beyond. Because they are approaching the subject from a global perspective, however, they are less able to account for the more fine-grained differences in the institutional setup of education and training systems in the Western world.

In this respect, historical institutionalism – or neoinstitutionalism more generally – may be superior (Hall & Taylor 1996; Pierson 2000, 2004; Steinmo *et al.* 1992; Thelen 1999). Theories of path dependency can explain why countries follow distinct development paths. Once a path is chosen, actors tend to stick with it, because changing the path would result in significant transaction costs (Pierson 2000, 2004). Institutions have feedback effects on the political process as well: actors whose political power is bolstered by existing institutions have an interest in the continued survival of these institutions (Pierson 2004: 36–7). Because of path dependency and the associated institutional "lock-in" effects, work in this tradition needs to "go back and look" (Pierson 2004: 47) at the historical origins of contemporary institutional arrangements, paying close attention to the fact that actors (or coalitions of actors) who supported the establishment of a particular institution at one point in time might not be the same ones that benefit from its continued existence in later periods. A well-known example of this is Thelen's historical account of the formation of training regimes, where she finds that unions initially opposed the establishment of workplace-based training regimes, only to become strong supporters in later years (Thelen 2004).

Historical institutionalism has been criticized on a number of fronts. One common criticism is that the claim of path dependency is overstated and does not fit empirical reality. In Pierson's analysis of Western welfare states, the conservative-corporatist type to be found in continental European countries is singled out as being particularly resistant to change and reform because of its many established veto points and powerful clientele groups (Pierson 2001: 446). Empirical studies of institutional change in "Bismarckian" welfare states, however, convincingly show that these welfare states *do* change in significant ways, although their changes proceed in various stages of reform and not in one single "big bang" (Häusermann 2010; Palier 2010).

Related to this empirical type of criticism, recent work on institutional change has drawn attention to theoretical inconsistencies in the first generation of theories in historical institutionalism (Hall & Thelen 2009; Mahoney & Thelen 2010; Streeck & Thelen 2005; Thelen 2003, 2004). The central problem is that theories of path dependency draw a stark distinction between periods of stasis, when the forces of path dependencies are at work, and periods of institutional breakdown (Streeck & Thelen 2005: 1). Path dependency is an excellent explanation for the forces that keep institutions in place once they have been set up, but it cannot explain *why* these institutions were established in the first place, nor *why or how* they might be transformed in incremental ways. In short: because they emphasize the impact of institutions on actors' choices, the early versions of historical institutionalism have no theory of action. This is why historical institutionalism should and can be combined with well-established actor-centered theories, such as power resources or partisan theory.

Classical power resources theory highlights the role of coalitions between trade unions and leftist parties in government as driving forces of welfare state development (Korpi 1983; Esping-Andersen 1990; Stephens 1979; more recently, but in a similar vein: Bradley *et al.* 2003; Korpi 2006). This perspective associates left-wing partisanship (powerful unions and social democratic parties) with the expansion of the welfare state in both the historical and the contemporary period. In its depiction of political conflict as a struggle between partisan coalitions of the left and right, however, power resources theory fails to explain the emergence and sustainability of cross-class coalitions. Such coalitions have been found to be the crucial supporting pillars of collective vocational training regimes, because the joint investment in vocational skills creates a form of mutual dependency between workers and employers (Busemeyer 2012a; Busemeyer & Trampusch 2012; Cusack *et al.* 2007; Thelen 2004).

The work of Kathleen Thelen is related to power resources theory in many ways, since Thelen has posited that the long-term survival of socioeconomic institutions depends fundamentally on the presence of supporting coalitions of actors (Thelen 2004: 290–1; Hall & Thelen 2009: 12). Actors make use of the "gaps" that necessarily emerge between institutions as abstract rules and the concrete implementation of those rules on the ground; as part of this process they are continuously engaging in institutional "re-creation" and inadvertently in institutional change as well, since changes in the balance of power between actors or their preferences can drive incremental changes in institutional frameworks that may lead to large-scale change in the long run (Streeck & Thelen 2005; Mahoney & Thelen 2010).

Thelen's coalitional approach is a significant advancement over previous work on theories of institutional change and classical power resources theory, because instead of conceptualizing political struggles over policy reforms in terms of epic battles between the left and right, Thelen advocates a fundamentally empirical approach. She pays close attention to the reconstruction of politico-economic coalitions in policy-making, arguing that the composition of these coalitions may sometimes run counter to *a priori* expectations. In this respect, Thelen's approach is quite similar to "actor-centered institutionalism," as put forward by Mayntz and Scharpf (Mayntz & Scharpf 1995; Scharpf 1997). The difference is that in actor-centered institutionalism, politics is conceived as a process of bargaining or mutual adjustment between individual or collective actors, whereas Thelen emphasizes the formation of *coalitions* of actors.

However, what has been missing in Thelen's argument is an appreciation of the role of partisan actors in general and government parties in particular as agents of institutional change. In her work on training regimes, Thelen argues that the state plays a crucial role in supporting the formation of different kinds of alliance between economic actors (Thelen 2004: 32), but that the interests of state actors do not seem to be determined by partisan politics as such. In later work, Martin & Thelen (2007) have noted that state actors in countries with a large public sector develop an interest in maintaining cross-class solidarity, because government bureaucrats have an incentive to cater to the interests of the low-skilled and the long-term unemployed: they too form part of the large sector of public employment (Martin & Thelen 2007: 16–17). Employers and unions in these countries also have an incentive to cooperate with each other in order to fend off the intrusion of the state (Martin & Thelen 2007: 17). Again, state actors feature as bureaucrats, not partisan actors. This may be helpful in explaining why cross-class solidarity and a large public sector develop a mutually reinforcing relationship over time, but it does not explain why countries have ended up with different degrees of state involvement in the political economy more generally and in systems of skill formation in particular.

In order to understand this, it is necessary to bring in partisan theory. Starting with Hibbs (1977), this theoretical perspective posits that differences in policy output occur when government parties cater to different electoral constituencies (Schmidt 1996). For example, leftwing parties will want to increase public spending to promote the interests of lower-income citizens, whereas rightist parties will prefer to lower taxes. Whereas power resources theory tends to regard government parties as the extensions of labor-market interest groups into the policy-making sphere, partisan theory gives government parties a certain degree of political independence from their electoral bases. Partisan actors are *both* office- and policy-seeking (Müller & Strøm 1999), in that they aim to implement certain kinds of policy even as they attempt to win electoral majorities by mobilizing their core electoral constituencies and appealing to the median voter.

In a certain sense, the blind spots of partisan theory are the mirror image of the coalitional approach. Whereas the coalitional approach focuses on the interaction between coalitions of economic actors and nonpartisan state actors, partisan theory glosses over the impact of organized interests on government policy choices. Power resources theory *does* take into account organized interests, but assumes coalitional patterns that reflect the underlying class cleavage, such as one of the unions and the left against the employers and the right.

A recent example of the application of partisan theory to the study of education policy is the influential work of Ansell (2008, 2010) and Boix (1997, 1998).[5] Both Ansell and Boix start out by deriving the expected interests of individual voters in different income classes with regard to institutional choices in education policy. For example, Ansell (2008: 200) argues that poor voters will prefer a privately funded elite system of higher education if access to universities is income-dependent, as they have no interest in subsidizing the education of the rich. The preferences of political parties are then derived from the preferences of the voter groups that the parties represent (Ansell 2010: 125); the choices of government parties thus reflect the (economic) interests of

---

[5] Other studies on the partisan politics of education include Busemeyer (2007, 2009b), Jensen (2011), Schmidt (2007), and Wolf and Zohlnhöfer (2009). The work of Ansell and Boix, however, is more rigorous in the application of classical partisan theory than these.

their core electoral constituencies. One theoretical weakness of this type of model is that it does not take into account the impact that organized interests have on the choices made by government parties in defining a range of feasible policy options.

In sum, existing theories have various blind spots that prevent us from developing a deeper understanding of the dynamics of institutional development in education and training systems and in contemporary political economies more generally. The VoC school of thought initially concentrated on identifying functional complementarities between education systems and adjacent institutional spheres and refrained from studying the origins of politico-economic institutions. Scholars have moved in this direction more recently, but I note a tendency to overestimate the importance of the long "shadow of the 19th century" (Iversen & Soskice 2009). Empirically, as Ansell (2010) has shown for the case of higher education, education systems start to diverge most clearly in the second half of the twentieth century. Partisan politics play an important role here, but in contrast to Ansell (2008, 2010) and Boix (1997, 1998), partisan conflict should not be depicted as a struggle between left and right. Instead, it is important to highlight the differences between Christian democracy and secular conservatism, especially in the field of education policy (Busemeyer & Nikolai 2010; Iversen & Stephens 2008). However, partisan politics alone is not a sufficient explanation. Ansell (2010) and Boix (1998) have focused on electoral politics and voters' preferences, but have not considered the role of organized interests, such as labor unions and employers' associations, in influencing education and training policies. Thelen's (2004) coalitional approach, in turn, focuses on the interaction between organized interests and state actors, but does not take into account the electoral arena and the role of partisan ideologies in shaping policy output. In order to fully understand the historical evolution of education and training systems, it is necessary to think more extensively about the interplay between partisan politics on the one hand and socioeconomic institutions and organized labor-market interests on the other.

Theoretical framework: partisan politics in context

The previous sections sketched out the contributions that existing theories can make towards explaining the institutional diversity of education and training systems. These discussions reveal comparative strengths and weaknesses. The VoC school draws a broad distinction between liberal economies and CMEs and is particularly well placed to elucidate the functional complementarities between education and training and adjacent institutional spheres. It fails to comprehensively explain the variety of skill regimes within the large group of CMEs, however: why has the Scandinavian development path been so different from the German one? The power resources approach and partisan theory emphasize the role of political struggles over the institutional design of educational institutions. These struggles and political conflicts occur because educational institutions, like welfare state institutions, affect the distribution and redistribution of economic resources. A significant shortcoming of these approaches, however, is their neglect of the institutional context in terms of economic coordination. Partisan theory, at least the classical version of it, essentially assumes that government parties will pursue the same policies in different countries. Taken to its logical extreme, this approach fails to account for how, and by how much, British Conservatives and German Christian Democrats have differed in their education policy. Partisan theory tends to dichotomize between left- and right-wing parties, treating Christian democrats as a middle category between the two.

The rest of this chapter develops a theoretical framework that emphasizes the role of partisan politics and power resources as explanatory factors while at the same time extending and modifying existing theory in three important ways. The first modification, to standard partisan theory, is to argue that political parties not only have preferences with regard to the content of policies, but also with regard to *how the political process should be organized*; that is, which interests should legitimately get access to policy-making. This extension captures a crucial difference between secular conservatives and Christian democrats and helps to explain their different approaches to education policy. The second modification is to give more credence to the *institutional context* and how it modifies the menu of options available to government parties when they pursue reform strategies. While government parties of the same family may have similar policy preferences initially, institutional contexts can change the relative costs and benefits of policy alternatives so as to make some policies feasible and others not. In the third and final modification, I posit that the *long-term balance of power* between partisan forces is more important than the short-term partisan composition of governments, simply because reforming social systems as complex as education systems takes a lot of time and political stamina.

The standard partisan model

I start my argument with a simple and by now fairly common model of how and why political parties differ with regard to their policy preferences. Going back to Hibbs (1977), the expectation is that political parties of the left and the right represent different electoral constituencies with different economic interests. In comparative welfare state research, this leads to the simple hypothesis that parties of the left, representing the economic interests of the lower income classes, will support more redistribution and a larger welfare state, whereas parties of the right will oppose these policies because they would require their constituencies in the upper income classes to pay higher taxes in order to finance the expansion of social policy.

Partisan theory can be and has been applied to the study of education policy (Ansell 2008, 2010; Boix 1997, 1998; Busemeyer 2007, 2009b; Rauh *et al.* 2011; Schmidt 2007; Wolf 2009). In general, and simplifying greatly, the findings that have emerged from this literature support the core claims of the theory (Schmidt 1996): that there are significant differences in policy output between left- and right-wing governments, and that left-wing governments are more likely to increase public spending on and expand access to education. Some of this literature (in particular Ansell 2008, 2010 and Boix 1997, 1998) has focused on the dichotomy between left- and right-wing parties, since these two party families are clearly the political representatives of voters in the lower and upper income strata, respectively.

Rather than formulating hypotheses about specific policies, such as spending, I would like to start with the more general claim that in education policy, political parties differ in how much they support or oppose educational expansion. Parties on the left are expected to promote educational expansion by creating opportunities to participate in education and obtain certificates, especially for those previously excluded from the higher levels of the education system. In contrast, parties on the right, if not outright opposed to educational expansion, are certainly more reluctant to promote it, instead attempting to slow down the general trend of expansion that set in after the Second

World War. I focus here on educational *expansion* instead of spending as such, and not just because Esping-Andersen (1990: 23) famously argued that political actors do not care about "spending *per se.*" More importantly, fostering educational opportunities for those previously excluded from participation in education can be achieved by various means; increasing education spending is just one way to do this, and not necessarily the most effective.

In principle, there are two different strategies by which to expand educational opportunities to previously excluded groups: the first is to expand access to higher levels of education for a wider share of the population, the second to expand the kinds of education more suited to the educational needs of those formerly excluded. The first strategy is associated with conflicts about expanding access to university education, whereas the second centers on the role of VET in the education system as a whole.

This is not simply a matter of choosing between the expansion of VET and higher university education, however. Because of the inherent complexity of the redistributive implications of educational investments, partisan preferences are *prima facie* ambiguous as well. For example, right-wing parties may support the expansion of VET as an educational alternative in order to "divert" the excess demand for educational participation away from higher education and towards other types of education. Furthermore, right-wing parties should have an interest in limiting access to higher education, in order to ensure their educational privileges, but they might be in favor of increasing spending on higher education anyway – as long as access continues to be limited – since such investment will benefit their electoral constituencies (Ansell 2010). The ambiguities are even more pronounced for left-wing parties. It could be expected that these parties will support general and vocational education, the types of education that will directly benefit the educational and labor-market needs of their constituencies (Ansell 2010; Boix 1998). On the other hand, left-wing parties may oppose the creation of separate and potentially dead-end educational tracks for their clientele and instead promote the opening up of access to academic higher education (Busemeyer 2009b). In short, and given these ambiguities, the specific policies supported or opposed by partisan actors will likely depend on the particular institutional context, delimiting the menu of feasible policy options, as I will argue in detail below.

The first obvious problem with the standard partisan approach is that it predicts the existence of *two* worlds of education regimes. Depending on how power is distributed between the left and right, one ideal-typical end of the underlying dimension will be a system with a high level of stratification and little educational mobility, while the opposite end will be a system with high levels of educational and social mobility and little stratification. However, the empirical evidence sketched out above and discussed in greater detail in Chapter 3 clearly confirms the existence of (at least) three different and distinct worlds. To understand the underlying reasons why this is the case is to step beyond simply observing the existence of "three worlds of human capital formation" (Iversen & Stephens 2008; see also Hega & Hokenmaier 2002; Willemse & de Beer 2012) and highlighting the obvious connections to the relative power of Christian democracy and social democracy.

First extension: preferences regarding the political process

The standard model of partisan theory focuses on the preferences of political parties in terms of policy content (which policies they promote or oppose). Because this approach disregards whether parties promote policies in order to get elected or to implement particular policy programs (cf. Müller & Strom 1999), the extension I propose is to think of parties as having not only specific policy preferences but also preferences with regard to *how the political process should be organized*. In particular, political parties and their ideologies may differ on two questions: Which interests should be granted access to decision-making (unions, employers, both, or neither)? And: Which forms of interest mediation between political and economic interests should prevail (pluralist, corporatist, or statist/hierarchical forms of interest mediation)? What is more, government parties can try to use policies as instruments to alter the balance of power between organized interests in the labor-market arena ("policies shape politics"). This expansion of perspective reveals stark differences in the ideological orientation of secular conservatives and Christian democrats.

The prevailing view in comparative welfare state research is that Christian democrats in government do increase levels of social spending and hence are not opposed to the welfare state on principle, as conservatives and liberals might be (Bradley *et al.* 2003; Esping-Andersen

1990; Van Kersbergen 1995; Wilensky 1981). Compared to social democrats, however, Christian democrats promote social policies that are less redistributive and are more transfer- than service-oriented. Thus, Christian democratic party ideology can easily be misunderstood as a middle class-oriented blend of conservatism and social democracy. Kees Van Kersbergen (Van Kersbergen 1995, 1999; Kalyvas & Van Kersbergen 2010) has convincingly argued that Christian democracy should be regarded as an ideology distinct from both social democracy and conservatism; he holds that the crucial difference between Christian democrats and other parties is their particular approach to the political process, which he calls the "politics of mediation" (Van Kersbergen 1999: 356). Historically, Christian democratic parties mobilized using the religious rather than the economic cleavage, so they had to establish procedures of interest mediation between different economic and social interests *within* their party organizations. This is why they ended up promoting interest mediation and "[c]ross-class coalitions" (Van Kersbergen 1999: 356) as a general principle of policy-making. A second important principle of Christian democratic ideology is that of "subsidiarity": delegating decision-making powers to autonomous civil-society associations to the greatest extent possible (Van Kersbergen 1999: 353).

In terms of the categories mentioned above, then, Christian democratic parties are expected to grant access to both employers' and union representatives and to support corporatist forms of interest mediation (Wilensky 1981) for the sake of maintaining cross-class compromise and cooperation. To a certain extent, Christian democratic government parties may pursue policies that seek to stabilize or create cooperation between unions and employers (e.g., passing laws that establish corporatist committees in charge of vocational training). But Christian democratic parties remain fundamentally on the "right" side of the partisan spectrum, meaning that despite their willingness to support cross-class cooperation they can be expected to grant business interests a certain privilege compared to unions. The influence of business interests and the connections between organized business and policy-makers in Christian democratic governments are likely to be very different from those in secular conservative governments, however. Christian democrats may be willing to delegate significant competences to corporatist bodies run by employers' associations and unions, but they expect employers to take over certain public responsibilities as well (Streeck & Schmitter 1985): in Christian democratic ideology, employers are given privileged access in return for their willingness to participate in the production of collective goods, such as vocational training.

Secular conservative parties are thought to differ significantly from Christian democrats in many respects. First of all, they do not subscribe to the principle of cross-class cooperation. Born out of the class conflict between capital and labor, secular conservative parties strive to minimize the influence of the left in general and unions in particular. Their preferred model of interest mediation tends to be pluralistic, based on the free competition of interests, but business interests can still expect a certain level of privileged access. Compared to Christian democrats, secular conservatives put less emphasis on the reciprocity between rights and obligations, perceiving themselves more as representatives of business interests in the policy-making arena than as a political force demanding that business contribute to collective goods. Secular conservatives may also design public policies with the goal of limiting and weakening the influence of unions, whom they consider their political enemy.

Finally, social democratic or socialist parties on the left can be expected to have different preferences with regard to the political process than do right-wing parties. Generalized expectations concerning leftist parties should be formulated in a very careful manner, since there is considerable variation in terms of ideologies across countries *within* the political family of social democracy (Merkel et al. 2006), and since partisan preferences with regard to process also depend on the institutional context (see below); in particular, whether the institutional context offers the opportunity for cross-class compromise. At one extreme, parties on the left are the representatives of the working class in the overarching battle between capital and labor: they give unions privileged access to policy-making, reject cross-class compromise, and are willing to use public policies to limit the influence of business (the pre-Blair Labour Party in the United Kingdom might serve as a rough real-typical example). At the other end, left-wing parties can become active supporters of cross-class compromise, understanding that the political sustainability of the universal welfare state model depends on broad supporting coalitions between different economic classes (Esping-Andersen 1990; Rothstein 1987). I would therefore argue that institutional context matters more in the case of social democratic parties, as a determinant of procedural preferences. The difference between Christian democrats and secular conservatives, by contrast, reflects inherent differences in terms of ideology.

Second extension: the role of institutional context

A look at the impact of institutional context will lead us to the second extension of the standard model in partisan theory. First, however, we must clarify what is meant by "institutional context." Here the concentration is on context in terms of socioeconomic institutions; that is, the prevailing level of economic coordination (Hall & Soskice 2001). As is well known from the VoC literature, high levels of coordination essentially entail a higher degree of cross-class and nonmarket-based cooperation between the organized labor-market interests. On the one hand, this implies differences in the patterns of interest mediation between LMEs and CMEs, as argued above, and shapes partisan preferences and strategies with regard to how the political process should be organized. On the other hand, institutional context also affects the menu of feasible policy options. In other words, economic coordination entails two aspects: one that is concerned with the collective organization – and ultimately also the power resources – of labor-market actors, such as unions and employers; and one that emphasizes the institutional constraints and complementarities.

In general, I posit that high levels of coordination contribute to making VET a sustainable educational choice and a worthwhile alternative to academic higher education for those making their way up the educational ladder. The conventional argument for why this is the case is that coordination allows labor-market actors to make credible long-term commitments to each other (Cusack *et al.* 2006; Finegold & Soskice 1988; Iversen & Soskice 2001). Employees, so the argument goes, demand some kind of insurance before they are willing to invest in occupation- or firm-specific skills, through either a generous welfare state or an employer's credible commitment to lifetime employment (Estévez-Abe *et al.* 2001; Iversen & Soskice 2001). Conversely, employers who invest in skill formation need assurance that employees will stay with the firm beyond the training period, so that the company can recoup its investment (Acemoglu & Pischke 1998).

A slightly different argument I would like to put forward here is that high levels of coordination also have an impact on the content of VET. The participation of employers' associations and labor unions in the design of VET curricula, both in the firm-based part and in the school-based component, ensures that the skills that are produced in the VET sector fit the needs of the employment system. When there is a high match between the skills taught in VET and the skills demanded on the labor market, choosing VET over general academic education becomes attractive, especially for those in the middle strata of the skills distribution. This is because a tight linkage between VET and the employment system enables smooth transitions from education to employment (i.e., low levels of youth unemployment) and increases the payoff on educational investment for those in the lower half of the skills distribution (Breen 2005; Gangl 2003; Wolbers 2007). When VET is not regarded as an educational dead end, but rather as a gateway to relatively attractive positions at the intermediate skill level, it increases the viability and sustainability of VET as a credible alternative to higher education. The existence of a well-developed VET system also changes labor-market structures: instead of the polarization between high-skilled services and low-skilled jobs that is often found in LMEs, CMEs have seen a strong segment of employment at the intermediate skill level (Marsden & Ryan 1990).

The cooperation between unions and employers' associations is a crucial point in the design of VET curricula. At a very general level, employers are expected to demand more specific skills (or at least a broad foundation of vocational skills with a strong specific component), whereas unions tend to favor broad skills. The simple reason for these differences in interest is that unions (and employees) have an interest in maintaining or increasing the labor-market mobility of employees, since labor-market mobility is related to bargaining power (Streeck 1994), whereas employers have an interest in minimizing the mobility of skilled employees (while maintaining the ability to fire the less-skilled ones), since this depresses employees' power to demand higher wages. The compromise that is likely to emerge from these interest-driven bargaining processes over the content of VET is one of occupational profiles that combine broad vocational skills with a firm-specific component. Incidentally, these types of "polyvalent" (Streeck 1996: 141) and yet specific skills have given a competitive advantage to firms engaging in "diversified quality production" (Streeck 1992), meaning high-end manufacturing and similar activities. Coalitions between unions and employers are also important in terms of political influence. Together, unions and employers can lobby policy-makers to continue supporting VET, since this type of education has traditionally been closer to the economic and organizational interests of labor-market actors than has higher education.

In the absence of cross-class coordination, by contrast, the linkage between VET and the employment system is weaker, decreasing the attractiveness of VET as an educational choice because of the less favorable labor-market outcomes. When the content of VET is mostly designed by employers, without the involvement of unions, there is a danger that training content becomes too specific. This decreases the attractiveness of VET from the perspective of employees/young people, because it does not increase labor-market mobility and the potential to invest in transferable skills. Conversely, when the state or the unions are the only ones in charge of designing the skills content, it may become too general and broad, decreasing the attractiveness of VET from the perspective of employers, who demand a certain degree of skill specificity. When unions are in charge of regulating access to training, moreover, they may abuse this position in order to limit the supply of skilled labor, so as to drive up wages (Thelen 2004).

It is important to remember that high levels of coordination as such are not a sufficient explanation for the variety of education and training systems in Western Europe. Although cross-class coalitions between unions, employers, and state actors are common in CMEs, the long-term balance of power between partisan actors remains an important factor. In other words, government parties can and do influence the politics of institutional change by selectively and carefully privileging certain organized interests, even when the general institutional framework may remain corporatist. This consideration of partisan power in corporatist settings implies a crucial change in perspective that distinguishes my approach from the classical power resources and VoC perspectives by building on and extending Thelen's coalitional approach (Thelen 2004; see also Hall & Thelen 2009). Unlike power resources theory, I acknowledge the importance of cross-class coalitions. Unlike the VoC school, I posit that cross-class coalitions may still be partisan in nature.

Third extension: long-term balance of power

Finally, I would like to draw attention to the role of time and timing. A common research design in quantitative studies of the effect of partisan politics on policy output is to include the current partisan composition of governments as an independent variable in regression models of some kind of policy output (cf. Schmidt 1996). Whereas early contributions to the literature were able to identify systematic partisan effects (e.g., Castles 1982, 1989; Schmidt 1982), more recent work has observed a weakening of these effects (Kittel & Obinger 2003; Kwon & Pontusson 2010), which might be explained by the constraining impact of globalization, a general convergence of party positions to the median, or other factors. A further explanation for the disappearance of partisan effects in the short term is the buildup of policy legacies and path dependency over time (Pierson 1994, 1996; Rose & Davies 1994). Thus, even in cases where parties come to government with a clear mandate to change policies, they often find it hard to do so because they need to deal with a large and ever-increasing set of entrenched interests and policy legacies.

In short, timing matters: the intensity of the impact of partisan forces on policy and institutional change is likely to vary across time. In the early phases of path formation, when institutional arrangements are still being established and are not yet fully developed, there is greater room for political agency (Pierson 2000). This means that partisan politics (or the balance of power between political interests) is likely to matter more during critical junctures of historical development.

How can we distinguish periods of path formation from periods of path consolidation, when large-scale change becomes increasingly unlikely? In broad terms, societal and economic development have proceeded alongside and in interaction with welfare state development. During the Industrial Revolution, the welfare state provided insurance against basic risks of health and safety and expanded to cover more and more life risks, such as unemployment and old age. The development of economies went along with a greater demand for education and skills (Goldin & Katz 2008), which led to the expansion of educational opportunities at the higher levels of the education system. The postwar decades in Western Europe were a critical period of path formation, in the sense that access to formerly elitist and closed post-secondary education systems was opened up to meet the increasing demand for education, both from business and from households. We can see from this that path formation occurs when the welfare state expands to address the new social needs and demands that arise from societal and economic development. The specific response of policy-makers to these new demands then depends on the balance of power between partisan interests.

A second point relates to the role of time, but not timing as such. Modern societies are extremely complex social systems. They are not mechanistic but organic in nature, which limits the leeway for policy-makers to influence societal developments or institutional change. Like "institutional gardeners," policy-makers can use their hedge trimmers by changing formal regulations such as laws and decrees. Formal legal change, however, does not directly translate into actual institutional change, because economic or other social actors can react to policy change in a manner that is very different from the policy-maker's original intentions (cf. Streeck & Thelen 2005). To provide a concrete example from the study of education systems: policy-makers can change the formal structure of education systems by creating a new educational pathway, for instance an apprenticeship-training track, but whether this educational pathway is actually accepted by employers and households is an entirely different matter. In open and democratic societies, educational choices are the privilege of individuals and their families. Policy-makers can only indirectly influence these choices, by manipulating the formal structure of educational institutions. Given this state of affairs, educational reform is a long-term project. Education is a central concern to many families. Structural changes in the education system usually need to be implemented over a period of several years, and large-scale change can only be implemented in a stepwise and incremental manner, in order to give individual households time to adjust. To put it another way: attempting to effect large-scale reforms in a short span of time is akin to political suicide and will most likely not succeed.

The upshot of this discussion of time and timing is that my empirical analysis will focus on the role of partisan politics and politico-economic coalitions in the formative years of the postwar decades, when critical decisions about the future development of education and training systems were being made. Futher, instead of paying too much attention to the short-term effects of the current partisan composition of governments, I will concentrate on differences in the long-term balance of power between different countries/regimes, which are expected to be more important for the development of education regimes. Of course, political parties may adopt their policy goals to changing circumstances in the long term. Parties' electoral constituencies can also change, reflecting changes in the social structures of societies. These problems are mediated by the fact that I focus on partisan conflict in the postwar period, which was characterized by tighter linkages between electoral constituencies and their representative parties. Partisan politics in the postindustrial age is more complex, because of the increased importance of value conflicts (Häusermann *et al.* 2013). Still, I would argue that basic differences between leftist and rightist parties that are related to fundamental issues such as inequality and redistribution are also discernible in the contemporary period and are rooted in the material interests and normative considerations of different electoral constituencies, even though these may have changed compared to the industrial age.

Putting the pieces together: hypotheses

The core argument for the following analysis is that different types of politico-economic coalition were responsible for shaping education and training policies during the critical juncture of the postwar decades. As a reminder, the core dimensions of variation are public involvement in education and training on the one hand and institutional stratification on the other (see Figure 1.1). The long-term dominance of one particular party family had an impact on the extensiveness and partisan nature of politico-economic coalitions, since parties have preferences with regard not only to policy content but also to how the political process should be organized. The prevailing institutional context in terms of economic coordination shaped the menu of feasible policy options. These propositions lead us to the following hypotheses/expectations:

Partisan politics in LMEs

In LMEs, cross-class coordination is expected to be largely absent. This also implies little coordination between government and labor-market actors in terms of corporatist forms of interest mediation. The scope of politico-economic coalitions is therefore quite limited, in line with the model of a majoritarian democracy (Lijphart 1999), with governing parties expected to occasionally reach out to friendly organized labor-market interests (unions in the case of left-wing parties and business groups in the case of conservatives), but otherwise governing by majority decision. Government parties from both sides may sometimes aim to expand VET instead of higher education, but they will do so for different reasons: conservatives are hypothesized to promote institutional stratification (i.e., diversion to VET) in order to lower the political pressure to open up access to higher education, while left-wing parties want to promote VET because it serves the educational needs of their core electoral constituency and helps unions to consolidate their membership base. When cross-class cooperation in VET is largely absent (or abolished for political reasons), however, VET will not become a viable and credible alternative to higher education, because it lacks the necessary institutional and political support. Partisan conflict is therefore hypothesized to center largely on the question of access to and financing of higher education in LMEs. Conservative parties are expected to be proponents of an expansion of private financing in order to slow down the expansion of access, and left-wing parties to promote public financing.

Partisan politics and cross-class coalitions in CMEs
Cross-class coalitions and corporatist forms of interest mediation are common in CMEs. Just because actors strive for consensual solutions, however, does not mean that partisan conflict is completely neutralized. Instead, the expectation is that different education regimes will be associated with different partisan cross-class coalitions, depending on the long-term balance of power between partisan forces.

A crucial distinction between conservative and Christian democratic ideology is that the latter actively promotes the formation of cross-class compromise (a "politics of mediation"; cf. Van Kersbergen 1999: 356) and the delegation of public obligations to corporatist decision-making bodies. Despite this, Christian democrats are still expected to favor the interests of organized business and upper-income strata over the interests of unions and workers, such that Christian democratic education policies will promote educational stratification by limiting access to higher education, diverting students from general academics to VET, and supporting segmented secondary school systems. These policies are very similar to conservative policies as far as their content is concerned; the crucial difference between them is related to procedural preferences. The cross-class compromise that Christian democrats encourage converts VET into a viable and credible alternative to academic education, because the institutional and political support for VET ensures that vocational degrees will have a high labor-market value in terms of employment security and wages. The close ties between organized business and Christian democrats mean that preference is given to those kinds of VET that are closer to the needs of employers, privileging firm-based apprenticeship training over school-based alternatives. Christian democrats are also expected to be less eager than conservatives to expand the private financing of education, because the diversion to VET lowers the pressure on the higher-education sector, and public spending on higher education then actually serves the interests of the wealthier sectors of the electorate, who already enjoy privileged access to that sector.

A different constellation is usually seen in CMEs where social democrats have long dominated in government. Unlike conservatives or Christian democrats, social democrats are expected to use any means available to promote educational expansion and mobility. This is primarily expressed by their strong public involvement in the financing and administration of education. Compared to left-wing parties in LMEs, social democratic government parties in CMEs actively support and promote cross-class coordination in the form of macro-corporatism (Rothstein 1987), which is often associated with the formation of formal or informal coalitions between parties in the political arena. The existence of cross-class alliances is hypothesized to contribute to the sustainability of VET as a credible educational alternative. In contrast to countries where Christian democrats dominate, however, countries where social democrats dominate are expected to promote school-based VET that provides broad qualifications and thereby increases the labor-market mobility of VET graduates.

Empirical strategy

The hypotheses and theoretical expectations outlined above will be tested against empirical evidence in the two chapters that follow, using a multi-method approach. One fundamental limitation and challenge in quantitative analyses of education policies is the general lack of good data (see Chapter 3 for a more detailed discussion). For this reason, it seems advisable to follow the advice of Rohlfing (2008) instead of Lieberman (2005): in other words, to start with small-N within-case studies before engaging in large-N statistical analysis. The purpose of the case studies (Chapter 2) is to explore in a relatively open and inductive manner the processes and causal mechanisms that led to the formation of different and distinct historical development paths in Western European education and training systems. At the end of Chapter 2, I restate and refine the theoretical expectations, which will then be analyzed in a broader sample of OECD countries using quantitative methods in Chapter 3.

For the case studies, I have selected the United Kingdom (England), Sweden, and Germany. These are selected as representative or typical cases (Seawright & Gerring 2008: 299) for the different welfare state regimes (Esping-Andersen 1990): liberal, social democratic, and conservative. All three cases had a relatively similar starting point in the years immediately following the Second World War (see Ansell 2010; Baldi 2012; Iversen & Stephens 2008 for a similar argument). They all had segmented and stratified secondary school systems, an elitist higher-education sector, and an existing tradition (even in Sweden) of firm-based apprenticeship and vocational training.

A further argument in selecting cases is that they should each have been dominated by a particular politico-economic coalition for a significant period of time. I therefore have sought a particular combination of outcomes on the dependent variable (education policy) of partisan politics (the independent variable). The primary goal is thus not hypothesis testing in the strict sense, but the illustration of a causal mechanism that links partisan politics to institutional choices, based on a deliberate selection of representative cases. The case selection is straightforward in Sweden and Germany, where social and Christian democrats each dominated governments for long periods of time. The situation is less clear-cut in the case of England, where the balance of power was more evenly distributed between the left and the right until the advent of Margaret Thatcher. There were various reasons, however, for looking at England instead of alternatives such as the United States. During the postwar years, the United States was expanding educational opportunities at the post-secondary level at a much faster clip than European countries. Furthermore, the United States never had anything approaching the UK tradition of apprenticeship training. This restricts the scope of the argument of this and the chapter that follows to Western Europe, as I have argued in the introduction, but

Chapter 3 will show that the core theses hold in a wider set of cases, covering the group of advanced democracies in the OECD world.

The case-selection strategy that I pursue here is somewhat problematic, in that it makes it hard to distinguish between the effects of partisan government in a narrow sense and more general country-specific effects that stem from a particular set of institutions or socioeconomic conditions. In simple words: did Sweden pursue an egalitarian education policy because it was governed by Social Democrats, or did the Social Democrats come to power there because of particular institutional and structural conditions? One way to gain traction in answering this question is to study within-case variation. While it is true that part of the reason these cases were selected is because they are all characterized by the long-term dominance of a particular party family, they do exhibit some changes in government, such as the advent of the social–liberal coalition in Germany in 1969 and that of the bourgeois coalition in Sweden in 1976. Analyzing differences in partisan government *within* cases helps to disentangle partisan effects from more general institutional effects. If institutional effects dominated, I would not observe any significant differences between governments of different partisan stripes within countries. If there *were* significant differences, as well as similarities in partisan ideologies across countries, this would support partisan theory. The empirical reality will most likely be a mix of both. Parties who are in the minority position in the long term (such as Swedish conservatives or German social democrats) will pursue policies different from their dominant predecessors once in government. The policies of these erstwhile minority parties will be similar to those promoted by their partisan brethren in other countries, but they will also reflect the prevailing institutional context. Jensen (2010), for instance, shows that right-wing parties are more cautious in engaging in welfare state retrenchment in the Scandinavian countries, because the welfare state is so popular. If the newly dominant party manages to stay in power for longer periods of time, however, it will become more assertive in implementing its policy program. This is another reason our focus should be on long-term partisan government instead of short-term effects.

2 | The politics of education and training reform
Case studies

In Chapter 1, I developed an analytical framework to explain the variety of education and training systems observed in Western European countries, with implications for the politics of education reform for the larger set of advanced industrial democracies. In brief, my argument emphasizes the importance of partisan power politics as a driving force of policy and institutional change, but adds three extensions to the standard model of partisan theory: the first paying attention to partisan preferences about how the political process should be organized, in addition to preferences related to policy content; the second taking into account the institutional and historical context in which partisan politics play out; and the third focusing on the long-term balance of power between parties rather than on short-term transitory effects.

Based on this framework, I expect to see major differences in the historical development of education and training policies in the United Kingdom, Sweden, and Germany. These cases have been selected as representative or typical (Seawright & Gerring 2008: 299) of the different welfare state regimes (Esping-Andersen 1990), in order to explore the causal mechanisms at work. My study of them recounts the most important policy developments in the three cases since the mid-twentieth century. This is followed by an analytical section in which I compare the takeaways from the case studies to my theoretical expectations.

The United Kingdom

The United Kingdom poses a number of problems compared to the other two cases. For one thing, the partisan balance of power is not as clearly in favor of one particular party family as it is in Germany or Sweden. Labour governed from 1945 until 1951, and then there was a long period of Conservative rule (1951–64). Labour governed again from 1964 until 1970 and from 1974 until 1979, but in both cases had to rely on small majorities or even minorities in Parliament. Conservative dominance was finally asserted during the premiership of Margaret Thatcher after 1979. Overall, then, the partisan balance of power in the postwar decades remained slightly tilted in favor of the Conservatives. Analytically, we must distinguish between effects that are due to the dominance of a particular party family in government (the Social Democrats in Sweden and the Christian Democrats in Germany) and those that result from some unspecified country-specific effect. The case of the United Kingdom is not as clear-cut in that respect as the other two, but it offers the opportunity to distinguish more clearly between partisan and country-specific effects through analysis of the *within-case variation*: changes in government policy after a change in that government's partisan composition.

A second complication (one that is probably causally related to the first) is that until Thatcher, the institutional character of the British economy was more that of a mixed economy than a pure LME (Hall 1992). Repeated but largely unsuccessful attempts to stimulate the economy with Keynesian demand-side policies and manpower planning (Perry 1976) conflicted with the tenacious legacy of a voluntarist and decentralized education system (King 1997). The Thatcher government then finally stripped away the institutional remnants of coordinated capitalism and turned Britain into a role model for neoliberal economic (and education) policies (Graham 1997). Britain's commitment to the path of a liberal skill-formation regime thus happened later than Sweden and Germany's, coming in the 1980s (Fuller & Unwin 2009) rather than the 1970s as in the other two cases.

A third hurdle is that because of its peculiar form of decentralization and devolution, the British polity is moving away from its historical status as a unitary state. Devolution is even more relevant in the case of education than in other policy fields, and the Scottish education system differs from the English one in certain nontrivial aspects. It follows that our case study is mainly concerned with policy development in England and Wales, although I will occasionally speak of the United Kingdom and/or Britain. In any case, the differences between England, Wales, and Scotland seem minor when compared to the other two international cases in the study.

For the purposes of this chapter, policy development in British education and training can be divided into three subperiods: first, the period of postwar consensus on educational expansion and institutional consolidation (1945–64); second, the period of increasing partisan conflict and crisis over the direction of post-secondary educational expansion (1965–79); and third, the period of neoliberal transformation of education and training policy (after 1979).

Postwar consensus and institutional consolidation (1945–1964)

The immediate postwar era in Britain was characterized by a widespread consensus between parties in matters of education policy. The legislative foundation of this consensus was the 1944 Butler Education Act, passed by the wartime coalition government after several years of consultation with societal stakeholders (Chitty 2004: 18). The progressive thrust of the Act was meant to achieve "secondary education for all" by, among other things, abolishing tuition fees for secondary schools. Both Labourites and Conservatives agreed on the desirability of expanding educational opportunities at the secondary level in the 1950s (Gordon *et al.* 1991: 62–4). This consensus was in part based on the fact that the Butler Act remained very vague with regard to the specific institutional design of secondary schools (Chitty 2004: 19). Although the postwar Labour government had instigated large-scale radical change in the British welfare state by establishing the National Health Service, it had remained rather timid with regard to reforming education. The implementation of the Act was largely left in the hands of the Local Education Authorities (LEAs), and Prime Minister Attlee himself did not support the comprehensive schools and favored maintaining public schools (which are, in fact, private schools in British parlance) (Lawton 2005: 49).

Since the Conservative government was even less eager to intervene in local affairs, the education systems had the character of a "national system, locally administered," based on "a benign partnership between central government, local government, and individual schools and colleges" (Chitty 2004: 21). The decentralized and essentially voluntarist character of the education system encouraged great variety in secondary schools, which effectively constituted a tripartite system: the elitist grammar and public schools, the new modern secondary schools, and the technical and trade schools. Access to the more prestigious types of state school was based on a competitive examination at age 11 (called *11-plus*) (Cheung & Egerton 2007: 201).

The Labour Party in opposition was initially divided on the issue. Assigning pupils to different schools on the basis of academic merit was regarded as an advancement over the previous system, where school choice depended on the discretion of teachers and parents (Baldi 2012: 1006). Over the course of the 1950s, however, critics of the tripartite system asserted a growing influence within the Labour Party, particularly after the Crowther Report (1959) and similar sociological research produced evidence that, controlling for academic ability, family background determined access to grammar schools (Baldi 2012: 1006–7; Gordon *et al.* 1991: 72; Lawton 2005: 57).

The climate of educational expansion penetrated both secondary and higher education. As in other countries, access to higher education was limited to a small minority of about 5 percent of a typical age cohort (Ansell 2010: 197), but public pressure to allow more young people to enter higher education mounted over the course of the 1950s, especially within the traditionally Conservative electoral constituencies in the upper middle class (Ansell 2010: 197). In 1963, a committee led by Lord Robbins recommended that access to higher education be opened to all who could benefit from it (Cheung & Egerton 2007: 196). The Conservative government implemented most of the recommendations from the Robbins Report and continued to support higher education institutions with public grants. According to Ansell (2010: 198), this seemingly progressive policy in fact benefited the Conservatives' electoral constituencies in the upper income classes (see also Gordon *et al.* 1991: 79), because even after the expansion, only a small minority of the relevant age cohort (about 15 percent) would enroll in higher education and therefore benefit from the public subsidization of universities.

VET remained disconnected from the general education system. The curricula of most secondary schools were still committed to a liberal arts education in preparation for university studies. The technical schools catered to those with low academic abilities and were oriented towards vocational skills. Unlike the German *Hauptschule*, however, they covered only a small share of the student population (about 4 percent of the secondary age group in 1958; see Chitty 2004: 25), so that there was effectively little to no vocational education in the general education system.

This made the matter of training primarily the responsibility of the economic actors themselves. As in other European countries, Britain had a tradition of apprenticeship training going back to medieval times (Perry 1976). The institutional setup of apprenticeship in the United Kingdom remained quite traditional until well into the postwar period: advancing from an apprentice to a journeyman was based not on the passing of externally administered exams, but simply on time served (Gospel 1994: 508–9). British unions are organized as crafts unions; that is, as unions of skilled workers in a particular craft or occupation. This differs from the industry-based organization of unions in Germany (Thelen 2004: 98–100). The nature of the UK system led unions there to develop an interest in limiting the supply of skilled workers so as to drive up wages: they used apprenticeship training as a gateway to skilled labor markets and enforced a strict separation between skilled and unskilled workers (Thelen 2004: 105–6). This is why the traditional system of apprenticeship training came under pressure in the postwar period, as demographic developments increased the need for more training opportunities. Critics also lamented the narrow nature of training, which was tied to a particular occupation and lacked reference to common standards (Gospel 1994: 508–9). The unions' hold on apprenticeship training also led employers to look for new ways to limit the role of skilled labor in production processes and effectively prevented the emergence of a lasting cross-class compromise on matters of training during the period of industrialization in the late nineteenth century (Thelen 2004: 107).

Despite the more contentious nature of training policies in Britain, unions and employers actually managed to come to a consensus immediately after the Second World War, when a joint report by the British Employers' Confederation and the Trades Union Congress (TUC) recommended that National Joint Apprenticeship Councils be established (Perry 1976: 49). Unions supported the establishment of collective institutions, but at the same time were careful to preserve their strong bargaining position in controlling access to skilled labor markets (Perry 1976: 60). British employers (as well as policy-makers) were increasingly worried about deficiencies in competitiveness compared to continental European countries such as France and Germany, and the issue of training and "manpower" policy was believed to be crucial in dealing with these problems (Corina 1975: 194). Nonmarket forms of coordination among employers were never as strongly developed in the

The politics of education and training reform

United Kingdom as in Germany, since British employers' associations remained voluntary in nature, in contrast to the statutory character of German Chambers of Industry and Commerce. But multi-employer bargaining in matters of wage policy was nevertheless common during the postwar decades, and it is believed to have been a crucial supporting factor for apprenticeship training (Gospel 1995: 41).

Demographic factors and the threat of youth unemployment continued to exert pressure on economic actors and policy-makers to reform the training system in the 1950s and early 1960s. The government refrained from intervening in industrial training at first; its position had been supported and confirmed by the report of the Carr Committee in 1958, and training was believed to fall under the purview of unions and employers (Perry 1976: 66). The ensuing debate, however, led to a transformation of the general political climate and government policy within just a couple of years.

In 1964, the Conservative government passed the Industrial Training Act, based on broad support from unions and employers, as well as the Labour Party in opposition (Perry 1976: 108, 125), reflecting a "general economic, social and ideological climate" (Evans 1992: 191) more favorable to expanding the role of the central state in manpower planning. The Act was considered "one of the largest-scale attempts at structural change in Britain" (Corina 1975: 195). It led to the establishment of a number of Industrial Training Boards (ITBs; 27 in total by 1969; see Perry 1976: 175), which were in charge of administering and financing firm-based training. To this end, ITBs were empowered to impose a training levy on firms in their own economic sector, the revenues of which would be used to subsidize out-of-firm training courses and the Boards' activities in devising training standards and supplying training materials. As bureaucratic organizations with a significant degree of autonomy from the government, ITBs developed their own practices over time, such that levy practices "became extremely variable across Boards, growing up in a haphazard way" (Corina 1975: 197).

If we disregard the implementation of the 1964 Act and look only at the formal set of institutions it created, we can see that the British training system after 1964 exhibits many characteristics of collective skill-formation systems (Busemeyer & Trampusch 2012), and in fact surpasses what Germany achieved a couple of years later with the enactment of the Federal Law on Vocational Education and

Training (the *BBiG*). Employers in Germany successfully fought against the introduction of a training levy in the 1970s, for example, because they feared that it would bring too much state intrusion (Busemeyer 2009c: 79–106). Nevertheless, the British ITB system retained a certain voluntaristic character in the sense that the Boards could not force firms to provide training, but were restricted to supporting the training efforts of individual firms through subsidies, the provision of training material, or the organization of out-of-firm training courses. The reform also did not establish a binding national framework of qualifications or occupational profiles, as happened in Germany – or much later, at the end of the 1980s, in the United Kingdom.

The case of the 1964 Training Act remains highly interesting, because it shows that policy-makers and economic actors in the United Kingdom did attempt to build up collective institutions in skill formation (as was the case in the United States at an earlier moment in its history; see Martin 2006). The British efforts to establish a collective skill-formation system were based on cross-class compromise between unions and employers, as well as between the Conservative government and Labour opposition. The partisan consensus proved to be short-lived, however, as will become clear in the next section. Furthermore, the pluralistic and fragmented character of industrial relations (their low degree of nonmarket coordination) prevented the short-term consensus between unions and employers from becoming sustainable in the long run. This shows the importance of the institutional context in terms of economic coordination as a constricting factor of partisan politics: as the ideological orientations of political parties rooted in class conflict became more influential in the years that followed, the partisan consensus in education policy proved to be transitory.

Increasing partisan conflict and crisis (1964–1979)

Starting in the mid-1960s, the postwar consensus on education policy, economic policy, and social policy came under increasing pressure, which was further aggravated by the massive economic crises of the 1970s and their high levels of unemployment and inflation. When Labour returned to power in 1964, one of the first actions of the new education minister, Anthony Crosland, was to issue Circular 10/65, which put more pressure on LEAs to establish comprehensive schools.

Despite his reputation as a "pace-setter" (Gordon *et al.* 1991: 82), Crosland granted LEAs considerable leeway in implementing the governmental directive. By this time, a bottom-up movement that favored comprehensivization based on "a coalition of parents, local politicians, and grassroots opinion" (Gordon *et al.* 1991: 189) was gaining momentum. As comprehensive schools spread more widely, especially in Labour-controlled LEAs, teachers at comprehensive schools became more influential within the Labour Party and contributed to transforming the party's formerly ambiguous stance on the issue into a more assertive position of support (Fenwick 1976: 114–15).

The issue of whether to promote comprehensive schools was now splitting the Conservatives (Knight 1990: 72). Centrist moderates such as Edward Boyle were supportive, because of comprehensive schools' general popularity. Margaret Thatcher, however, was radically opposed to comprehensivization. When she came into power as minister of education with the change of government in 1970, one of her first actions was to rescind Circular 10/65, but this did not stop the expansion of comprehensive schools (Fenwick 1976: 147; Gordon *et al.* 1991: 193). One obvious indication of the breaking up of the partisan consensus on education reform was the so-called "Black Papers," published beginning in the late 1960s by a group of Conservative educationalists representing the "Establishment Tories" (Ansell 2010: 199). The Black Papers criticized certain aspects of comprehensive education and the general expansion of access to higher education (Lawton 2005: 85).

Perhaps this is one of the reasons why Labour acted more cautiously and refrained from enacting more large-scale reforms once it was back in government in 1974. According to Lawton (2005: 96), the period of Labour government between 1974 and 1979 must be regarded as an "education failure": "[Prime Minister] Wilson seemed to be uninterested in the details of school education; [Prime Minister] Callaghan was interested, but adopted a technicist, unsocialist stance, neglecting to consider the importance of education for society as a whole rather than simply concentrating on the needs of industry." In 1976, Prime Minister James Callaghan gave a famous speech at Ruskin College at Oxford University that is widely regarded as a "turning point" in British education policy (Lawton 2005: 91), because it marked "the end of the period of educational expansion" (Chitty 2004: 44) and contained a challenge for schools to provide more skills that were directly relevant to industry. In reality, however, the ensuing "Great Debate" on education reforms produced a large number of reports and White Papers, but little concrete policy output until the advent of the Thatcher government (Gordon *et al.* 1991: 95–6).

The Labour government of the 1960s also introduced a binary system of higher education institutions: "an 'autonomous' sector consisting mainly of old and new universities and colleges of advanced technology (which acquired university status in 1966–7); and a 'public' sector under local authority control and represented by the leading technical colleges and the teacher-training colleges, to be known in future as colleges of education" (Chitty 2004: 164). The Labour government set up "30 polytechnics intended to provide advanced vocational education and respond to local labor market and industrial research needs" (Cheung & Egerton 2007: 196). Lord Robbins, who a couple of years earlier had forcefully advocated the expansion of access to higher education, expressed concern about this new Labour policy at a conference in 1965:

> I just can't understand what has happened. Here you have a Labour government which is attempting, for good or bad, to introduce the comprehensive principle into the schools, which I think is the right thing to try to do provided that it is done with good sense and prudence. At the same time they are deepening the existence of lines of division in higher education and actually announcing as a matter of policy, which has never been announced before, that these divisions are to be permanent. They are making the system more hierarchical than ever before. (Cited in Gordon *et al.* 1991: 240; see also Chitty 2004: 164)

From a redistributive perspective, however, the Labour policy of promoting vocational education at the tertiary level made sense. Instead of expanding academic universities, which catered to children of the upper income classes, the new type of higher education institution could potentially attract new groups of students from more disadvantaged backgrounds. What is more, the new polytechnics would be placed under the direct control of LEAs, whereas the traditional universities remained largely autonomous, giving state actors less control over their admissions policies. The price for this differentiation was, of course, that polytechnics were regarded as "subordinate institutions" compared to the traditional universities (Gordon *et al.* 1991: 241).

The Labour government of the 1960s was also responsible for establishing and developing further the ITB system (Evans 1992: 208). Critics of the system grew louder towards the end of the 1960s, after ITBs had been set up for most economic sectors (with the notable exception of banking and finance). Small firms in particular chafed under the levy-grant system (Perry 1976: 273). Once the Conservatives took over, they commissioned a review of the ITBs, which together with the related Green Paper actually recommended the wholesale abolishment of the levy-grant system (Perry 1976: 285), as could be expected from a business-friendly Conservative government. The Confederation of British Industry (CBI), on the other hand, preferred to keep the ITB structure as the "lesser of two evils," since unions had been pressing for a more centralized approach to training policy for a long time, and with increasing success (Perry 1976: 292). As a consequence, the 1973 Employment and Training Act retained the levy-grant system in principle but made it much easier for firms to opt out. More specifically, "the criterion for exemption [from the levy-grant scheme] was a firm's training activity measured in terms of its own needs; and only if these were deemed not to have been met would a liability for a levy arise" (Perry 1976: 301). Given this ability to define their own needs, individual firms could more or less decide by themselves whether to participate in the scheme or not, causing the levy-grant system to be "effectively abandoned" in 1973 (Lee 1989: 158). The Act also established the Manpower Services Commission (MSC), fulfilling long-held demands by unions for a more centralized approach to training policy (Evans 1992: 18) and resulting from the CBI finally coming around to lending its support (Perry 1976: 301).

Another major change in the British training system was the decline of traditional apprenticeship training. This change, at least in the beginning, happened not as a consequence of policy-making, but due to structural changes in the economy. The decline of traditional manufacturing and the rise of the service economy led to a severe downfall in the number of apprenticeship places, from 218,000 in 1970 to 73,000 in 1985 (Lee 1989: 159). Union attempts to limit access to the skilled labor market and drive up wages triggered adversarial reactions by employers and the government (Lee 1989: 159). As wage-bargaining institutions became increasingly fragmented in character, moreover, the wages of apprentices began to approach those of unskilled employees, making employers less willing to invest in the training of young workers (Marsden & Ryan 1990, 1991). Confronted with high levels of youth unemployment, the newly founded MSC started sponsoring specific labor-market programs such as the Youth Opportunities Programme (YOP). These would be massively expanded in the 1980s.

In hindsight, the 1970s can be regarded as the onset of a critical juncture. This had less to do with Callaghan's Ruskin speech, however, than with the changes that happened in the field of training policy: the effective abandonment of the short-lived collectivist levy-grant scheme in 1973, the decline of traditional apprenticeship training, and the setup of publicly sponsored labor-market programs to deal with youth unemployment in a voluntarist framework. All of these trends would become much more pronounced in the 1980s.

Neoliberal transformation of education and training policy (1979–1997)

As far as general schooling goes, the 1988 Education Reform Act (ERA) is widely regarded as a "historically significant" milestone, "because it represents the culmination of a break with the consensus politics of education which had prevailed from 1944 to 1979" (Lawton 1992: 59–60). The ERA fundamentally changed the role of LEAs by shifting "power away from LEAs to the central authority, contrary to the established tradition of avoiding too much centralized control" (Lawton 1992: 47). In the old system, "[c]ontrol over the content of education was left, instead, in schools in the hands of head teachers, who in turn tended to leave what went on in the classroom to individual teachers" (Ainley 2001: 458). Based on the general mistrust of public administrators and officials common in neoliberal ideology, the ERA was aimed at centralizing control over the provision of education on the one hand and maximizing opportunities for choice by strengthening the role of consumers (in this case, parents and students) on the other (Gingrich 2011). The result was the emergence of a more complex governance structure (Ainley 2001). The Act also created a new, privileged class of "grant-maintained" schools, which were funded directly from the central government and operated independently of the local control of LEAs. Grammar schools (and former grammar schools) were overrepresented in the group of schools that applied for this new status (Gingrich 2011: 138–9).

The Conservative government also committed to deeply transforming the higher education system. Williams considers the period between the end of the Second World War and the advent of the Thatcher government the "golden age" of British universities, because they then enjoyed a considerable degree of autonomy and were generously financed by public funds (Williams 2004: 243). The early years of the Thatcher government saw massive cuts in spending on higher education, and the government used the purse strings to effect changes in the universities (Williams 2004: 244). As the share of core funding via maintenance grants from the central government fell from 70 percent in the 1960s to just over 30 percent in the mid-1990s (Cheung & Egerton 2007: 200), the universities turned to new sources of revenue, such as research contracts, short courses, and conferences, as well as student fees. These fees, however, were initially still paid by the central government and administered through the local authorities (Cheung & Egerton 2007: 200).

Changes in the funding mechanism fueled competition between universities for students and research funding. As student fees became a more important source of revenue, universities could effectively increase their funding by admitting more students, which led to "an explosive expansion of student numbers" (Williams 2004: 247) in the late 1980s and early 1990s (Mayhew *et al.* 2004: 66). After the ERA of 1988 upgraded the status of polytechnics, the 1992 Further and Higher Education Act finally abolished the binary structure of the system by putting the former polytechnics and universities under the same funding scheme, taking control over the former polytechnics away from local authorities (Cheung & Egerton 2007: 198). Although the system was now less stratified in formal and legal terms, a *de facto* hierarchy of higher education institutions quickly developed, which was much more pronounced than before and was determined by the relative successes of institutions in attracting good students and research funding (Cheung & Egerton 2007: 199). Responding to the large increase in student numbers in the early 1990s, the government introduced a cap on the maximum number of students to be admitted in 1994/95 (which was removed again in 2001/02; Mayhew *et al.* 2004: 69). This is a nice example of partisan differences in the promotion of educational expansion: the Conservative government initially expanded access to higher education, but then restricted it once a critical threshold had been reached. The (New) Labour government, in turn, abolished that restriction.

The Conservative government fundamentally transformed vocational training policies as well, although some changes had begun in the 1970s. The Thatcher government, however, decisively and deliberately cleared away the institutional remnants of coordinated capitalism and collective approaches to skill formation in particular, and thus firmly consolidated the British development path as a liberal skill regime. Youth unemployment remained persistently high in the early 1980s, which persuaded the government to keep the MSC alive for the moment (Evans 1992: 45). But instead of reviving the collective ITB scheme, the Thatcher government sought to abolish the training boards (Finn 1987: 135) and expand training measures, with a strong focus on fighting youth unemployment. The general aim of Conservative training policy was to minimize the role of unions by undercutting the traditional apprenticeship system in particular, as well as by getting rid of the institutional legacy of collective skill-formation institutions in order to give individual employers more flexibility to make their own decisions about training (Dingeldey 1996; Evans 1992: 152, 209; King 1993: 215).

The MSC, which was established in 1973 as a genuinely tripartite institution, with equal participation of unions, employers, and state actors, was increasingly used by the Conservatives as a labor-market agency to sponsor programs for unemployed youth (Evans 1992). With its New Training Initiative (NTI), the MSC initially proposed a collective approach to solving the problem of youth unemployment. The government's version of the NTI, published as a White Paper in 1981, strengthened the workfare component by threatening to withdraw benefits to youths who did not accept the training opportunities offered by the MSC's programs (Finn 1987: 154–5). The YOP, mentioned above, had by this time become quite unpopular with youths, because it suffered from problems in the quality of training. Nevertheless, a tripartite task force at the MSC proposed to introduce a new version of the YOP in 1982 – the Youth Training Scheme (YTS) – which was accepted and supported by the government as a concession to unions and employers (Finn 1987: 158). The YTS provided employers with funds to train people under the age of 18 for one year (this was extended to two years in 1986), guaranteeing a period of thirteen weeks of off-the-job training (seven weeks in the second year). Area Manpower Boards (AMBs) under the auspices of the MSC were responsible for administering and monitoring in-firm training, but the actual provision of training was outsourced to a number of training providers. These could be individual employers, but were more often groups of employers, further colleges of education, or commercial training companies. The number of youths participating in the YTS in the 1980s and the sum of public funds devoted to it were significant, although not as high as in the German apprenticeship system (Ryan & Unwin 2001). At the peak of its power, in 1986, the MSC had a budget of more than £2 billion, of which about £850 million was spent on the YTS (Evans 1992: 83). Indeed, by some measures it proved a successful short-term remedy for youth unemployment: an estimated 60 percent of trainees either stayed with their initial training sponsor or found employment elsewhere (Lee 1989: 161).

But the scheme was heavily criticized by unions and the youths themselves. In 1985, about 200,000 pupils in over sixty towns protested against the YTS and the proposal to make it compulsory (Finn 1987: 182). One widely uttered criticism of the scheme was its focus on quantity of training, instead of quality. While the MSC and its AMBs were formally in charge of monitoring, these organizations did not in fact have the necessary administrative capacities to effectively monitor the implementation of the scheme on the ground (Finn 1987: 175). Neither were there any clearly defined standards on the content of training to be provided, because the original MSC task force had pursued a strategy tantamount to "black boxing": "Black boxing meant that what trainees do on work placements is not directly vetted but placed largely at the discretion of the trainee's employer. It is constrained only by agreed 'end-product' criteria which the MSC has found difficult to enforce" (Lee 1989: 166).

The lack of standards resulted in a huge variation in the quality of training provided. At the top of the hierarchy were manufacturing firms, which used the opportunity to replace traditional apprenticeship training schemes with new YTS-sponsored training (Lee 1989: 164). Firms in the service economy were at the low end of the hierarchy, effectively using YTS trainees as a source of cheap labor without formally investing in skill formation ("bogus training") (Lee 1989: 165). All in all, the YTS marked a "watershed in the transition from the employer-led style of apprenticeship to a State-led approach"

(Fuller & Unwin 2009: 413; see also Unwin 1996) in the financing and provision of training as labor-market policy, even though the stated policy goal had been to promote employer involvement and leadership.

The government's strategy to undermine traditional apprenticeship training and replace it with employer-led, but government-sponsored, training schemes started with the YTS scheme and was carried to the next level by the reforms of the late 1980s. The continued electoral success of the Conservatives, coupled with union criticism of the YTS scheme, "ended any government willingness to maintain tripartite links with unions and employers" (King 1993: 226–7) and effectively dissolved the tripartite MSC; it was transformed into a Training Agency within the Department of Employment. In fact, this step was long overdue, because "the MSC had enjoyed a quite anomalous existence during the first decade of the Thatcher government, explicable mainly because it solved problems during a difficult era of transition which other agencies were unable to address" (Evans 1992: 127).

In 1988, the government established Training and Enterprise Councils (TECs, called Local Enterprise Councils in Scotland) as the successors to ITBs. Unlike ITBs, TECs were private companies in charge of both local economic development and vocational training, with the latter often confined to a secondary role (King 1997: 398). TECs were dominated by representatives from industry; neither unions nor other stakeholders such as local authorities had a statutory right to be included. TECs received funding from the central government for training programs and then acted as managing agencies in outsourcing the provision of actual training (King 1993: 232–3). They lacked the power to intervene in firms' training practices, however. Since the voice of organized labor had already been marginalized, firms could "continue with their own training in traditional voluntarist style (advantaged by the weakening of trade unions)" (King 1997: 401). Thus, even though TECs were supposed to be employer-led organizations of self-governance, they very much depended on continued government support (Keep 2006: 51) and represented a less *dirigiste* and more voluntarist approach to training policy (Coffield 1992; Evans 1992: 127, 138).

The government began developing a system of National Vocational Qualifications (NVQs) to make training quality and standards more uniform. Industrial training organizations (ITOs) were created by the state; these were supposed to develop NVQs, but their relationship with the TECs remained unclear, leading to conflicts and competition (Evans 1992: 181). NVQs were awarded by a central body, the National Council for Vocational Qualifications (NCVQ), and later the Qualifications and Curriculum Authority (QCA). The new system reflected an output-oriented and modular approach to training, in the sense that trainees and training firms were free to combine training modules as they pleased and to accumulate qualifications by demonstrating the ability to perform skills as stipulated in the NVQs. This stands in contrast to the occupational principle (*Berufsprinzip*) at the core of the German training system, which values broad training in occupational skills (Pilz 2009: 59–60). The British NVQ system instead allowed employers to pursue a "cafeteria approach" to skill formation (Ryan & Unwin 2001: 110), selecting only those training modules required for the immediate task at hand.

In addition to setting up labor-market programs, the Conservatives also promoted vocational education in the general schooling system, in the spirit of "new vocationalism" (Skilbeck *et al.* 1994; cf. Knight 1990: 151). Without consulting the MSC, the government announced the Technical and Vocational Education Initiative (TVEI) in November 1982, an attempt to increase funding for vocational education in schools for students between the ages of fourteen and eighteen (Finn 1987: 166–7). Vocational skills acquired in a school-based setting were to be certified in the form of General National Vocational Qualifications (GNVQs), which were meant to prepare students to acquire a broader set of vocational skills in an occupational field than were available from the narrower NVQs. Critics interpreted the TVEI as an attempt by the Conservative government to reestablish a quasi-tripartite system: "The independent sector has been strengthened and subsidised through the Assisted Places Scheme, which by 1985 was supporting 20,000 pupils. Within the state sector, an academic elite will be separated from a middle tier doing something like TVEI; and the bottom 40 per cent will be suitably differentiated and offered a curriculum which no doubt will more adequately prepare them for employment, or more realistically for places in the two-year YTS" (Finn 1987: 171).

In 1994, the John Major government engaged in yet another attempt to reform the training system by introducing the successor to YTS (which had briefly been renamed Youth Training, YT), known as

Modern Apprenticeship (MA). MA signaled a certain change in the government's perception of the value of apprenticeship training. The goal was to increase the supply of intermediate level skills at the third level of the NVQ framework, which was supposed to correspond to the level of German apprenticeship training (Steedman 2011: 1) and promote employer involvement in the financing and provision of training (Gospel & Fuller 1998: 5–6). Although MA was deemed to perform better than YTS in terms of completion rates and quality (Gospel & Fuller 1998), the number of young people in high-quality apprenticeships remained low compared to Germany: Ryan & Unwin (2001) have estimated that 13.6 percent of a typical age cohort entered apprenticeship in the United Kingdom in 1998, compared to 62.9 percent in Germany. This means that 0.50–0.67 percent of employees were apprentices in the United Kingdom, compared to 4.42 percent in Germany (Ryan & Unwin 2001: 101).

Consolidation of the liberal skill regime (after 1997)

Despite the consistently high levels of reform, rebranding, and relaunching of training schemes in the 1990s and beyond, the politico-economic and institutional logic behind them remained essentially unchanged after the critical juncture in the mid-1980s (Finegold & Soskice 1988; Gospel & Fuller 1998; Keep 1999; King 1997; Ryan & Unwin 2001: 111). Even the New Labour government did not fundamentally change the basic logic of the system, neither in the general education system nor in training policy (Gleeson & Keep 2004: 58; Keep 2006: 60). The key assumption underlying New Labour's social investment strategy was the idea that public investment in the supply of skills would boost international competitiveness and at the same time help low-skilled individuals to gain access to education and training, lowering social inequality (Keep & Mayhew 2010; Payne & Keep 2011: 1) and redefining the purpose of education in economic terms (Wolf 1998).

As for training policies, the Labour Party had abandoned its commitment to the collective levy-grant scheme shortly before coming into office and instead supported the creation of Individual Learning Accounts (ILAs) (King & Wickham-Jones 1998). Hence, the Labour Party had turned away from collective approaches to skill formation based on cooperation between the organized labor-market interests towards supporting more individualistic and voluntarist instruments such as individual learning subsidies. Although the New Labour government envisaged a somewhat stronger role for unions, it remained committed to "voluntary partnerships," instead of genuine social partnership (Keep 1999: 324), and kept the basic employer-dominated infrastructure of the training market in place. The TECs were replaced with the Learning and Skills Council (LSC) and Local Learning and Skills Councils (LLSCs) in 2001, but employers remained the interest group with the "highest level of representation" in these (Gleeson & Keep 2004: 44).

The focus of training policy continued to be on combating youth unemployment. Shortly after coming to office, Tony Blair initiated a series of initiatives intended to integrate more young people into the labor market. Prominent examples of these were the "New Deal for Young People" program and Foundation Apprenticeships below the level of MAs, which in fact represented a recurrence of the labor-market programs of the 1980s (Ryan & Unwin 2001: 111). Public subsidies were used to sponsor low-quality and lightly regulated training programs for youths; once again, increasing the quantity of training opportunities was more important than addressing quality concerns (Fuller & Unwin 2011: 191). The fundamental structures of the British "training market" (Ryan & Unwin 2001: 107) were left in place, since a multitude of public, private, and semi-private training providers had to compete for public subsidies. It should be mentioned, however, that in 2009 the outgoing Labour government passed the Apprenticeships, Skills, Children and Learning Act, which established the National Apprenticeship Service, an entity designed to convince employers to participate in training, and created an entitlement to apprenticeships for young school-leavers (Steedman 2011: 3).

With regard to general schooling policies, the Labour government continued along the lines set out by the Conservatives, fostering more competition and choice in the education marketplace (Lawton 2005: 134). Political parties are generally expected to differ in their motivations for privatization and decentralization: whereas parties of the right are more inclined to promote market-based reforms for ideological reasons, the left may support decentralization and privatization of education in order to maintain middle-class support and legitimacy for the continued provision of social services in the public or quasi-public domain (Gingrich 2011: 38, 136). Whatever the reason, New Labour largely accepted the principles of market-based reforms, renaming the grant-maintained schools created by the Conservatives in the 1980s "foundation schools." The new administration expanded the powers of central government to enforce the national curriculum and school inspections (Bache 2003: 303, 305), making the role of LEAs even more circumscribed. It also established "academies," a new type of school that was still publicly funded but could attract additional private sponsors and was free from the governance and regulation of LEAs. Academies were initially set up in poor neighborhoods to provide educational opportunities for disadvantaged children (Gingrich 2011: 142). Once the coalition of Conservatives and Liberal Democrats came to power, however, a new Academies Act was passed in 2010 that significantly expanded the number of academies in order to promote the more general process of decentralization and privatization (Taylor-Gooby & Stoker 2011: 9, 11), even though public opinion, and that of teachers' unions in particular, was generally critical of these reforms (Hatcher 2011).

Significant changes also occurred in the financing of higher education, but these were entirely path-dependent; that is, they reinforced the character of the English system as a liberal skill regime. In 1998, the Blair government decided to allow universities to charge tuition fees of up to £1000 per year (in 2004, this was increased to £3000). This increase in the private share of financing was accompanied by an expansion of subsidies (grants and loans) to low-income families (Harrison 2011: 452), softening the blow. Most importantly, the Blair government adopted the goal of increasing the enrollment rate in higher education to 50 percent of an age cohort (Ansell 2010: 200–1). This indicates that VET as an educational alternative was officially written off by a Labour government that was instead eager to expand access to academic higher education for children with disadvantaged backgrounds. This dynamic continued even more forcefully after the change in government; the coalition government of Conservatives and Liberal Democrats passed a motion in 2010 allowing universities to charge tuition fees of up to £9000 per year. This brought the share of private spending on education in the United Kingdom to the same level as found in the United States (OECD 2012: 257).

The coalition government tried to resuscitate apprenticeship training. Appealing to the "beauty of craft skills" (Fuller & Unwin 2011:

196), the new education minister Michael Gove set out to secure a central place in the government's agenda for the promotion of apprenticeship training (Payne & Keep 2011: 10). As has been argued by Fuller & Unwin 2011: 200), "apprenticeship training as a pathway for young people is astonishingly under-utilised in the UK despite the policy rhetoric and investment afforded to it over the past few years." In 2008/09, about 5 percent of 16- to 18-year-olds were in apprenticeships (and most of them in less ambitious level-2 qualifications; cf. Fuller & Unwin 2011: 200; Payne & Keep 2011: 13), compared to close to 50 percent in countries such as Denmark, Germany, and Switzerland. In line with Conservative policies of the 1980s, the new coalition government has continued the "employer-led" approach to training (Fuller & Unwin 2011: 202), meaning that there is no strong push to organize a cross-class compromise on training that would include a strong voice for unions. The new government allocated public funds to promote apprenticeship training, but according to Payne & Keep (2011: 10), the sums are "relatively small beer" compared to the investments in YTS in the 1980s. Because of this, the government has appealed to employers "mainly through exhortation and voluntary pledges" (Payne & Keep 2011: 27) to promote investment in skills, maintaining the British voluntarist tradition in training policies. The much-debated Richard Review of Apprenticeships has adopted a similar tactic, by arguing that "[t]he solution lies in shifting the power over designing and developing apprenticeship qualifications to employers" (Richard 2012: 7). The 2011 Education Act by the coalition government rescinded the entitlement of young people to an apprenticeship or other qualification that had been introduced in the 2009 Act (Steedman 2011: 3).

All of this is further evidence that after the critical juncture of the mid-1980s, the British system became firmly committed to the path of a liberal skill regime, largely because "the vast bulk of employers have to date been unwilling to support the development of a vibrant, high-quality workbased route for new entrants to the workforce" (Payne & Keep 2011: 13; see also Steedman 2011). The distinguishing feature of this regime is a market-based approach to the provision of education and training, allowing individual employers a large degree of flexibility to define the content and standards of training. The system also promotes competition for public funding among a variety of training providers (Steedman 2011: 4). In contrast to Germany, where firms have integrated training into their regular work processes, the large majority of British training providers are companies or colleges specialized in supplying out-of-firm training. The role of unions in the governing bodies of the British training system is marginal. One consequence of this is that NVQs are narrow in scope, since each employer or group of employers can have its individual training programs certified as an NVQ (Keep 1999: 334–5). Even though the dominant policy approach of the last thirty years in the United Kingdom has been to promote employer leadership in training policy, employers there are confined to "a subordinate, supportive role as recipients of public subsidy and delivery agents for an ever-growing list of schemes the government has designed for them with little or no real employer input" (Keep 2006: 56). British employers take on less responsibility for the training of young people than do German employers, but they continue to have influence over government policies and the design of vocational qualifications – a regime that Gleeson & Keep (2004: 50) call "voice without responsibility."

Sweden

In many ways, Sweden and its universal welfare state represent a counter-model to the liberal British system. Comparative welfare state research puts the social democratic welfare state at the opposite end of the spectrum from the liberal model (Esping-Andersen 1990). When it comes to education policy, however, there are some interesting parallels between the two cases, which also distinguish them from the German development path. As above, I divide the reconstruction of the process of policy development in the Swedish education system into three subperiods: first, the period of the construction of the comprehensive education system (1945–75); second, the period of consolidation (1975–90); and third, the period of reform in general schooling (after 1990). This attempt at periodization would seem to imply a significant degree of reform and transformation, but the Swedish system was actually much less prone to constant attempts at reform and transformation than the British case. The basic institutional features of the system were established by the early 1970s and have since remained remarkably stable (Arnesen & Lundahl 2006).

The construction of the comprehensive education system (1945–1975)

Immediately after the Second World War, the Swedish education system was still as elitist and segregated as most other European education systems at the time: "Most children only received a six- or seven-year education, which provided them with basic skills in counting, reading and writing. Secondary and higher education were reserved for a minority, which typically came from the wealthier classes and aimed at forming an elite" (Hudson & Lidström 2002: 34; see also Hickox & Lyon 1998: 32). Only 5 percent of a typical age cohort passed the *Studentexamen* required for university admission (Härnqvist 1989: 18). Over the ensuing decades, the old elitist system was transformed into a comprehensive education system with the goal of eliminating educational inequalities and opening up access to higher levels of education. This "Nordic model of education" was considered an integral component of the "Nordic welfare state" (Antikainen 2006: 240) and was very much tied to the political dominance of social democracy (Antikainen 2006: 240, cf. also Aasen 2003; Wiborg 2010).

Even though the balance of power favored the left, the educational reforms of the postwar period were based on a broad consensus between the major political stakeholders. Crucial coalitions had been formed in the 1930s in both the political and the labor-market arenas, following a long period of industrial conflict: in 1933, the Swedish Social Democrats (SAP) and the Agrarian Party formed a "red–green" coalition, which became a crucial driving force behind the universal welfare state model (Manow & Van Kersbergen 2009: 27; Wiborg 2010). In 1938, the leading organizations of trade unions (Landsorganisationen i Sverige, LO) and employers' associations (Svenska Arbetsgivareföreningen, SAF) passed the historic Saltsjöbaden or Basic Agreement, which led to the institutionalization of class compromise and is considered to be a historical turning point in labor-market relations (Ball & Larsson 1989: 3–4). These far-reaching agreements between the major political stakeholders set the tone for the predominant style of policy-making in the postwar period – one that was consensus-oriented, and in fact "positivist-rationalist": "Parliamentary commissions were established to undertake a careful collection of views, evidence and research, to initiate investigations and experiments and canvass opinions. Commission reports were then subject to widespread consultation with interested groups" (Ball & Larsson 1989: 10). The consensual and rationalist character of policy-making was accompanied by the emergence of a broad cross-class coalition in support of reform, under the ideological and political leadership of the Social Democrats (Aasen 2003: 110; Hickox & Lyon 1998: 27). The coalition included the major labor-market actors (LO, SAF, and the white-collar union Tjänstemännens Centralorganisation, TCO) and most of the major political parties (Ball & Larsson 1989: 7).

When the Social Democrats came to power in the 1930s, educational reform was not particularly high on their agenda; other economic and social problems were considered to be more pressing (Paulston 1968: 10, 60). Members of the working class did not care much about secondary schools at the time, since these were regarded as the domain of the upper and middle classes (Paulston 1968: 62). After the Second World War, however, education rose to the top of the reformers' agenda. The process of rational policy-making had already started during the war, with the establishment of the Expert School Committee in 1940, whose majority recommendation was to maintain the segregated and differentiated school system (Paulston 1968: 95). In the ensuing political debate, the SAP came out as the strongest supporter of comprehensive schooling; the Liberals were less supportive and the Conservatives were openly opposed (Paulston 1968: 95). The Agrarian Party had sided with the Conservatives in this question before 1932, but now changed its position to become the SAP's main ally: "Because of the plight of rural education at the war's end and its many fundamental problems caused by the very nature of a dual system of education, the farmers in general warmly concurred with the sentiment for longer common schooling but, as usual, balked at the thought of increased costs" (Paulston 1968: 96).

Another committee was established in 1946: the Political School Commission. In contrast to the Expert School Committee, the membership of this group came from the major political parties (Paulston 1968: 109) and was thus well placed to come up with a viable political solution to the school reform debate. The Commission submitted its report in 1948, recommending that compulsory schooling be extended to nine years and that comprehensive schools be introduced at the secondary level (Paulston 1968: 113). This was the starting point for

The politics of education and training reform

the decades-long process of constructing the comprehensive education system, setting in motion a period of cautious and local experimentation with the new comprehensive schools (Härnqvist 1989: 20). Following these experiments, legislation in 1962 introduced the nine-year comprehensive basic school (*grundskola*) as the standard. By this time, comprehensive schools had already spread significantly, to cover about a third of the compulsory school population (Härnqvist 1989: 20). There was isolated but sometimes vocal opposition against the introduction of comprehensives from grammar-school teachers and the Conservative Party in the 1950s, but it remained ineffective (Husén 1965: 182, 186–7; Lundahl 1990: 163; Paulston 1968: 128; Rothstein 1996: 160). The move towards comprehensivization was supported by a number of popular movements, such as the Workers' Educational Association (ABF) and trade unions. Their goal was to eliminate educational inequalities both between economic classes and between urban and rural areas (Hudson & Lidström 2002: 35). The popular support for the comprehensive education system – also expressed in surveys of public opinion (Husén 1965: 187) – was so widespread that it is now regarded as a "self-evident consequence of society's democratization and the development of the welfare society" (Hudson & Lidström 2002: 35).

The introduction of the nine-year *grundskola* was only the first step towards the full comprehensivization of the system, however. The next was to overcome the traditional tracking of students into different types of school at the upper-secondary level. Until the reform of upper-secondary education in 1969, the traditional grammar school (*Gymnasium*) existed alongside a number of technical, commercial, and trade schools with a more vocational orientation (Härnqvist 1989: 25). The 1969 reform integrated the various parts of upper-secondary education into one comprehensive school, the *Gymnasieskola* (Härnqvist 1989: 26). The obvious purpose of this reform was to reduce the distinction between academic and vocational education in order to promote educational mobility. But the institutional legacy of the old system can be recognized in the structure of the new one, in which three- to four-year academic programs, the "vestiges of the traditional university entrance studies formerly provided by the gymnasium" (Opper 1989: 140), were run in parallel with a number of two-year academic and vocational programs. The upper-secondary education system conferred about 80 to 100 final qualifications in different occupational fields (Busemeyer 2009a: 392; Opper 1989: 140–1), signaling a relatively high degree of vocational specificity. One crucial difference from the German system was that all upper-secondary programs in Sweden, in principle, allowed students to continue studying at the tertiary level (Opper 1989: 141), a clear expression of the social democratic goal of promoting educational mobility.

The 1969 reform, which came into force in 1972, was a critical point in the history of VET in Sweden. It firmly established the priority of school-based training over other forms. But the path towards school-based VET was by no means the only one the country could have taken, even if apprenticeship training in Sweden may never have had the same relevance as it did in Germany (or the United Kingdom, for that matter). In the critical period of the 1930s, when the foundations of the welfare state were laid, the governing coalition of Social Democrats and farmers also delved into the field of VET policy; the ruling coalition wanted to expand state financial support for apprenticeship training in order to prevent youth unemployment (Nilsson 1983: 33). Both employers and unions in this era were against increased state involvement in matters of apprenticeship training, albeit for different reasons. Because of their opposition, the state itself set up and financed a number of vocational schools, particularly in areas of the country where unemployment was high (Nilsson 1983: 33). The government decided to expand the number of regional workshop schools following recommendations from a parliamentary commission in 1937; these "remained the backbone of the vocational school system for 30 years, especially during the 1950s" (Nilsson 1983: 34), until they were replaced by integrated upper-secondary schools. By the early 1960s, 6,700 students were enrolled in 38 vocational schools (Nilsson 1983: 34). According to Lundahl (1997: 93), the total number of students in state-sponsored vocational schools was actually as high as the number of apprentices in 1945 (about 10,000). As in Germany, employers and unions had successfully lobbied for the establishment of a national board for apprenticeship training and were strongly involved in the administration of the training system between 1944 and 1970, although the system was on a smaller scale than that in Germany (Crouch 1992: 38; Nilsson 2011; Rothstein 1996: 103). The number of apprentices declined significantly after 1945, however, so that by twenty years later they totalled about 2,000, while enrollment in vocational schools had by then expanded to 75,000 (Lundahl

1997: 93). The strong increase in enrollment in vocational schools can be explained by the government's attempt to promote vocational education, a response to the realization that VET had become too important to be left in the hands of employers alone (Nilsson 1983: 36). State subsidies for full-time courses in vocational schools were significantly increased in 1955, and paved the way for the later integration of VET into secondary education, although dual apprenticeships remained important and popular until the end of the 1960s (Nilsson 2011). Social Democrats and unions, fearing that apprentices could be exploited as cheap labor by employers, advocated integrating VET into the secondary school system instead (Crouch 1992: 38).

Before the big reform of the late 1960s, both unions and employers were wary of too much state intrusion into the field of vocational training: "SAF and the LO argued that preparatory vocational training in the compulsory school should be the responsibility of the State, whereas substantial parts of VET proper should be planned by and take place within industry, which could provide advanced machinery, modern methods and real working conditions" (Lundahl 1997: 94). A drop in enrollment in vocational education in the 1960s, however, was "pivotal" in securing the backing of labor-market actors for the 1969 reform (Opper 1989: 153). Unions were generally more willing to support the integration of VET into upper-secondary education, because they valued the contribution of the reform towards the goal of promoting educational mobility (Lundahl 1997: 95; Nilsson 2011: 28). SAF was "the more reluctant party and argued that VET had become too broad and general at the expense of a focused goal" (Lundahl 1997: 95). Employers supported the reform because they wanted to make sure that the general education system produced a sufficient number of graduates with a vocational education, even if it was less specific than they would have liked. The dominance of large export-oriented firms and the absence of small and medium-sized enterprises (compared to Denmark) also helped to stabilize school-based VET in Sweden. Large firms were more willing to hire school leavers with broad occupational skills, which could be complemented with on-the-job training in firm-specific contexts (Crouch 1992: 38). Compared to a purely statist system (e.g., France), employers retained some influence over the design of vocational curricula in schools (Crouch 1992: 39).

The 1969 reform was considered a success, "both as a combination of adjustment to the second phase of industrialisation and as a response to social demand for greater equality between different types of vocational education and between the vocational school system and the corresponding system for academic education" (Nilsson 1983: 38). Enrollment in upper-secondary education expanded significantly between 1971 and 1981, from 75,000 to 106,000. The vocational tracks proved a very popular choice with students: enrollment increased from 24,000 to 49,000, compared to an increase from 30,000 to 41,000 in three- to four-year academic programs (Nilsson 1983: 40).

Consolidation and conflict (1975–1990)

Bureaucratic obstacles hampered the implementation of the comprehensive school model for a long time. Conflicts and administrative dualism in the National School Board between proponents of the grammar schools and those of the elementary schools continued to slow the realization of the comprehensive model, for example by preventing the formulation of common teacher training standards (Rothstein 1996: 97, 157). At the same time, the introduction of comprehensive education moved from upper-secondary to tertiary under the social democratic government of Olof Palme. As was the case in VET, higher education was increasingly regarded as the building block of a nationally unified, centrally administered, and rationally planned political economy and welfare state (Elzinga 1993: 197). The Social Democrats lost power to a bourgeois coalition that governed from 1976 to 1982, but many of the reforms begun in the early 1970s were taken up again later on, in part because the nonsocialist coalition did not have strong parliamentary support. The university reform of 1977, in particular, eliminated distinctions between academic and vocational tertiary education by abolishing the binary system and forming a new unified *Högskola*, as well as by upgrading the professional status of welfare professions (Elzinga 1993: 217). The 1977 reform was also an attempt to promote applied instead of basic research, so as to maximize the contribution of higher education to the development of the political economy (Elzinga 1993: 207–8). In spite of these structural reforms, however, participation in higher education did not expand significantly during the 1980s (Jonsson & Erikson 2007: 116).

Regarding the general schooling system, the nonsocialist government did not transform "education in a neo-liberal direction to any large extent" (Lundahl 2002: 690), but it did start a process of decentralization from the central to the local level that would continue on a small scale throughout the 1980s. Examples of decentralization included granting more responsibility to local authorities in matters of financing, transforming governance modes from hierarchical steering to goal- or output-oriented governance, and increasing choice options for parents (Lindblad & Wallin 1993: 79). This early wave of decentralization was a reaction to popular criticism of the overly bureaucratic and centralized system of the 1970s, which, amplified by the Conservative party, focused on topics such as the lack of discipline and academic standards in comprehensive schools (Lundahl 1990: 156). This is an interesting parallel to the debate in the United Kingdom triggered by the Black Papers. At the same time, the Swedish Conservatives display similarities to Christian democratic ideology on matters of education policy. For instance, they supported early streaming of pupils onto different tracks, a stronger separation between academic and vocational education at the secondary level, and a closer connection between VET and the labor market (Lundahl 1990: 160–1). Like British Conservatives, however, Swedish Conservatives lack a strong commitment to the corporatist "politics of mediation" (Van Kersbergen 1999: 356).

In contrast to the radical decentralization reforms of the British Conservative government in the 1980s, which emphasized choice and competition, the driving force behind the early Swedish efforts at decentralization was an attempt to increase the participation and influence of local stakeholders, such as local policy-makers, teachers, and parents, in the governance of education. When the Social Democrats regained power in 1982, the government engaged in a process of careful decentralization in reaction to mounting evidence that citizens felt a lack of influence in public schooling (Björklund *et al.* 2005: 2; Bunar 2010a: 6; Klitgaard 2008: 490). Significant political momentum for the decentralization of education policy came from the political left demanding more local flexibility in the implementation of new pedagogical concepts (Aasen 2003: 114). As a consequence, the government delegated responsibilities for primary schools to municipalities and increased local stakeholders' ability to influence the content of teaching. A significant reform occurred in 1989, when municipalities were put in charge of personnel matters and a new funding scheme was introduced: in the new regime, the central government would give subsidies in the form of lump-sum payments to the municipal governments, greatly increasing the autonomy of local decision-makers (Björklund et al. 2005: 2; Hudson & Lidström 2002: 45; Klitgaard 2008: 490; Lundahl 2002: 691). The extent of decentralization was limited overall, in part because of the intense conflict within the Social Democrat party between the reformers who supported decentralization and the "true believers" who preferred the old, centralized model (Klitgaard 2008: 489). The result was a "cooperative model" of decentralization (Mons 2004), in which the local level gained more autonomy but the central state remained committed to, and strongly involved in, certain matters, such as national-curriculum standards and school inspections (Bunar 2010a: 7; Hudson & Lidström 2002: 46).

VET in Sweden went through a period of consolidation and simmering conflict in the 1980s. In 1976, shortly before leaving office, and confronted with the rising problem of youth unemployment (as in the United Kingdom and Germany), the social democratic government had set up a parliamentary commission to reform upper-secondary education. The goal of this reform was to further erode the differentiation between the academic and vocational tracks in the newly integrated upper-secondary school system. The incoming nonsocialist government weakened this aspect of the reform, but the parliamentary commission's report in 1981 effectively remained committed to the goal, proposing a common structure for educational programs so that they would all contain both academic and practical components (Lundahl 1997: 97). Not surprisingly, the SAF strongly opposed this reform, especially the proposed extension of the role of basic vocational education, because employers wanted VET to more closely reflect the needs of industry (Crouch 1992: 39–40). The unions opposed the reform, too; in their view, the proposal did not go far enough towards abolishing the differences between academic and vocational education (Lundahl 1997: 97). Such widespread opposition to the reform led the government to abandon it. This example shows that in CMEs, such as Sweden, government attempts to promote policy change against the joint opposition of employers and unions will likely fail.

For the remainder of the 1980s, the institutional structure of upper-secondary education followed the stipulations of the 1972 reform, but the political debate on reforming the system continued. Employers and unions began criticizing the system's strong orientation towards school-based forms of VET and its lack of linkages to the labor market. They also feared that vocational education would be neglected, as an increasing number of young people opted for academic education (Lundahl 1998: 43). The next push for reform was a joint effort by the social partners: they set up yet another commission in 1984 (working via the Joint Industrial Training Council set up in 1944), which in 1986 recommended extending the length of VET from two to three years and expanding workplace-based components of training (Lundahl 1997: 98). The social democratic government implemented some of these proposals, but on a small scale (Lundahl 1998: 43). For example, a new agreement in 1984 between the government, educational authorities, and social partners introduced apprenticeships as a potential VET route in upper-secondary education. The number of apprentices in 1984 and thereafter remained very low, however, amounting to about 10 percent of total enrollment in vocational tracks at upper-secondary level (Opper 1989: 147); that is, roughly 4 percent of a typical age cohort at the time.

The Conservative party was a strong supporter of apprenticeships and wanted apprenticeships to become the dominant form of VET at the upper-secondary level (Lundahl 1997: 98). The employers were less enthusiastic, wondering whether firms could provide the kind of broad occupational skills that would be required (Lundahl 1997: 98). Unions, in turn, wanted to keep apprenticeship training in a marginal position, because they feared education would become subordinated to the needs of employers (Lundahl 1998: 47). In sum, despite increased support among the important stakeholders for increasing workplace-based components of VET in principle, the system essentially remained stuck on its development path of a statist skill regime.

Decentralization and reform (after 1991)

The bourgeois government coalition that was in charge from 1991 until 1994 followed a more market-oriented ideology and accelerated the decentralization of the governance of education (Aasen 2003: 129). The nonsocialist government attempted to increase the role of private, independent schools in particular, which traditionally had a very marginal position (accounting for 0.2 percent of enrollment in the early 1980s; cf. Klitgaard 2008: 489–90). The Social Democrats, despite strong internal conflicts, had already taken the first steps in this direction in the late 1980s: the new financing mechanism mentioned above distributed public funds to *both* public and private schools, according to local needs (Klitgaard 2008: 490–1). The nonsocialist government, however, went beyond that by giving private schools the legal right to receive public funds amounting to 85 percent of the average costs of a public school student and allowing schools to charge tuition fees for the remaining 15 percent (Klitgaard 2008: 492). This new regime was effectively a voucher scheme for independent schools because it was complemented by the introduction of school choice, meaning that parents could now freely choose among public (and independent) schools within their municipality, although students were sill allocated to schools on the basis of residence (Björklund *et al.* 2005: 6). Other policy changes included transferring employer responsibility for teachers (eventually including wages) from the central to the municipal level, introducing a new curriculum, and establishing more flexibility to adapt the curriculum to local needs (Arreman & Holm 2011: 227). Interestingly, the social democratic government after 1994 by and large did not reverse these policy reforms, although it did enact some form of recentralization in terms of regulation and oversight (Gingrich 2011: 154). First, it lowered the level of subsidies to private schools to 75 percent of average per-student costs in public schools. Then, it increased subsidies to 100 percent of the average, but prohibited private schools from levying additional fees (Klitgaard 2008: 492). This policy was passed against the wishes of organized interests (especially teacher unions) and can best be understood as an attempt by reformist Social Democrats to cater to the interests of the middle class, which demanded more opportunities for choice in education (Klitgaard 2008: 492).

Can the decentralization and privatization reforms of the 1990s be considered as path-changing reforms? First of all, empirical research on the reforms indicates that their effects have been rather small. "Surprisingly or not, just 17 years after the reform was enacted, it seems that it has not managed to bring decisive changes (either positive or negative) into the educational system. [. . . M]ost researchers and evaluators still claim that the outcomes in terms of segregation, costs, and achievement at the national level are ambiguous or at best visible but small" (Bunar 2010a: 13, see Björklund *et al.* 2005 for a similar conclusion). Even so, the share of post-16-year-old students in independent schools has increased to 20 percent (as of 2008), and the share of upper-secondary schools that are independent has increased to 40 percent of total (2007/08; cf. Arreman & Holms 2011: 235). Many of these new independent schools have a vocational orientation. While they may be run by commercial companies, they are still entirely publicly financed and are not allowed to charge tuition fees (Arreman & Holms 2011: 226; Bunar 2010b: 49). Furthermore, "free" schools have to comply with the national curriculum and are subject to public inspections and regulations (Bunar 2010b: 49, 53–4). Most importantly, free schools can decide whether to accept students from other districts, but "no one's application can be turned down based on his or her ability, level of achievement, gender, ethnicity, religion, or social background" (Bunar 2010b: 53). The prohibition on selecting students based on academic ability prevents private schools from becoming overly selective organizations catering to the academically gifted. In sum, as Bunar (2010b) argues, the Swedish school system has become more competitive and decentralized, but competition plays out in a highly "controlled school market" (Bunar 2010b: 49), pervaded by an "ideological legacy" (Bunar 2010b: 56) that emphasizes equity and equality in education. In a similar manner, Aasen (2003: 145) argues that the reforms of the 1990s can be interpreted as a "renewal of social-democratic progressive education to meet new challenges" and "an effort to defend the Scandinavian social democratic political model."

With regard to VET, the outgoing social democratic government passed a large reform of upper-secondary education in 1991. This was further spelled out in the 1994 reform of the national curriculum, which took up a number of proposals developed by the social partners in the reform debate of the 1980s. More specifically, the new system consolidated the number of courses or tracks at upper-secondary level into seventeen national programs, thirteen of which had a vocational orientation. All of them conferred a basic eligibility for studying at a higher education institution and all had a common core of general subjects. The length of VET courses was also increased, to three years (cf. Arreman & Holm 2011: 228; Lundahl 1997: 98–9; Lundahl *et al.* 2010: 49–50). The reform further blurred the line between academic and vocational education. It also greatly expanded access to higher education: nowadays, almost all students from lower-secondary education proceed to secondary education (Lundahl 2002:

692). The Conservative government fueled the expansion of higher education with the passage of the Higher Education Act in 1993, which also increased the autonomy of individual universities with regard to admissions (Ansell 2010: 203).

There is also evidence of a "new vocationalism" at work: the reform was intended to increase the share of instruction in the workplace to 15 percent of scheduled time in vocational courses (Lundahl 1997: 98–9). The coalitional dynamic behind the 1991 reform is interesting: The reform was largely supported by LO and SAF, because its purpose was to increase the relevance and attractiveness of VET (Lundahl 1997: 100). The Conservative and Liberal parties were opposed, however, because the reform further blurred the distinction between academic and vocational education, as mentioned above (Lundahl 1998: 49; 2010: 50). More recent reforms by the current bourgeois government coalition have gone in the direction of reinstating the distinction between academic and vocational education (Lundahl *et al.* 2010: 56).

The Swedish case shows that the transformation of education systems from the elitist and class-based models of the past to the comprehensive and universalist social democratic variant has taken a long time, despite the long-term dominance of Social Democrats and their allies in government. The early 1970s can be regarded as a critical juncture, in which VET was fully integrated into the secondary school system, setting Sweden on the path towards a statist model of skill formation. Significant reforms happened after this period as well, in particular the decentralization reforms of the 1980s and 1990s, but the fundamental institutional structure of the Swedish system has remained largely stable since the integration of VET.

Germany

One important difference between the German case and both Sweden and the United Kingdom lies in German political institutions, which have implications for the politics of education and training reform. Sweden and the United Kingdom are both unitary states, whereas Germany has a long tradition of federalism. In contrast to other federalist countries such as the United States, Canada, and Switzerland, however, German-style federalism has a strong unitary tendency,

The politics of education and training reform

which Erk (2003) sees as a consequence of the "nonfederal" character of German society. The different levels of government in Germany often share responsibilities and competencies in policy-making: there is no clear separation of powers. Members of the second chamber of parliament, the *Bundesrat*, are delegates of the *Länder* governments, not elected senators as in the United States. This institutional setup causes regular friction between two different kinds of cleavage: first, conflicts between the federal level and the *Länder*, and second, partisan conflicts between the two large partisan blocks (the Christian Democrats and the Social Democrats, with the Liberal Party aligning with one or the other until the rise of the Green party in the 1980s). Thus, party competition interacts with distributional conflicts across levels of government (Lehmbruch 2000), contributing to joint-decision traps (Scharpf 1988) and incremental policy change. If policy change is to occur, it requires the support of informal or even formal grand coalitions (Schmidt 2008) between the two large partisan blocks, particularly when the *Bundesrat* is captured by the party in opposition in the *Bundestag*. In many policy fields, moreover, the government has delegated important powers to corporatist bodies, or "private interest governments" (Streeck & Schmitter 1985). In order to achieve significant policy change, therefore, the formal or informal grand coalitions in the partisan arena have usually been complemented by cross-class coalitions in the labor-market arena. In recent years, however, there have been indications that coalitional patterns are becoming more varied. The erosion in membership of intermediate associations such as trade unions and employers' associations, as well as the increasing distance between corporatist actors and professional politicians, has led to a more contentious, less consensus-oriented style of policy-making (Busemeyer 2012a; Häusermann 2010; Trampusch 2009; Vail 2007).

This institutional setup has an important consequence for the politics of education and training reform: policy-making powers in the field of education policy are largely in the hands of the state (*Länder*) governments. Therefore, the study of Germany requires that more attention be paid to the multilevel nature of the policy-making structure than in the other cases. Nevertheless, there are several arguments in favor of studying Germany as a whole instead of as individual *Länder*. First, as Erk (2003) points out, and as will become clear below, there is significant horizontal and vertical coordination between the *Länder* and the federal government in matters of education policy. Although nontrivial differences across the *Länder* remain, there is a high level of horizontal coordination, resulting in a much more unitary education system than would be expected of a federal country. Second, the relative power of the federal government varies across educational sectors. With regard to general schooling, the *Länder* are clearly the dominant players, but the federal government has more policy-making powers in the fields of VET and higher education. The political context on the federal level is thus much more important in these sectors, where the federal government has often acted as the agenda-setter and pacemaker for large-scale reform attempts.

The following discussion identifies three periods of policy development: first, a period of reconstruction and restoration (1945–65); second, a period of expansion and only partially successful reforms (1965–82); and third, a period of consolidation and incremental adaptation (after 1982). It needs to be emphasized that this attempt at defining periods is mostly motivated by pragmatic concerns. Compared to the United Kingdom and Sweden, in Germany there is less evidence of a clear separation between periods as a consequence of changes in government, because policy developments across subsystems of the education system developed on different timescales (especially in the field of VET; see Greinert 1998: 58). The incrementalism of policy change in general also implies less stark differences in terms of policy across time periods. Unless noted otherwise, "Germany" refers to West Germany from 1949 until 1990, and thereafter to reunified Germany.

Reconstruction and restoration (1945–1965)

Without a doubt, the end of the Second World War marked a significant watershed in the political and historical development of Germany. The large-scale destruction of cities and property, millions of refugees from the East, the redesign of political institutions, and the denazification of the public sector were immediate and pressing problems. In these times of extreme uncertainty, policy-makers often turned to established institutions and policies of the prewar era, or, in some cases, left the existing institutions in place. Instead of a large-scale break with the past, there was a great deal of institutional continuity, particularly in the field of VET (Greinert 1998; Thelen 2003, 2004).

The policy legacies that policy-makers were confronted with go back to the roots of the German education and training system in the nineteenth and early twentieth centuries. Prussia was among the first countries to enact compulsory schooling, in 1763, although this regulation was difficult to implement and enforce at the time (Herrlitz *et al.* 1998: 52). Access to prestigious positions in the Prussian bureaucracy was tied to school certificates, in particular the *Abitur* – the school-leaving certificate of the academic track of secondary education, the *Gymnasium* (Herrlitz *et al.* 1998: 34; Thränhardt 1990: 178). As a consequence, access to higher levels of education became an important factor in class politics. One element in Bismarck's attempts to fight off the rising power of the working and middle classes was the limiting of access to universities and *Gymnasien* through increased tuition fees (Herrlitz *et al.* 1998: 76). These efforts were complemented by efforts to channel the educational aspirations of the rising classes into new alternative tracks. A new middle school below the level of *Gymnasien* but above the common school (*Volksschule*) was established (the predecessor of the modern-day *Realschule*), preparing the children of the bourgeoisie for intermediate-level clerk positions in the public and private sectors (Herrlitz *et al.* 1998: 76, 132). In 1897, the government passed the "Handwerkerschutzgesetz," which is widely regarded as an important cornerstone of the apprenticeship system because it protected the privileged position of craft chambers to regulate, monitor, and administer apprenticeship training in firms in the crafts sector; this was entrenched by further legislation in 1908 (Greinert 2006: 500; Thelen 2004: 43). As Thelen (2004: 44–53) has pointed out, this was aimed at convincing the craft sector (the *petite bourgeoisie*) to align themselves with the authoritarian regime instead of the rising labor movement. Because of this legislation, German unions could not effectively use apprenticeship to control access to skilled labor markets, as British unions had. The unintended consequence of this constellation was that it triggered the rise of industrial unions, instead of craft unions, which in later periods facilitated the formation of cross-class consensus in matters of skill formation.

The Weimar period was significant in two respects. First, the enactment of the 1920 school law (Reichsgrundschulgesetz) symbolized a preliminary school compromise between Conservatives and the supporters of educational reforms promoting a more comprehensive education system (Mitter 1991: 156). It introduced a four-year basic school for all children, whereas before the *Gymnasien* and other higher schools had their own basic schools. This progressive element was counterbalanced by the more conservative three-tiered structure of the education system at post-primary level, consisting of the *Volksschule*, the *Realschule*, and the *Gymnasium*.

The second legacy of the Weimar period was the establishment of a collective and essentially voluntarist approach to VET, based on coordination between firms in the crafts and industry sector (cf. Greinert 1998: 62–86; Thelen 2004: 53–89). Because previous legislation had essentially given the crafts sector a monopoly over apprenticeship training, industry interests now aimed to expand their own control over the content of training and the certification of vocational skills. The Deutscher Ausschuß für Technisches Schulwesen (DATSCH), founded in 1908 by the associations of the engineering and machine-making industries, developed training curricula and exams and thus contributed to standardizing training content across the economy. In 1925, the DATSCH teamed up with the peak employers' associations to establish the Arbeitsausschuß für Berufsbildung (Working Committee for Vocational Education). Once trade unions had been officially recognized as partners in collective wage bargaining, they too tried to expand their influence over vocational training. Employers were initially in favor of cross-class compromise, supporting the establishment of the Zentralarbeitsgemeinschaft der industriellen und gewerblichen Arbeitgeber und Arbeitnehmer Deutschlands in 1921, a committee of employer and trade union representatives concerned with enacting comprehensive legislation. This effort at cross-class coordination fell apart at the end of the 1920s, however, when the industry and crafts sectors joined forces to fend off state legislation of this domain of employer-led self-governance (Greinert 1998: 86).

Both of these legacies became important during the immediate postwar period. As Ellwein puts it: "When the educational establishments were reopened in the postwar period, immediate concerns and needs were foremost; getting things off the ground was the order of the day. There was little time for reflection on the problems of established institutions and future needs. People turned to existing institutions and continued along these lines" (Ellwein 1998: 89, author's translation). One new actor in the education policy arena was, of course, the American military government. The US occupying power promoted educational reform in the name of democratic reeducation, because it was believed that Germany's elitist education system had contributed to the rise of the Nazis (Herrlitz et al. 1998: 160, 163). The United States was successful in promoting a new set of educational institutions in Japan that were modeled on the US system of comprehensive secondary education (Heidenheimer 1997: 55). In Germany, however, these attempts mostly failed. A progressive, reform-oriented coalition of Social Democrats, trade unions, associations of teachers from the *Volksschulen*, and the US military government was pitted against a conservative coalition of Christian Democrats, universities, teachers from the *Gymnasien*, and churches (Herrlitz et al. 1998: 164; Thränhardt 1990: 188). The conservative coalition gained considerable legitimacy from the support of the Catholic Church, which was less tainted by the Nazi legacy and which derided the proposed educational reforms as "unchristian" (Herrlitz et al. 1998: 164).

Some *Länder* governments made use of the head start gained by virtue of their constitutions having been enacted before the Federal Basic Law was passed in 1949. In particular, *Länder* governed by the SPD, such as Berlin, Hamburg, Bremen, and Schleswig-Holstein, passed a series of educational reforms in the years following 1945. By 1953, most of these reform attempts had been rolled back, and the three-tiered structure of the secondary school system was fully reinstated across all of West Germany (Thränhardt 1990: 189). One reason for the rollbacks was the losses suffered by the SPD in *Länder* elections of the early 1950s, perceived as being a consequence of the school reforms (Schmidt 1980: 93; Wiborg 2010: 552–3). A more indirect, but probably more lasting reason for the unpopularity of the comprehensive school model is that it was introduced in East Germany as the "fundamental school type of the unified socialist educational system" (Mitter 1991: 157). The exploitation of the comprehensive school by the socialist regime in the East contributed to its delegitimization as a reform model in the West. A further factor may have been "national policy discourses" (Baldi 2012: 1000); that is, the dominance of conservative thinkers in educational research who emphasized the validity of the "fixed-ability approach" tied to the segmented school system.

The peculiar character of German educational federalism is evidenced by the fact that the central coordinating organization was actually established *before* the founding of the Federal Republic in 1949. The Ständige Konferenz der Kultusminister der Länder in der Bundesrepublik Deutschland (Kultusministerkonferenz, or KMK, for short) was established in 1948 as a voluntary association of the education ministers of the German *Länder*. Because the KMK is a forum for voluntary horizontal coordination between the *Länder*, decisions must be unanimous, which often results in gridlock and lowest-common-denominator policies (Thränhardt 1990: 182–3). Nevertheless, the KMK has issued hundreds of decisions and recommendations over the decades, which although formally voluntary are regularly implemented by the *Länder*. The KMK is thus crucial in creating and sustaining a unitary framework in the federalist education system. The agreements of Düsseldorf (1955) and Hamburg (1964), for example, defined the core features of the German three-tiered education system and remain in force today.

Once the central features and institutions of the education system had been restored and consolidated, no further large-scale structural reform attempts were made for the rest of the 1950s or much of the 1960s. The Christlich Demokratische Union Deutschlands (CDU) staunchly defended the three-tiered structure of secondary education and justified it with religious references to the divine order of an organic society, based on the principle of differences between individuals (Faulstich 1977: 94), which contrasted sharply with the secular and egalitarian comprehensive school model promoted by left-wing partisans. The 1950s also saw conflicts over the survival of confessional (religious) schools, which cumulated in a popular referendum in Bavaria in which the Christian Democrats (organized into the party of the CSU in Bavaria) faced a coalition of liberals and Social Democrats who advocated ending confessional schools (Thränhardt 1990: 194–5). After this struggle, purely confessional schools were abandoned, but private schools with ties to church authorities and largely financed by the state survived.

The SPD increasingly became a supporter of the comprehensive school model, albeit probably a less enthusiastic one than its Nordic neighbors (Faulstich 1977: 98–102; Schmidt 1980: 92). Comparing the effects of partisan government at the *Länder* level, Schmidt (1980: 59, 63) found that SPD participation in government was associated with higher levels of education spending and participation, as well as more concern for primary, lower-secondary, and vocational schools.

Education policy was not a particularly important topic for trade unions in the 1950s, when economic and social policy issues were more pressing (Schmidt 1980: 128, 135).

In 1953, the Deutscher Ausschuß für das Erziehungs- und Bildungswesen (German Committee for the Education System) was established as an advisory committee. Half of its members were educators, the other half academics and business experts. The committee produced a significant number of reports and recommendations, but these did not have any sustainable impact (Hepp 2011: 96). Compared to similar committees and commissions in the United Kingdom and Sweden at the time, its recommendations were rather cautious and conservative. In its Rahmenplan zur Umgestaltung und Vereinheitlichung des allgemeinbildenden Schulwesens (Framework for the Reform and Unification of the General School System), the committee expressed continued support for the three-tiered structure of secondary schooling (Herrlitz et al. 1998: 168). Its proposals were minor: to extend the four-year primary school by two years and to ease transitions between the different tracks of the secondary school system (Herrlitz et al. 1998: 169–70).

In VET, the overarching topic was again the restoration of prewar institutions, meaning the quasi-voluntarist and employer-dominated system of apprenticeship training (Thelen 2004: 240–58). Immediately after the end of the war, various Chambers of Industry and Commerce coordinated to reinstate the prewar training curricula and to accept only training in recognized training occupations (Greinert 1998: 68). The successor to the DATSCH, the Arbeitsstelle für Betriebliche Berufsausbildung (ABB) was established in 1953 under the aegis of the Bundesverband der Deutschen Industrie (BDI), one of the two main employers' associations. The CDU-led government passed two smaller pieces of legislation that supported the system of employer-led self-government: the 1953 Handwerksordnung (Crafts Ordinance) and the 1956 Gesetz zur vorläufigen Regelung des Rechts der Industrie- und Handelskammern (Law on the Preliminary Regulation of Chambers of Industry and Commerce). These pieces of legislation reinstated and reinforced the Chambers' powers to monitor, implement, and design training, without expanding the participation rights of trade unions in these semi-public and employer-dominated institutions (Lemke 1969: 1305). They also reaffirmed the distinction between training in the crafts and in the industry sectors, which continued to be subject to different regulatory regimes. As Bismarck had done before him, Adenauer saw the continued protection of the privileges of the crafts sector as an effective instrument by which to support small and medium-sized businesses (*Mittelstandspolitik*; Stratmann 1990b: 80–1), which were needed to carry out postwar reconstruction and fight surging youth unemployment.

Employers' associations were closely aligned with the Christian democratic government. Deliberately taking up a popular campaign slogan of the CDU in the 1957 campaign (*"Keine Experimente!"* – "No experiments!"), the German Association of the Industry and Commerce Chambers (Deutscher Industrie- und Handelstag, DIHT) staunchly defended the principle of self-governance of employer associations in matters of training policy, pointing to the high level of training standards (DIHT 1958: 1). The ideology of German employers' associations was also deeply influenced by religious concerns, which differentiates them from secular conservative or liberal business associations in other countries. The peak employers' association published two pamphlets in the early 1950s that highlighted the importance of the religious underpinnings of the German variety of democratic capitalism in the form of the social market economy (Baethge 1970: 61–2). In an echo of Catholic social doctrine, the education of young people was considered to be an important obligation for employers (Baethge 1970: 63).

The trade unions were less satisfied with the quality of training than were employers. They renewed their prewar demand for the establishment of a comprehensive legislative framework of firm-based training. In 1950, there were about 900 recognized training occupations (*Ausbildungsberufe*), which was taken by trade unions as an indication of the narrow and overly firm-specific nature of apprenticeship training (Stratmann 1990b: 85). The unions called for broader vocational education with stronger theoretical foundations, more involvement in training decisions in the workplace, and a training levy to address the disparity of investment in skill formation between training and nontraining firms (Greinert 1998: 84).

Towards the end of the 1950s, unions prodded the SPD to become more active in the field of VET. The Deutscher Gewerkschaftsbund (DGB, the German Federation of Trade Unions) presented its own proposal for a law on VET in 1959 (Greinert 1998: 87). Following the initiative of the SPD, the *Bundestag* unanimously passed a motion

(*Entschließungsantrag*) in 1962 to push the CDU-led government to begin work on a proper law proposal (Stratmann 1990c: 148). Ludwig Erhard, the new chancellor, stated his opposition to state intervention in the field of VET and his support for the principle of self-government by associations (Stratmann 1990c: 148–149). The federal government officially responded to the motion in 1964 (one year after the deadline), stating that it was not yet able to present a proposal because of the "extreme complexity of the matter" (cited in Greinert 1998: 87, author's translation). Serious reform of the VET institutional framework would have to wait until the first CDU-SPD grand coalition came into power in 1966.

Expansion and reform (1965–1982)

Like other European countries, Germany went through a phase of massive educational expansion in the 1960s and 1970s. Before the 1960s, higher education policy was fully in the hands of the *Länder* governments, without the intervention of the federal government. Universities went through a phase of denazification and turmoil immediately after the end of the war, but by and large, their governance model remained that of the prewar years and became a textbook case of academic oligarchy (Clark 1983). Like the governance model in VET, the principle of self-government (in this case: of university professors and their faculties) is today still deeply entrenched, although the ministerial bureaucracies of the *Länder* have intervened quite heavily in the recruitment of professors, as well as in management and financing issues.

The involvement of the federal government was very limited in the beginning, but expanded significantly during the 1960s and 1970s, in response to the massive increase in student numbers. In 1950–55, only 3.4 percent of a typical age cohort was students. This share increased to 5.4 percent in 1960–65 and to 11.7 percent in 1970–75 (figures from Heidenheimer 1997: 236). The *Länder* governments were unable to deal with this surge alone, because many of them lacked the resources to establish new universities on their own. The grand coalition therefore passed a reform of the Basic Law in 1969, which enumerated new "Joint Tasks" (*Gemeinschaftsaufgaben*) to the *Bund* and the *Länder*, in particular the building of new universities, educational planning, research funding, and educational subsidies, and provided a general competence for the federal government to enact a legal framework for higher education (Hepp 2011: 112–13).

This constitutional reform opened the door to a massive expansion of the federal government's involvement. After the grand coalition collapsed in 1969, a new government coalition between the SPD and the liberal FDP attempted to push forward an agenda of significant reforms in many policy fields and to do away with the conservative legacy of the Adenauer era (Schmidt 1980). Facilitating educational opportunities for previously excluded segments of the population was a central element of this progressive, social–liberal reform agenda. By holding the purse strings, the federal government could influence the speed and specific guise of the expansion of higher education. In 1971, the SPD-FDP government passed legislation granting educational subsidies to low-income students for the first time (Bundesausbildungsförderungsgesetz, BAFöG). In 1973, 46 percent of students received at least some subsidies for their living expenses under this law (Hepp 2011: 164). In 1976, the government passed framework legislation for the higher education sector (Hochschulrahmengesetz) that upgraded the status of universities of applied sciences (*Fachhochschulen*) to the level of universities proper; this included detailed regulations that prompted resistance on the part of the *Länder* and universities.

In line with the prevailing zeitgeist, the government initiated a large-scale venture into educational planning. The Deutsche Bildungsrat (German Education Council) was founded in 1965 as the successor to the ineffective Deutscher Ausschuß. This time, the group consisted of both academics and government representatives, in order to achieve a tighter connection to policy-making. The Bund-Länder Kommission für Bildungsplanung und Forschungsförderung (BLK) was established in 1970, following the constitutional reform of 1969. Its institutional setup was different from that of the KMK: in the BLK, the federal government had the same number of votes as the *Länder* taken together. Decisions were made by qualified majority rule. This meant that on the one hand, no decision could be made against the will of the federal government, while on the other, if a majority of *Länder* governments supported the position of the federal government, qualified majority decisions could be passed. Until 1976, the SPD (alone or in coalition with the FDP) ruled in a majority of the *Länder*, in addition to being in charge of the federal government. The social–liberal coalition was able to use qualified majority decisions to move forward with its reform agenda, even with the opposition of those *Länder* governments in which the CDU dominated.

There were bitter ideological conflicts in the BLK from the beginning (Hepp 2011: 138). The SPD had by then become a strong supporter of integrated comprehensive schools, whereas the CDU continued to oppose them. The main task of the BLK and the Bildungsrat was to develop a comprehensive educational plan for the whole system (*Bildungsgesamtplan*), which they managed to do in 1973 despite the bitter conflicts. A central feature of this plan was the integration of VET into the general school system (more on this point below). The Bildungsrat also recommended that forty integrated comprehensive schools be established as part of a pilot program (the social–liberal coalition had a majority on this committee, just as in the BLK), about fifteen to twenty years after the United Kingdom and Sweden had started similar projects. This recommendation was supported by the KMK in 1969, and the BLK was put in charge of monitoring and evaluating these experiments. In the years that followed, the *Länder* governed by the SPD established comprehensive schools on a much larger scale than the *Länder* governed by the CDU or the CSU, where comprehensive schools remained isolated experiments. Even in those places where a significant percentage of students attended comprehensive schools, however, the old three-tiered structure, in particular the *Gymnasium*, was not abolished, effectively resulting in a four-tiered structure (Heidenheimer 1997: 98–100; Hepp 2011: 214; Mitter 1991: 157). The BLK published its report on the comprehensive schools in 1982. By then, the tide had turned: the CDU *Länder* fully reverted to the three-tiered system and successfully pushed to dismantle the Bildungsrat in 1975 (Heidenheimer 1997: 98–9). The FDP had become a less ardent and reliable supporter of comprehensive schools than it had been in the early 1970s (Schmidt 1980: 105). The project of comprehensive educational planning was mostly abandoned after the change in the federal government in 1982 (from the social–liberal coalition to a coalition of the Christian Democrats and the FDP) and the change in the majority of the *Bundesrat* in 1976 (Mäding 1985).

Unlike the other educational sectors, the field of VET experienced a critical phase of path formation in the 1960s and 1970s. Shortly before the grand coalition came to power at the end of 1966, the SPD formally submitted a proposal for a VET law to the *Bundestag*. The CDU/CSU/FDP government coalition followed up with its own proposal shortly thereafter. The two different proposals strongly reflected the divergent interests of trade unions and employers' and crafts associations (Offe 1975: 57). The various organizations clashed during the public hearing of the proposals in 1967, and the grand coalition then decided to speed up the process by merging the two proposals and passing the Law on Vocational Education and Training (Berufsbildungsgesetz, BBiG) in 1969 (Greinert 1998: 87).

The reactions to the adoption of the BBiG were mixed. While trade unions had lobbied for the establishment of a comprehensive legal framework for firm-based VET, the law fell short of their expectations ("Restoration instead of reform," Lemke 1969: 1303, author's translation; see also Faulstich 1977; Kuda & Mignon 1982). The law fundamentally did not question the autonomy of training firms in their decision to participate in apprenticeship training and to influence its content. Unions had also lobbied for the establishment of publicly controlled training funds (financed by a training levy) in order to create a redistribution of funds from nontraining to training firms, none of which became law. The extensiveness of the remit of the BBiG was limited as well, because the crafts sector was allowed to keep its own regulatory scheme for apprenticeship training (Offe 1975: 59). Finally, the law only regulated the firm-based part of apprenticeship training, over which the federal government had exclusive lawmaking powers; the school-based part of training fell into the domain of the *Länder*. Employer representatives were largely satisfied with the law, but the unions were not (Offe 1975: 71). As Thelen (2004: 262) has argued, the law "brought greater unity to the previously disparate legal framework" but did not fundamentally change the existing system of self-governance (see also Lipsmeier 1992 for a similar assessment).

The impetus for a "reform of the reform" started to grow after the change in the political makeup of the federal government in 1969 (Stratmann 1990a: 179). That same year, the Bildungsrat published an evaluation of the existing apprenticeship system that was critical of the lack of systematic and theoretical training and cited the danger of apprentices being misused as cheap labor (Deutscher Bildungsrat 1991). The SPD-FDP coalition in the federal government paid particular attention to promoting VET in its agenda for educational reform, demanding that training no longer be treated as the "stepchild of education policy" (Bundesregierung 1974a: 24, author's translation). In

The politics of education and training reform

its initial ambitious proposals for reform (Bundesregierung 1974b), the government wanted to expand public oversight of firm-based training and strengthen the quality and theoretical underpinnings of training curricula by establishing foundational training courses. It also proposed to establish a training levy system and fully integrate VET into the new comprehensive secondary school system. Unions were generally very supportive of these proposals, but, unsurprisingly, employer representatives of all stripes and the Christian Democrats were hostile to them (Busemeyer 2009c: 80–8). The government backed down from its initial proposals when employers threatened to boycott apprenticeship training (Baethge 1983: 148). Faced with increasing youth unemployment after the oil crisis, changing demographics, and a shift in administration (from Brandt to Schmidt in the chancellorship and Dohnanyi to Rhode in the education ministry), the government passed a much watered-down reform in 1976. This legislation still allowed the government to impose a training levy (which it never did), but only under exceptional circumstances, such as in the case of a severe lack of apprenticeship places. More ambitious proposals to expand public oversight in training were effectively abandoned. In 1980, the Federal Constitutional Court declared even this watered-down reform unconstitutional, and therefore void – not because of the substantive policies it contained (the training levy was not the problem), but because the federal government had failed to consult with the *Länder* in the *Bundesrat* with regard to some administrative issues (Busemeyer 2009c: 92–5). The government then passed yet another diluted version of the law in 1981 (the Berufsbildungsförderungsgesetz, BerBiFG), which did not contain any provisions concerning the training levy and mostly served to establish the Federal Institute for Vocational Education and Training (Bundesinstitut für Berufsbildung, BIBB). Despite its initially ambitious plans, therefore, the social–liberal government largely failed to implement large-scale reform in VET (Baethge 1983).

At the same time, the institutions of the VET system continued to develop and evolve "below the radar of national legislative politics" (Culpepper 2007: 183). Once unions realized that large-scale policy reforms would be impossible, they turned their attention to promoting their interests via corporatist bodies and at the firm level (Greinert 1998: 99; Kuda & Mignon 1982: 66). A complex framework for the regular upgrade and reform of training occupations was established in the 1970s. The BIBB came to occupy a central place in this framework, managing the coordination between employers and unions on the one hand and between the federal and *Länder* levels on the other (Busemeyer 2009c: 97). Unions were on more equal footing with employers in this framework than in their partially subordinated position in the local Chambers, and they used their newfound power to press for broader and more theory-oriented training occupations. Common demands for a solid foundational education led to the enactment of the school-based Vocational Foundation Year (Berufsgrundbildungsjahr, BGJ). The KMK decided to implement the BGJ in 1972, and the federal government passed legislation to ensure that apprentices would get credit for it during their regular apprenticeship. Towards the end of the 1970s, it became clear that employers had found effective ways of getting around this regulation, for example by only taking apprentices who promised not to demand recognition for their prior study (Busemeyer 2009c: 102–3; Stratmann 1990a: 192). It was for this reason that the BGJ (and similar instruments set up in the following years) never posed a fundamental challenge to the principle of employer autonomy in training decisions.

Consolidation and incremental adaptation (after 1982)

The 1980s and 1990s were a period of consolidation and, at best, incremental adaptation of the education system. This is most clearly the case in VET, the education sector in which the influence of the federal government is the greatest. When coming to power in 1982, the head of the new government coalition of Christian democrats and liberals, Chancellor Kohl, proclaimed a "spiritual and moral turnaround" ("geistig-moralische Wende"), signaling a break with the reform-oriented and progressive spirit of the previous government. The new federal education minister, Dorothee Wilms (CDU), blamed the SPD for having turned education policy into a "political battlefield" (Wilms 1983: 59, author's translation) and neglecting VET in favor of a focus on the expansion of higher education. According to Wilms, employers did not need that many university graduates and would have preferred more skilled workers instead (Wilms 1983: 65). There were too many unemployed academics already, she said, and the "educational illusions" (Wilms 1986: 12) from the 1970s surmising that these academics would create their own demand on the labor market were wrong. Wilms insisted that the dual system of apprenticeship training and the differentiated three-tiered system of secondary schooling should be preserved as they were (Wilms 1983: 86; 1986).

Demographics in Germany contributed to a high demand for apprenticeship places in the late 1970s and early 1980s, as also happened in the United Kingdom. Rather than threatening employers with the imposition of a training levy, however, as the previous government had done, the Kohl government refrained from direct intervention, instead asking employers' associations and the Chambers to lean on firms to expand the number of available training slots (Busemeyer 2009c: 106–7). This appeal to the spirit of corporatism was effective in significantly increasing the number of training slots, especially in the crafts sector, during the first half of the 1980s. The government's thank-you for this engagement on the part of employers was to refrain from pushing any structural reforms in VET:

Vocational education and training has developed in an organic and successful regulatory framework, which must be preserved. The broad distribution of responsibility on the *Bund*, the *Länder*, and the social partners, the privilege of individual educational and vocational choices, the autonomy of firms and other suppliers of training, the dismissal of statist-bureaucratic demand steering, as well as the orientation on the principles of subsidiarity, plurality, and competition are likely to meet the challenges that vocational education and training is facing in the coming years. (Deutscher Bundestag 1989: 1–2, author's translation)

In this new political constellation, the repeated demands from unions and the SPD to introduce a training levy and other more far-reaching structural reforms fell on deaf ears (Busemeyer 2009c: 111–15). Trade unions largely continued their strategy of pushing for incremental reforms within the confines of the corporatist framework that had been established to update and reform training occupations (Hilbert et al. 1990; Streeck et al. 1987). Of crucial importance in this respect was the reform of training occupations in the metal and electrical industry; the bargaining between unions and employers on this lasted more than ten years and did not finish until 1988. The final agreement on reform was a great success for the unions. It reduced the total number of occupational profiles in the metal/electrical field, which guaranteed broader training instead of narrow, firm-specific skills acquisition. The reform also largely phased out so-called "staged apprenticeships," which initially were meant to promote foundational training but in fact allowed employers to lay off apprentices after the first stage, resulting in reduced training and lower pay. The Christian democratic government was highly committed to the principles of corporatism and self-government through "private interest governments" (Streeck & Schmitter 1985). It did not intervene strongly in the process of training reform and instead assumed the position of a neutral arbiter in the background (Hilbert et al. 1990: 55), mediating conflict between the social partners.

The 1980s were a tranquil period of consolidation in general schooling and higher education as well. Individual *Länder* progressed on their own specific paths with regard to the expansion of comprehensive schooling. The government did pass higher education legislation in 1985 that allowed for greater differentiation in the system and granted more autonomy to individual universities, but it was not until much later, at the end of the 1990s, that significant steps were taken to move away from the oligarchic model of governance in higher education and towards a more deregulated and market-oriented one (Hepp 2011: 155).

The dominant topic of the 1990s is obvious: educational institutions in the new eastern *Länder* had to be reformed and integrated into a unified framework. As in other spheres of the welfare state, this was largely a story of institutional transfer from the West to the East; reunification was certainly not used as an opportunity to implement large-scale reforms of existing institutions. Because the comprehensive school (polytechnische Oberschule, POS) had been the central form of secondary schooling in the GDR, it suffered a steep drop in legitimacy after reunification. The new *Länder* all opted for a more differentiated system, but significant differences emerged between them according to the political constellations at the beginning of the 1990s (Hepp 2011: 214; Overesch 2007; Stern 2000; Von Below 2002). Brandenburg (governed by the SPD) favored the establishment of comprehensive schools, but also kept the popular *Gymnasien* alive. Mecklenburg-Vorpommern (where the CDU was in charge for most of the 1990s) was the only *Land* that maintained the classical West German three-tiered system. Saxony established a two-tiered system, with the traditional *Gymnasium* as one pillar and a merged *Realschule* and *Hauptschule* (called *Mittelschule* or "middle school") as the other (Edelstein & Nikolai 2013).

Institutional transfer in the field of VET was not as easy as in other parts of the welfare state. The formal legal and institutional framework was transferred quite quickly and easily through such actions as establishing Chambers and creating regulations on the recognition of vocational qualifications awarded in the GDR. The dual system of apprenticeship training had evolved and developed within an institutional ecology of intermediate associations in the West, however, which could not be easily transplanted or created from scratch in the eastern *Länder* (Culpepper 2003; Johnson 1995). Large state-owned firms had been the central pillars of the vocational training system in the GDR. When these firms went bankrupt after reunification, there was no viable crafts sector that could take over apprenticeship training: the federal government and *Länder* governments had to step in by heavily subsidizing firm-based, school-based, and out-of-firm training (Busemeyer 2009c: 132–3). Initially regarded as a short-term measure, public subsidization of training at a much higher level than in the West has become an important and lasting feature of VET in the new *Länder*.

The 2000s were a period of more heightened reform activity than the 1980s and 1990s, due in part to the more activist stance of the red–green government coalition (SPD and Greens) that came into power in 1998, but also to important international developments such as the Bologna Process and the PISA debate, as well as the 2006 institutional reforms of the federalist structure. According to Hepp (2011: 69–70), partisan politics in education policy-making has now become less ideological and more oriented towards problem-solving, especially compared to the 1970s (although Overesch (2007) reached the opposite conclusion when comparing Germany to Finland). The PISA shock in the early 2000s resurrected the debate about structural reforms of the three-tiered system. Regardless of ideological debates, increasingly practical concerns have provoked a number of *Länder* to merge the two lower tiers (*Hauptschule* and *Realschule*), essentially following the example of Saxony in the early 1990s (Edelstein & Nikolai 2013). As expansion of access to higher levels of education has continued, the lowest tier (*Hauptschule*) has become an increasingly unpopular choice. Demographic changes (a decrease in the number of pupils) and general fiscal pressures have made the costs of maintaining three different school types oppressive, especially in rural areas. Merging the two lower tiers into semi-comprehensive schools (labeled differently in different *Länder*) and maintaining continued independence of the academic *Gymnasien* has become a general trend, and a potential solution to the decades-long conflict over school structure. Although this trend represents a cautious movement towards the comprehensive model, a full-scale comprehensivization of the system seems very unlikely – especially the abolishment of the *Gymnasien* – because it would face significant political opposition from middle-class voters.

The Bologna Process triggered a surprisingly far-reaching process of internationalization and deregulation of the higher education sector (Voegtle *et al.* 2011). For example, the structure of a large majority of study programs was changed from the traditional four- or five-year diplomas to the internationally more common two-cycle structure of bachelor's and master's degrees. By contrast, the attempts by the red–green government to prohibit tuition fees and establish junior professorships as an additional career pathway to full professorship (instead of the traditional *Habilitation*) were ruled unconstitutional by the Federal Constitutional Court because they infringed on the autonomy of the *Länder* (Hepp 2011: 157). There is nevertheless a general trend towards introducing market-oriented governance mechanisms in higher education (Kamm & Köller 2010). Such mechanisms include strengthening the autonomy of universities, introducing cost–benefit budgeting, and establishing new university boards that feature representatives from industry and other stakeholders. For a rather brief period in the 2000s, various *Länder* governments introduced tuition fees at the comparatively low level of €500 per semester. Because tuition fees were always introduced by Christian democratic governments and then revoked once the Social Democrats regained power (Kauder & Potrafke 2013), by 2014 no *Land* will require the payment of fees.

As for VET, German governments of different stripes have promoted the flexibilization and differentiation of the training system by doing such things as allowing firms more leeway in implementing training profiles and waiving or abolishing regulatory policies (Busemeyer 2009c, 2012; Deissinger & Hellwig 2005). These reforms have proceeded in an incremental manner, but may end up producing a significant change in the character and institutional logic of the system, making it more attuned to the needs of training firms than of unions or young people (Thelen & Busemeyer 2012). For the moment, however, the reforms have also helped to maintain the popularity of the system with employers (Bosch 2010; Hassel 2007), and the core of the training system in the export-oriented parts of the economy remains very stable. One negative side effect of this stability is the rise of the so-called "transition system," which is a complex and uncoordinated arrangement of school- and workplace-based training measures, reminiscent of UK-style "make-work" schemes. Similar to developments in social and labor-market policy (Palier & Thelen 2010), this differentiation between a stable core and increasingly precarious transition paths for low-skilled youths at the periphery amounts to a form of dualization (Busemeyer 2012a,b).

Analysis: partisan coalitions, economic coordination, and the politics of education reform

The previous sections sketched out the historical development of education policy in three cases: the United Kingdom (England and Wales), Sweden, and (West) Germany. These case studies are typical or representative of the three worlds of welfare capitalism (Esping-Andersen 1990), but they can also be regarded as diverse cases in the sense of Seawright & Gerring (2008: 300). The purpose of this section is to reflect on the extent to which the analytical framework developed in Chapter 1 is applicable to these case studies before it is applied within the broader context of a comparison of OECD countries in Chapter 3. I will pull together the crucial elements of the three case studies under two headings. I will first discuss the extent and continuity of institutional change, as well the importance of critical junctures in the postwar period for the development of upper and post-secondary education. I will then examine the role of partisan conflict and apply the extended model of partisan theory sketched out above to the cases at hand.

Critical junctures in the postwar development of upper and post-secondary education

The notions of critical junctures and punctuated equilibria were prominent features in the early generation of scholarship in historical institutionalism (Steinmo *et al.* 1992; Thelen 1999). But as Streeck and & Thelen (2005: 1) have pointed out, drawing a "sharp distinction between long periods of institutional stasis periodically interrupted by some sort of exogenous shock that opens things up" is too simplistic a picture of the complex process of institutional change in advanced political economies. To a significant extent, both the distinction between institutional change and stability and the definition of a "critical juncture" depend on how much the observer "zooms in" on the process of institutional development. If one studies large-scale change in polities (e.g., constitutional reforms or revolutions; Skocpol 1979), as the early work in historical institutionalism did, the punctuated-equilibrium model might be the appropriate one, and critical junctures are critical in the sense of being relatively short episodes of radical change. In advanced political economies, however, the institutional density and complexity is much higher than in preindustrial societies. In such a setting, large-scale policy change is always less likely than incremental change (Streeck & Thelen 2005).

This does not necessarily imply, however, that the notion of critical junctures cannot be applied in a meaningful way in these cases. By "zooming out" of the cases studied above, it is possible to identify certain time periods in which the potential for reform was higher than in others. These windows of opportunity open up when policy-makers face different options for the institutional development of a previously underdeveloped policy field. Indeed, compared to primary and lower-secondary education, as well as other social policies, upper-secondary and post-secondary education was an underdeveloped policy field that had not yet been fully institutionalized in European countries in the postwar period. Over time, the institutional density of policy fields increases and the window of opportunity for reform closes, because, as Pierson (2000: 253) has written, events that happen earlier in a chain of path-forming events have more significant implications than events that occur later.

We can thus distinguish different stages in the process of path formation, which can be called *path initialization, path formation*, and *path consolidation*. The concept of critical junctures is most meaningful in the second stage, when switching to alternative paths is still a politically feasible option.

Path initialization refers to the idea that policy legacies matter even in the relatively early stages of path formation. But policy legacies do not fully determine future events, and path switching could and did occur in the three cases studied above. While the cases had relatively similar policy legacies in the immediate postwar period (in comparison to countries like the United States and Japan), it is obvious that there were some significant differences. Even early on, the status and importance of apprenticeship was probably higher in Germany than in Sweden, although Sweden still had an apprenticeship system, whereas the ideological appeal of the universal welfare state model was stronger in Sweden. These facts can of course be taken as foreshadowing later events, but there is room for political action and conflict. The "shadow of the 19th century" (Iversen & Soskice 2009) may be long, but it is not endless. The case studies in this chapter have shown that there were significant political struggles over the institutional design of education systems in the 1950s, 1960s, and 1970s, and that these had strong implications for the future development of education systems.

The second stage, *path formation*, occurs when decisive choices are made about the design of institutions, choices that with hindsight can be identified as critical junctures. It is important to emphasize, however, that path formation during critical junctures is still a *process*, which may happen over an extended period of time. Rarely does one single instance of reform change development paths completely. Large-scale reforms, by contrast, proceed through various stages before they result in significant institutional change (see, for instance, the long process of comprehensivization in the Swedish system). It follows that the long-term balance of power between partisan actors matters more than the short-term partisan composition of governments. But it is not only partisan politics that matters: the long-term political sustainability of a chosen path depends on the congruence between the policy reforms and the socioeconomic context; that is, the institutional setup of the political economy and the interests of labor-market actors. When there is a hegemonic partisan coalition and the congruence between policies and socioeconomic institutions is high, path consolidation happens earlier and development paths are more sustainable over time. Critical junctures should thus not be conceptualized as brief periods of large-scale change, but rather as windows of opportunity that can be open for a longer stretch of time. Policy-makers may need to enact several steps of policy reform during such a stretch, each of which might look incremental at first sight, but which taken together will add up to a significant degree of institutional change over time (Streeck & Thelen 2005: 8).

Each of this chapter's cases went through a critical juncture, but the specific timing varied. In the case of Sweden, the construction of the Nordic model of education started under social democratic hegemony in the 1950s and lasted roughly until the 1970s. The crucial reform of upper-secondary education in 1972 had a lasting, path-shaping impact. The integration of VET into the general secondary school system contributed to the phasing out of workplace-based forms of apprenticeship training, leading large companies to make changes to their personnel strategies. The promotion of educational mobility within the egalitarian education system exacerbated academic drift towards higher education to a greater extent in Sweden than in Germany.

The critical juncture in Germany happened in the 1960s and 1970s. The 1969 law on VET stabilized and institutionalized the dual system of apprenticeship training and its core features, especially the dominance of firm-based training over school-based forms. The prewar three-tiered secondary education system had been restored by the 1950s, but the real window of opportunity for reforms opened up after the social–liberal coalition came into government. This coalition started out with an ambitious reform agenda that prioritized education. The prevailing zeitgeist greatly favored the creation of a comprehensive education system similar to the Swedish one; important components of the government's plans included integrating VET into the secondary school system and strengthening school-based forms of VET. The failure of most of these policy reforms indicated a consolidation of the specific path of institutional development, characterized by a strong and deeply institutionalized separation between academic and vocational education at the secondary and post-secondary levels.

The UK is a less clear-cut case, and not only because the Conservatives had a less hegemonic position than the Christian Democrats in Germany or the Social Democrats in Sweden. That being said, the Conservatives in Britain were certainly more influential than Labour during the postwar decades, particularly after 1979. The system could be considered a hybrid case until 1979, since it combined certain features of the Scandinavian and German models and added these into a more conservative and elitist model. As in Sweden, comprehensive schools spread throughout the 1960s and 1970s, but independent private schools survived as well. Like in Germany, apprenticeship training continued to be important in the manufacturing industry, and it was actually a Conservative government that passed the collectivist 1964 Industrial Training Act and expanded access to higher education in the early 1960s. The Thatcher government was crucial in setting the United Kingdom on a liberal-conservative development path, both in education and in welfare state policies more generally, making the 1980s the critical juncture for the British case. The 1988 Education Act introduced the principles of competition and choice into the general school system. The collectivist and corporatist institutional framework of the training system was dismantled; vocational training came to be regarded by both the government and employers as a social policy program for unemployed youths, instead of an investment in skilled labor. Once VET had ceased to be a viable route to secure and well-paid employment, academic drift came to be even more pronounced in the United Kingdom than in countries such as Sweden.

The third stage, *path consolidation*, is reached when the dominant political and economic actors adapt their preferences and strategies to reflect the institutional status quo. This does not preclude any kind of institutional change, but the fundamental structure of institutions will rarely be challenged, and change is bound to reflect existing policy legacies to a stronger extent than in the previous phase of path formation. As a consequence, partisan conflict matters less in this later stage, especially short-term changes in the partisan composition of governments. While it is true that studies comparing the policies of different governments over time within individual countries will always find differences that are related to the different electoral constituencies of political parties, the range of feasible policy options decreases because of path dependencies.

The case studies include numerous examples of path consolidation. In the United Kingdom, for example, the New Labour government of the mid-1990s and early 2000s largely continued along the lines of its Conservative predecessor. New Labour did not go back to the collective, corporatist approach to training policy of the 1960s and 1970s, but kept the voluntarist, employer-led framework in place instead. It also continued to promote choice and decentralization in the area of school policy. The coalition government likewise continued along the path set out by New Labour, particularly in higher education policy and with respect to establishing new kinds of schools independent of local authorities. Despite its newfound enthusiasm for apprenticeships, the coalition government did not return to the collective approach of the 1960s either, but stuck with the liberal voluntarist system.

The most significant educational reforms in Sweden were the decentralization and privatization reforms of the 1990s. These reforms did introduce more competition into the Swedish education system, but the case study shows that this change did not yet pose a fundamental challenge to the political and normative logic of the Nordic model of education. Most tellingly, the political conflict was about the division of power between localities and the central government in governing the education system, *not* about the place of VET in the education system, the reintroduction of apprenticeship training, access to higher education, or other aspects that would have represented far-reaching changes. The fundamental characteristic of the Swedish education system today remains in place: a statist and integrationist model of skill formation in which VET is fully integrated into the upper-secondary school system.

A similar conclusion can be drawn for the case of Germany. This country has gone through a period of intensified reform activity in the last decade, but its fundamental characteristics have been maintained. The red–green coalition initiated a number of significant reforms in the welfare state, and the education system – particularly higher education – went through a phase of internationalization. The privileged status and importance of dual VET (apprenticeship) has remained unchallenged, however, and is supported by most influential political actors, including unions. This is why the red–green coalition did not take up the more ambitious plans of the social–liberal coalition of the 1970s to fully integrate VET into secondary schooling. Although there is a trend towards slowly changing the structure of schools from a three-tiered to a two-tiered structure, a full-scale comprehensivization along Swedish lines is politically unfeasible for the foreseeable future.

Partisan politics in context

As documented in Chapter 1, there now exists a large and growing literature on the partisan politics of education (Ansell 2008, 2010; Boix 1997, 1998; Busemeyer 2007, 2008, 2009b, 2012a; Castles 1989, 1998; Jensen 2011; Nikolai 2007; Rauh *et al.* 2011; Schmidt 1980, 2002, 2007; Wolf 2009; Wolf & Zohlnhöfer 2009). Partisan preferences can vary across a number of policy dimensions, such as the preferred level of public or private investment in education, the distribution of resources across educational sectors (early childhood, compulsory, academic, and vocational education), the relative importance of education vis-à-vis other kinds of social policy, and the preferred governance model, including preferences concerning which kinds of organized interest should be involved. In this chapter I have concentrated on two aspects: the division of labor in financing education (commodification) and the stratification of education in terms of institutions.

I will now apply the theoretical framework – essentially an extended partisan model – developed in Chapter 1. I will first comment briefly on similarities and differences in partisan preferences across country cases, and then discuss the extensions to the standard partisan model proposed above. I have already discussed the third extension (i.e., the focus on long-term balance of power instead of the short-term partisan composition of governments, covered in the previous section). In this section, I concentrate on the two remaining extensions: the discussion of partisan preferences about the political process in addition to policy content, and the role of the institutional context, particularly in terms of economic coordination.

The case studies reveal some similarities in partisan preferences across countries. Finding these similarities (independent of context in terms of institutions and idiosyncratic party-specific ideological and organizational legacies) can be taken as support for the general model of partisan theory. At a very general level, left-wing parties are in favor of expanding access to higher levels of education for their core electoral constituencies in the lower half of the income and skills distribution. This also implies a preference for strong state involvement in the financing and administration of education, such as increases in public spending and individual subsidies for students, and a determination to limit educational stratification. For example, in all three countries the social democratic parties have become strong supporters of the model of comprehensive schooling, although the German Social Democrats have been less effective in implementing this preference because of the disadvantageous balance of power. Right-wing parties, by contrast, care less about educational expansion and are more supportive of private involvement in the financing and administration of education; they have strong preferences for a differentiated education system with extensive tracking. In this regard, the ideology of Christian democrats is not all that different from that of the secular conservatives. In all three countries, bourgeois parties have been the defenders of the traditional segmented school system, which also implies restricted access to higher education and a strict separation between VET and general schooling. Again, the bourgeois parties have been more or less successful in defending this model, depending on the balance of power (the Swedish conservatives' opposition to the comprehensive secondary school was ineffective, for instance).

In sum, the standard model of partisan theory assumes that different political parties of the left and of the right have similar policy preferences regardless of the context, and that differences between country cases emerge solely because of differences in the balance of power between partisan families. The standard model should work best in the early stages of path formation, before institutional legacies and contexts begin to shape the range of feasible policy options. One extension to this standard model is to argue that political parties have preferences with regard not only to policy content but also to how the political process should be organized. Whereas secular conservatives aim to minimize the influence of labor (Wolf 1998), Christian Democrats pursue a "politics of mediation" (Van Kersbergen 1999: 356). This has implications for the range of feasible policy options. As mentioned above, there are some similarities between conservative and Christian democratic ideology with regard to policy content, such as a preference for a segmented secondary school system and elite universities that is justified by the organic division of labor in society. The most important difference, however, may be the approach to apprenticeship training. British Conservatives, especially after 1979, regarded collective institutions such as the levy-grant system and the training boards as infringing on the autonomy of individual firms, and they did not hesitate to use the policy reforms of the wage-bargaining and training system in the 1980s to weaken the influence of trade unions. The German CDU, by contrast, pursued a corporatist policy approach that encouraged cross-class compromise and, to a certain extent, deliberately granted influence to union voices. The Christian democratic approach to training respected employers' autonomy to train as they wished, but at the same time demanded that they carry out their duty to train young people. Following the principle of subsidiarity, intermediate associations have been given a central role in the management and operation of the training system, even as the state remains a neutral moderator in the background, ready to intervene if necessary.

As expected, the case studies revealed some diversity within the social democratic family with regard to procedural preferences. In Britain, political parties are inclined to coalesce with and grant privileged access to those economic interests that belong to their electoral constituencies (business in the case of the Conservatives and unions in the case of Labour). In principle, parties are less keen on engineering cross-class consensus, which may be related to the majoritarian nature of the United Kingdom's political institutions and the liberal character of the economy. However, we also saw that there was a time when Labour and the Conservatives were able to form a broad coalition supporting education reforms in the immediate postwar period, for example in the case of comprehensive secondary schools and in the establishment of the levy-grant system in training. The consensual period ended decisively when Thatcher brought back the "class warfare" spirit. New Labour then tried to appeal to business interests while still maintaining ties to the unions, which could be interpreted as a cautious attempt to create some sort of cross-class compromise. In both Sweden and Germany, social democratic parties have historically been more open to the notion of corporatist bargaining.

The comparison between Germany and Sweden on the one hand and the United Kingdom on the other leads to the next issue: even though political parties may be willing to promote cross-class compromise, their ability to do so depends on the organizational foundations of labor-market actors and the institutional setup of the economy. Partisan politics does not happen in a societal vacuum, but is embedded in and interacts with institutional contexts. The linkage between political parties and organized labor-market actors varies across countries. This goes back to the old distinction between pluralist and corporatist systems of interest mediation (e.g., Lehmbruch 1979; Schmitter 1979), which is reflected in the recent differentiation between LMEs and CMEs (Hall & Soskice 2001). In LMEs, the coordination among economic interests follows the market logic; this implies a pluralistic conception of interest mediation. It is less likely that unions and employers' associations will engage in the formation of sustainable cross-class coalitions, nor is it likely that organized economic interests will enter into close alliances with state actors or partisan policy-makers, institutionalized in corporatist bodies. In contrast, corporatism is strong in

CMEs. This includes both the monopolization of functional representation via peak associations and tight linkages between these associations and the policy-making system. In sum, the concept of economic coordination entails two aspects: coordination among organized economic interests in the labor-market arena and coordination between these interests and policy-makers in the political arena.

Socioeconomic institutions are also associated with particular patterns of democratic decision-making (Lijphart 1999). Where coordination is low, as is the case in majoritarian Westminster democracies, policy-makers may be able to effect more significant policy change, but given the lack of coordination, it is an open question *ex ante* whether this policy change will actually lead to real change. If there is no congruency between the policies and the institutional context, they will remain ineffective in triggering real institutional change. Where coordination is high, policy-makers can hardly pass policies against the joint opposition of organized interests; instead, they must engage in the formation of politico-economic alliances that span the gap between the policy-making and labor-market arenas. Once agreement on policy reform is reached, however, it is more likely to lead to real institutional change that is sustainable in the long run.

In the United Kingdom, an LME, the formation of a sustainable cross-class coalition was not feasible in the long run. The low level of coordination in both the business and labor camps led to pluralist forms of interest mediation and relatively weak peak associations, with little influence. It thus prevented the establishment of representative monopolies, which would have been necessary for the establishment of a viable system of private-interest government via associations (Streeck & Schmitter 1985). The tumultuous 1970s, with their high levels of strike activity, delegitimized and put an end to earlier attempts to establish corporatist institutions in training and manpower policy more generally. The wildcat strikes during the Winter of Discontent (1978–79) are a good example of policy-makers' failure to coordinate with organized economic interests: although Labour was in government at the time, it could not prevent unions from striking. The lack of coordination between labor-market interests and policy-makers may also explain the government's repeatedly unsuccessful attempts to promote apprenticeship training (Finegold & Soskice 1988; King 1997; Ryan & Unwin 2001). Because policy-makers cannot credibly commit labor-market actors to long-term strategies of skill formation, employers will refrain from investing in skills beyond short-term needs and unions will be unwilling to accept lower wages for apprentices, which would be a necessary condition for skill investments by firms (Marsden & Ryan 1991).

On the other hand, cross-class coalitions are a hallmark of CMEs. A well-known argument in the literature is that coalitions between employers and unions in matters of skill formation and social policy are important historical foundations of the institutional framework of CMEs (Cusack *et al.* 2007; Mares 2003; Martin & Swank 2008, 2012; Swenson 2002; Thelen 2004). What is less appreciated in the literature, however, is that there can be different types of cross-class coalitions, depending on which partisan actor is the *formateur* during the critical juncture (Busemeyer 2012a). Cross-class coalitions can be more or less encompassing, and policy-makers as political and partisan actors can selectively grant privileged access to certain kinds of organized interest.

In Sweden, the hegemony of social democracy was a consequence not only of the strong position of the SAP in parliament and government, but also of the extraordinary power of the trade-union movement. As is well known, employers responded to the threat of organized labor by establishing extensive coordination mechanisms on their own (Martin & Swank 2012; Swenson 2002), and the 1938 Saltsjöbaden agreement laid the foundation for sustainable cross-class compromise and macro-corporatist wage bargaining. Nevertheless, employers' associations were the weaker partners in this cross-class coalition. In the 1950s and 1960s, the Social Democrats' preference for statist solutions and the unions' worries about apprentices being misused as a cheap source of labor led to the dismantling of the institutional legacies of firm-based apprenticeship training from the postwar era. The 1972 reform of upper-secondary education was supported by both unions and employers, but the SAF would have preferred a much stronger linkage of VET to the workplace (Lundahl 1997: 95). Once the path was selected, however, labor-market interests adopted their strategies in the same way as the political parties had done. When Swedish conservatives promoted the resuscitation of apprenticeship training in the 1980s, the SAF was initially supportive, but it then became quite reluctant, because employers had already adjusted their recruitment strategies and were not willing or able to invest in broad occupational skill formation (Lundahl 1997: 98). Unlike the unions in Germany, Swedish unions have strongly supported the integrated secondary system and school-based VET.

The German case is different from the Swedish one. Here, the *formateur* of the cross-class coalition was the Christian Democratic Party, not the Social Democrats. In this case, business interests had a privileged position compared to unions. The passing of the BBiG in 1969 provides a good example of the specific bias of this variety of cross-class coalition. The law did not fundamentally challenge the privileged position of training firms in training matters, even though the SPD was a formal member of the government coalition. Unions were very much part of the social–liberal reform coalition of the 1970s, but this coalition eventually failed because of effective opposition from employers, who were threatening to withdraw from apprenticeship training in a time of rising youth unemployment. After this critical juncture passed, unions changed their strategies, working through corporatist institutions at the firm and industry level, as well as the complex institutions set up to reform training occupations. Unions have since become strong defenders of firm-based training over school-based alternatives (Busemeyer 2012a), even more so than the SPD.

These cases are excellent examples of how actors adopt their strategies and preferences once a critical juncture has passed. They also demonstrate how "policies shape politics" (Pierson 2005: 37–9). German trade unions supported the establishment of a more statist skill-formation regime in the 1970s because they hoped this would increase their political influence in the administration of the system. The prevailing dominance of firm-based apprenticeship and the continued central role of Chambers of Industry and Commerce in the governance structure of this system crushed the unions' aspirations. In the United Kingdom, the Thatcher government's use of training policies to break the influence of trade unions was even more blatant.

Preliminary conclusions and outlook

Chapter 1 laid out a theoretical framework meant to explain the observed variety of education regimes in Western European countries. The case studies in this chapter have applied this theory to the three cases of the United Kingom (England), Sweden, and Germany. The main findings can be summarized as follows: partisan conflicts do matter, and reflect the distributive power struggles over the institutional design of education systems, but the standard model of partisan theory needs to be extended. First of all, the case studies revealed that each case went through the three stages of path initialization, path formation, and path consolidation. Critical choices about the design of educational institutions happened during the second stage, when policy alternatives remained politically feasible, but the ultimate defeat of such alternatives set in motion a process of path consolidation, locking in the development path and defining the fundamental characteristics of education regimes. Because large-scale change takes time, the notion of critical junctures needs to be broadened to take into account that critical junctures are more akin to windows of opportunity for reform, which may remain open for a significant amount of time. It is less the short-time frame that defines the "criticalness" of critical junctures, then, but the fact that choices undertaken during this period have long-term implications for future development paths. A first extension to the standard model of partisan theory is thus to pay more attention to the long-term balance of power between partisan forces and how this varies across countries, rather than focus too much on the short-term effects of changes in the partisan composition of governments.

A second extension is to take into account that political parties have preferences not only about the content of policies but also about how the political process should be organized and which interests should gain access to policy-making. I have argued that this extension reveals a clear distinction between secular conservatives of the British kind and Christian democrats, which is reminiscent of the debate in welfare state research about the distinctiveness of Christian democratic social policy (Van Kersbergen 1995). Conservative parties are strongly opposed to the notion of cooperating with unions, and in the British case have even used training and labor-market policies to marginalize union influence. In contrast, Christian democratic parties promote corporatist forms of interest mediation, including giving a voice to unions.

The extent to which cross-class compromise is achieved depends not only on the willingness of political parties to foster compromise but also on the institutional structure and the organizational foundations of labor-market actors. In LMEs, class conflict dominates, whereas in CMEs, cross-class compromises between unions and employers are more common. Political parties can and do try to influence the partisan logic of cross-class coalitions, however, tilting the balance slightly more in favor of those economic interests that are closer to their electoral constituencies.

What is the upshot of these discussions, and how are they related to the topics discussed in the remainder of the book? The key to understanding the linkage between education, employment, and the welfare state more generally is to recognize the importance of the survival of VET as an educational alternative to academic higher education. Where VET has declined as a viable alternative for middle-class children, as in the United Kingdom, the focus has shifted to higher education, contributing to skills polarization and higher levels of inequality. Where VET has survived as a popular and politically viable alternative, a stronger compression of skills and income has resulted, creating lower levels of inequality, as will be shown in detail in Chapter 4. This effect is particularly strong for school-based forms of VET that are fully integrated into the secondary school system (e.g., in Sweden), because this opens up routes to social and educational advancement for children from the lower classes. The dominance of workplace-based types of VET (apprenticeships) in countries such as Germany has contributed to keeping segregated secondary school and elitist higher education systems alive and politically viable, as long as school leavers from the lower tiers have access to good apprenticeships and decent jobs afterwards. The high degree of institutional stratification in this system also helps maintain willingness among employers to invest in apprenticeship training, since they do not have to fear that apprentices will abscond to universities after their training has finished. In short, the survival of VET has had deep implications for the expansion of higher education and the institutional structure of secondary school systems.

3 | *Worlds of skill formation*
Cross-national quantitative analysis

In this chapter, I continue along the lines of the previous one by expanding the comparative lens from the three selected case studies to a broader set of advanced industrial democracies in the OECD world. Chapter 3 consists of three distinct parts. In the first, I present descriptive statistics on the variety of educational institutions in Western welfare states. In the second, I present a number of simple scatterplots and cross-sectional regressions on the institutional and political determinants of the various characteristics of education regimes. In the third I look at multivariate regression analyses.

Descriptive statistics

This section starts with a broad overview of the institutional characteristics of education regimes in the OECD world. First, I would like to go back to Figure 1.1 (reprinted as Figure 3.1), which represents the distribution of cases along the two broad dimensions of commodification (i.e., the division of labor between public and private in the financing of education) and educational stratification. This graph provides initial support for the notion of three distinct worlds of education: we can observe the expected clustering of countries. Table 3.1 presents a more qualitative summary of the core characteristics of the different regimes, building on the insights from the case studies in Chapter 2 and the pertinent literature on worlds of education (Allmendinger & Leibfried 2003; Busemeyer & Nikolai 2010; Crouch *et al.* 1999; Hega & Hokenmaier 2002; Iversen & Stephens 2008; Lynch 1994; West & Nikolai 2013; Willemse & de Beer 2012). Table 3.2 provides more detailed statistical data to back up the qualitative statements. The grouping of countries into different clusters (liberal, collective, statist, mixed) is mainly done for presentational purposes at this point. Since I am interested in broad cross-national comparisons,

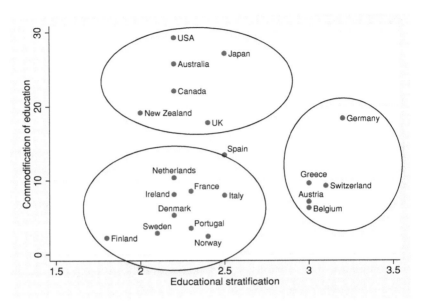

Figure 3.1 De-commodification and stratification in education systems

Table 3.2 presents average values for the recent period (1997–2008), for which high-quality and standardized comparative data are available in the OECD Education Statistics Database (Columns 2 through 5). For some countries, the OECD provides data for earlier years, which will be used in the quantitative multivariate analyses later in this chapter. I refrain from extending the period of analysis beyond 2008 because the global economic and financial crisis had significant effects on policy and economic output in some of the countries under observation and less severe effects in others. This might potentially bias the average values, particularly for short time series such as these. Therefore, the main purpose of this data presentation is to capture cross-national differences in the 2000s before the onset of the crisis.

One continuing problem in the OECD data is the lack of convincing quantitative measures of the variety of VET systems, particularly with regard to the distinction between school-based and workplace-based systems. The OECD does publish data on enrollment patterns in upper-secondary education (Indicator C1.2 in the *Education at a Glance* series), which distinguishes between enrollment in general (or

Table 3.1 *The diversity of education and training systems in OECD countries*

	Overall investment in education	Private share of funding	Public investment in higher education	Stratification of the secondary school system	Dominant type of vocational training	Extensiveness of vocational training	Relationship between education and social policy
Anglo-Saxon countries, e.g., the United Kingdom	High	High	Medium	Low	Market-based; on-the-job training	Low	Education as social policy
Scandinavian countries, e.g., Sweden	High	Low	High	Low	School-based	High	Education as part of the welfare state
Continental European countries, e.g., Germany	Medium	Low (except for firms in vocational training)	Low	High	Workplace-based; dual training	High	Institutional and political separation

Table 3.2 *Selected quantitative indicators, cross-national averages, 1997–2008*

Country	Public spending on education, percentage of GDP	Private spending on education, percentage of GDP	Percentage of education spending that is public	Percentage of population with at least upper-secondary education (15- to 64-year-olds)	Employer involvement in VET	Public commitment to VET
Liberal skill regimes						
Australia	4.3	1.4	74.6	61.6	0.00	0.06
Canada	5.1	1.2	78.5	82.3	−0.95	−1.81
Ireland	4.3	0.3	91.7	59.1	−0.97	−1.86
New Zealand	5.5	1.3	80.1	72.1	n/a	n/a
United Kingdom	4.8	0.8	82.2	67.1	−0.16	−0.63
United States	5.0	2.0	71.1	87.3	n/a	n/a
Statist skill regimes						
Finland	5.9	0.1	97.8	74.5	−0.24	0.23
Iceland	6.4	0.6	90.5	60.1	n/a	n/a
Norway	6.2	0.2	97.6	82.9	0.13	0.09
Sweden	6.4	0.2	97.2	80.6	−1.03	0.57
Collective skill regimes						
Austria	4.3	0.3	93.3	76.9	1.23	0.81
Denmark	6.7	0.4	94.5	76.8	1.68	−0.13
Germany	4.3	1.0	81.4	83.3	1.65	0.13
Switzerland	5.5	0.5	90.8	82.4	1.66	−0.14

Mixed skill regimes

Belgium	5.5	0.3	93.8	61.4	−0.97	1.51
France	5.7	0.4	91.4	65.2	−0.16	0.43
Greece	3.7	0.5	91.5	52.2	−1.09	−0.58
Italy	4.5	0.3	92.5	45.2	−0.92	−1.10
Japan	3.5	1.3	73.1	82.4	n/a	n/a
Netherlands	4.5	0.4	89.8	67.9	−0.22	1.86
Portugal	5.5	0.2	96.5	23.2	n/a	n/a
Spain	4.3	0.7	86.4	41.3	n/a	n/a

academic) tracks on the one hand and enrollment in vocational tracks on the other. Additional data are given on the share of upper-secondary students in vocational programs that combine school- and workplace-based training; that is, dual apprenticeships. Unfortunately, these data have a number of problems. There are a lot of missing values, particularly with regard to the share of apprenticeship training. This is largely a consequence of the inherent complexity of some VET systems, such as the British one, where training is offered by a multiplicity of training providers, ranging from vocational schools via private training providers to regular employers. Because the OECD data are based on enrollment shares, they also miss important qualitative differences between education and training systems. To pick an extreme example, the share of students in vocational education in Australia (47.5 percent) is similar to that in Denmark (46.5 percent; all values for the year 2010; OECD 2012: 332). While it is well known that VET in Australia plays a larger role than in other Anglo-Saxon countries (Toner 2008), the similarity in enrollment shares glosses over important qualitative differences in the institutional setup between the Danish and Australian skill regimes.

To mitigate the problem of missing data, we conducted a survey among VET experts in a large number of OECD countries in order to come up with better measures. Additional information on the survey can be found in Busemeyer & Schlicht-Schmälzle (2014). Initially, we approached 193 experts in 23 OECD countries, and we ended up with 99 completed questionnaires, which we used to construct measures of two core dimensions of variation in VET systems (see also Busemeyer 2009a; Busemeyer & Iversen 2012; Busemeyer & Trampusch 2012; Martin 2012): the involvement of employers in skill formation and the degree of public commitment to the provision of VET. The first measure captures the extent to which employers are involved in the provision of training – mostly in the form of dual apprenticeships – and in the governance of these schemes. The second measure relates to various characteristics of the education system, such as the extent to which vocational qualifications are certified and the amount of public subsidization of VET. These two dimensions are not as strongly correlated as could be expected (the bivariate correlation is 0.23). They capture essential differences between the statist and the collective skill regime. The two measures in Table 3.2 are standardized; they have a mean of 0 and a standard deviation of 1.

What are the core characteristics of the different worlds of skill formation? The liberal regime combines medium levels of public expenditure with above-average levels of private education spending. A large share of private education spending is made up of tuition fees for higher education. In sum, the overall levels of educational investment are clearly above the OECD average. This pattern is particularly pronounced in the United States, Canada, New Zealand, and Australia. The United Kingdom and Ireland are somewhat different. Higher education institutions in the United Kingdom are mostly public, and thus strongly dependent on public subsidies, but the governance of higher education is market-oriented because these institutions are highly autonomous. The significant increase in tuition fees in recent years has made the UK system more similar to the North American countries with regard to financing mechanisms (Ansell 2010). Ireland is different again from the other countries because it is still in the process of catching up. The share of the working-age population (15- to 64-year-olds) with at least an upper-secondary education is significantly lower in Ireland than in other countries, hinting at the legacy of a low-skill economy struggling with brain drain. A common characteristic of the liberal Anglo-Saxon countries is that levels of both public commitment to and employer involvement in VET are below average. Australia is a partial exception because apprenticeship training there survived in particular economic sectors, such as construction, longer than it did in the United Kingdom. This also speaks to the peculiar character and generally more robust system of Australian industrial relations (Gospel 1994; Toner 2008). Compared to continental European countries, the education systems of liberal skill regimes are much less institutionally stratified. In all of these countries except Ireland, secondary education is mostly provided in comprehensive high schools. Post-secondary education centers on academic education in colleges and universities. Some of these may have a vocational orientation (such as the American community colleges), but the systems are generally geared towards providing general and transferable skills (Busemeyer 2009a; Estévez-Abe et al. 2001).

Japan shares many characteristics with liberal skill regimes (see also Busemeyer & Nikolai 2010), including low levels of public expenditure combined with above-average levels of private education spending, the dominance of general education at the secondary level in comprehensive high schools, and the central position of academic education at the post-secondary level (Dore & Sako 1998). Some of these similarities can be traced back to the influence of the United States as an occupying power in the immediate postwar years. A crucial difference between Japan and the liberal countries, however, is that Japanese employers are much more involved in skill formation (Thelen 2004). Skill formation is provided in a more firm-specific context than in collective skill systems, and the mechanisms for the authoritative certification of vocational skills that would ensure job mobility between firms are less developed (Estévez-Abe et al. 2001). Japan is therefore usually classified as a segmentalist skill regime (Busemeyer 2009a; Busemeyer & Trampusch 2012; Thelen 2004).

In many ways, statist skill regimes are the opposite of liberal regimes: they are characterized by above-average levels of public spending on education, but below-average levels of private spending. But beyond these apparent differences, there are a number of interesting commonalities. Looking at total levels of education spending, for example, the liberal and statist regimes are roughly even: where liberal regimes draw on private sources for additional funding, statist systems inject more public funds (Wolf 2009; Wolf & Zohlnhöfer 2009). As in most liberal countries, the percentage of the population with at least an upper-secondary education is strongly above average (with the exception of Iceland, as a catch-up country). Another similarity is the spread of comprehensive education as the dominant form of secondary education, which implies a desire to overcome the segmentation between academic and vocational education and to promote educational mobility. A crucial difference between the statist and the liberal regime, however, lies in the treatment of VET. Compared to its low status in the liberal world, VET remains an important and viable educational alternative to general academic education in the Scandinavian countries. This is evidenced by the large difference between the statist and the liberal regime type that we found in our measure of public commitment to VET. Employers are much less involved in the provision of skill formation than in collective skill regimes, because VET is largely provided in vocational schools or in the form of dedicated tracks in the integrated comprehensive school system.

Finally, the collective skill regimes exhibit medium to below-average levels of public spending on education. Levels of private education spending are higher than in the Scandinavian countries, for reasons which include that in some cases, such as Germany, employer contributions to apprenticeship training also count as private education spending (Heidenheimer 1996; Wolf 2009). The population share with at least an upper-secondary education is above average too, indicating a broad distribution of educational credentials. Whereas liberal skill regimes such as the United States and Canada achieve high scores on this indicator as a result of high levels of college enrollment, the collective skill regimes have a competitive advantage in the provision of intermediate-level skills related to well-established VET systems. Compared to the other worlds of skill formation, employers are much more involved in the provision of skill formation. The level of public commitment to VET is only middling, however. These two aspects are related because collective skill-formation systems are based on the principle of corporatist self-governance, which implies a certain self-restriction on the part of state actors against getting involved (Busemeyer & Trampusch 2012). Levels of public commitment to VET are higher in Austria than in the other countries because school-based VET is more important there (Graf *et al.* 2012).

Denmark and the Netherlands are interesting cases that combine elements of different skill regimes. Denmark displays much higher levels of public spending on education than do other countries in the collective skill-formation regime, and its secondary education system is less stratified and more integrated. Compared to other Scandinavian countries, the degree of employer involvement in skill formation is much higher in Denmark, since dual training is the dominant form of VET at the secondary level (Nelson 2012). The Dutch system, by contrast, privileges school-based VET (indicated by its high level of public commitment to VET), but apprenticeship training has become an important part of the secondary education system since its resuscitation in the early 1980s (Anderson & Oude Nijhuis 2012). As in other continental European countries, the secondary system remains more stratified institutionally and the level of public spending on education is merely average.

The Belgian and French education systems are in many ways similar to the Dutch system: VET remains important, but it is largely provided without strong firm involvement, although French policy-makers have been trying to use various means to get employers to commit (Culpepper 2003). The governance mechanisms in these education systems are very much state-centered. The French education system remains highly centralized, the Belgian system less so after the transition towards a federalist system in the 1990s. Nevertheless, both countries exhibit significantly higher levels of public spending on education than their German-speaking neighbors, in part because of their extensive systems of early childhood education.

Finally, a case can be made to group the southern European countries into a cluster of their own (see, e.g., Allmendinger & Leibfried 2003). The discussion over whether there should be a "fourth world of welfare state capitalism" for southern European countries is a repeating topic in comparative welfare state research (Esping-Andersen 1999; Ferrera 1996). The data in Table 3.2 show that these countries have a number of things in common: below-average levels of public and private spending on education and, as a corollary, below-average shares of the working-age population with at least an upper-secondary education. Employer involvement in VET and public commitment to VET are likewise low in those cases for which we have data (Greece and Italy), potentially accounting for the exceptionally high levels of youth unemployment in these countries.

The grouping of countries in Table 3.2 is deliberate and therefore to a certain extent arbitrary. As an alternative, Figure 3.2 presents the results of a hierarchical cluster analysis. Cluster analysis is a simple but highly illustrative tool of descriptive statistics that calculates the relative distances between cases in the multidimensional space defined by the variables entered into the analysis (in this case, I used the Ward method for calculating differences). The downside of hierarchical cluster analysis is that the clustering can be very sensitive to the inclusion or exclusion of additional cases and/or variables. The findings should be treated with caution and used merely as a descriptive illustration of what has been said so far. In order to determine the relative robustness of the clusters identified in the analysis, I ran two different specifications. In the first, I included a large set of variables, namely all variables contained in Table 3.1 (except the public spending share; this does not provide any new information because I included both public and private education spending as individual variables). In the second, I used a reduced set of variables: the public share of education spending, public commitment to VET, and employer involvement in VET. These variables, in my view, capture the essential dimensions of variation in the institutional setup of education and training systems (commodification and stratification). Because two of the variables included in the analysis are the same, the results of the cluster analysis are not that

Worlds of skill formation

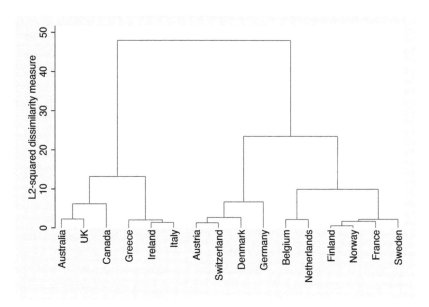

Figure 3.2 Results of a hierarchical cluster analysis of countries

different from one another. Figure 3.2 presents the findings from the analysis using the larger set of variables.

Importantly, the cluster analyses confirm the existence of three broad clusters of countries. The statist skill regime is made up of Finland, Norway, and Sweden, joined by France. Belgium and the Netherlands are related to this cluster on a higher level, confirming their intermediate position between the statist and the collective world; not only are they close to one another, but they are also not that far from the statist group. The collective skill regime consists of Austria, Denmark, Germany, and Switzerland. Their cluster is connected to the statist group at a higher level, which makes sense, since this is the large group of CMEs. The liberal countries in the sample, Australia, the United Kingdom, and Canada, also form a cluster of their own. Somewhat surprisingly, they are quite close to the southern European countries (Ireland is actually grouped together with Greece and Italy). The explanation for this group of strange bedfellows may be that the educational pathways in VET in all of these countries are either underdeveloped or nonexistent compared to the other country clusters.

It can be argued that at a general level, the different worlds of skill formation relate to the different conceptions of how education and the welfare state are connected (Allmendinger & Leibfried 2003; Allmendinger & Nikolai 2010). In the liberal world, the promotion of education might be considered a functional equivalent to social policy in securing against the vagaries of the labor market. As Heidenheimer (1981: 269) has argued, the differences in the relative emphasis on education versus social insurance policies in Europe and the United States could simply be "the cores of alternative strategies pursued by emerging welfare states": essentially different means to achieving the same end. In a liberal political culture that values individual freedom and choice over collective forms of social insurance, education may even be regarded as the morally superior solution to the problem of labor-market uncertainty, because it rewards individual effort and limits collectively enforced redistribution.

The liberal world shares with the Scandinavian statist world the notion that education should be considered part of the welfare state. Whereas in liberal countries education may be regarded as the functional equivalent of redistributive social policies or a substitute for these, in Scandinavian countries it is conceived as an essential element of the universal model of the welfare state: in other words, as a complementary addition to social policy. Another important difference is that in the more liberal regimes, the placing of academic (often even liberal arts) education at the top of the hierarchy of educational alternatives has prevented and delegitimized the establishment of more practical or applied types of secondary and post-secondary education, which could have benefited those in the lower half of the academic skills distribution. Whether due to the lingering legacies of elitist and stratified education systems or the explicit influence of unions and employers, VET has remained a viable educational alternative in Scandinavian countries. In contrast to continental Europe, however, and in line with the notion of a comprehensive model of education, VET in Scandinavia is also supposed to facilitate educational mobility for low-skilled youths and enable them to ascend the educational ladder.

In the collective skill systems of continental Europe, the spheres of education and welfare state policies are politically and institutionally separated. The conservative welfare state model implies a delegation of responsibilities to corporatist, self-governed, semi-public

Worlds of skill formation 135

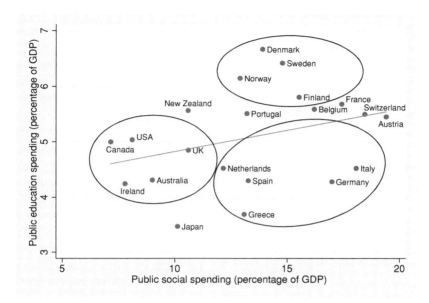

Figure 3.3 Public spending on educational institutions and social policies as percentage of GDP, average values 1997–2008

institutions that are eager to defend their autonomy against intrusion by the central government. In a number of federalist countries in this cluster (Germany, Austria, Switzerland), the asymmetrical distribution of policy-making competencies for education and social policy may have exaggerated this separation.

Figure 3.3 is a simple way of demonstrating the relative emphasis put on education in the different worlds of skill formation. The x axis shows the level of public social spending, broadly defined (but excluding education, of course) as a percentage of GDP. The y axis displays the level of public education spending, also as a percentage of GDP. The positive slope of the fitted regression line indicates that the public provision of education can generally be regarded as a complement to, rather than a substitute for, a well-developed welfare state. Residual welfare states do not compensate for their low levels of social spending with above-average levels of public education spending. Conversely, generous welfare states are also more likely to funnel a significant amount of public investment into the education system. More interesting than this general trend are the departures from it. The liberal cluster (the United States, Canada, New Zealand, the United Kingdom, and Australia) is exactly where we would expect it to be: these countries combine low levels of public social spending with medium levels of education spending. If we add private education spending to public spending, of course, some of the countries move up to the level of the Scandinavian countries. This indicates a strong emphasis on education. The Scandinavian cluster exhibits high levels of both social and education spending. These countries' position above the regression line indicates that they have a strong relative emphasis on education (i.e., levels of education spending are even higher than would be expected given the respective levels of social spending). Finally, a number of continental European countries (southern European countries in particular, but also Germany and the Netherlands) exhibit a certain bias that favors social policy provision to the detriment of public investment in education, as indicated by their position below the regression line. In this picture, the southern European states cluster together with the typical representatives of the conservative welfare state model, although there are other continental European countries such as Belgium and France that are between the Scandinavian and the Continental cluster. In any case, the borderlines of these clusters should not be drawn too sharply; they are sensitive to the inclusion of different cases and variables.

Political and institutional determinants of educational institutions: bivariate analyses and scatterplots

I now present a series of bivariate analyses and scatterplots that provide a first test of the theoretical expectations developed in Chapters 1 and 2. I will concentrate on the main independent variables of interest: partisan politics and economic coordination. Alternative explanations and additional control variables will be discussed in the third part of this chapter. In this section, I am interested in broad cross-national comparisons, as well as in how partisan legacies of the postwar decades are related to the contemporary institutional setup of education and training systems. The underlying assumption that I have to make is that changes over time within countries will be less pronounced than cross-national differences. All dependent variables analyzed in the following section are defined as average values for the contemporary period (1997–2008) for which the OECD has provided high-quality comparative data.

Worlds of skill formation 137

As is common in the literature, I use the cabinet share of different party families to measure their influence on policy output. This indicator is more problematic in the case of education than in other social policies because it measures the partisan composition of national governments, despite the fact that the provision and administration of education, especially in federalist countries, is usually delegated to lower levels of government, such as state governments in the United States or *Länder* governments in Germany. In the present case, therefore, the indicator should be regarded as a more general measure of the balance of power between party families over longer time periods. For the bivariate analyses, I use the dataset provided by Schmidt (2003), because this covers the entire postwar period and differentiates clearly between the party family of Christian democrats and others (social democrats, conservatives, and liberals). I calculate long-term averages of the cabinet shares of different party families (1945–2000). To measure differences in economic coordination, I use the encompassing index of economic coordination in labor relations developed by Hall & Gingerich (2009: 456–8). This indicator combines information about the prevailing level and degree of wage coordination (both of which are related to the centralization of wage bargaining), as well as labor turnover (a measure of labor mobility). Higher values indicate a stronger degree of coordination.

I start out by analyzing the political and institutional determinants of the first of the two dimensions depicted in Figure 3.1: (de-)commodification in terms of the public/private division of labor in education financing. Differences in the private share of education financing are strongly related to the size of the welfare state (Figure 3.4). Higher levels of social spending are associated with a higher public share in the financing of education, and vice versa. Without necessarily implying a causal relationship in one direction or the other, this negative association clearly indicates an empirical correlation between the differences in the institutional setup of the education system and the welfare state.

Partisan legacies are another important determinant of the public/private division of labor in education financing (Figure 3.5; see also Wolf 2009; Wolf & Zohlnhöfer 2009). The private share of education spending is considerably higher in countries where conservative parties have occupied a larger share of cabinet seats in the postwar period. The participation of social democratic parties in government, by contrast, is strongly associated with lower levels of private spending. The

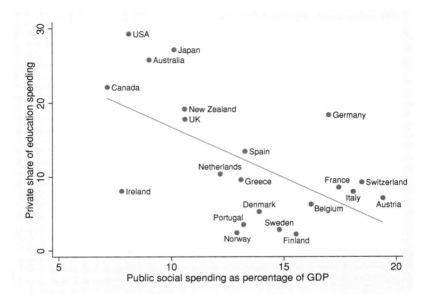

Figure 3.4 Private share of education funding and public social spending, 1997–2008

influence of Christian democratic parties is not as clear-cut as in the other two cases; the association between the Christian democratic cabinet share and the private spending variable is negative, as in the case of social democrats, but it is relatively weak.

These results can be confirmed in simple cross-sectional regression analyses using long-term averages (Table 3.3). Even when we control for levels of social spending (and are aware that government partisanship and social spending are themselves correlated), the historical partisan composition of governments matters. Models 1 to 4 in Table 3.3 look at the share of private education spending, whereas Models 5 to 8 analyze the spending share for tertiary higher education only. Private spending on higher education amounts to roughly two-thirds of total private education spending (Wolf & Zohlnhöfer 2009: 231), making it more significant than private spending on primary and secondary education. In any case, the effect of partisan government on the division of labor between public and private sources is very similar regardless of whether we look at all levels of education or at higher education only. On the other hand, there is no apparent association between

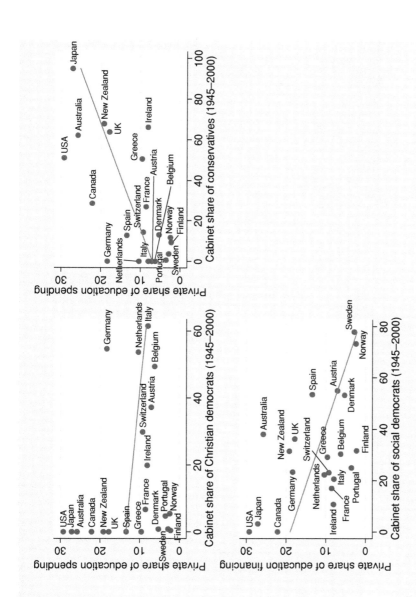

Figure 3.5 Partisan politics (1945–2000) and private share of education spending (1997–2008)

Table 3.3 *Partisan politics, social spending, and private share of education spending, cross-sectional regression analyses*

	(1)	(2)	(3)	(4)	(5)	(6)	(7)	(8)
Dependent variable	\multicolumn{4}{c}{Private share of education spending, all levels of education, average 1997–2008}	\multicolumn{4}{c}{Private share of education spending, tertiary education only, average 1997–2008}
Public social spending, % of GDP	−0.599 (0.500)	−1.563** (0.571)	−1.069** (0.422)	−1.287* (0.716)	−2.145** (0.995)	−3.845*** (1.092)	−2.926*** (0.826)	−3.492** (1.562)
Cabinet share of conservatives, long-term average	0.141*** (0.0486)				0.242* (0.125)			
Cabinet share of Christian democrats, long-term average		0.0576 (0.0823)				0.112 (0.155)		
Cabinet share of social democrats, long-term average			−0.152*** (0.0524)				−0.275** (0.120)	
Economic coordination in labor relations				−1.698 (9.626)				−0.0884 (20.17)
Constant	16.29* (8.051)	32.06*** (7.649)	31.13*** (6.428)	30.31*** (7.222)	43.89** (15.55)	71.39*** (14.89)	69.50*** (13.01)	69.46*** (14.98)
Observations	21	21	21	20	21	21	21	20
R^2	0.482	0.373	0.487	0.362	0.553	0.489	0.565	0.508

Robust standard errors in parentheses
*** $p < 0.01$, ** $p < 0.05$, * $p < 0.1$

the private share of education spending and the degree of economic coordination. This is not surprising, since the latter is hypothesized to be more relevant with regard to VET in terms of the distribution of students across different tracks.

As well as affecting the division of labor in education spending between public and private sources, partisan politics matters with regard to the *level* of public investment in education. The simple cross-sectional regressions in Table 3.4 look at the statistical association between the long-term averages of the cabinet share of conservatives, Christian democrats, and social democrats on the one hand, and public spending on educational institutions for all levels of education, for higher education, and for VET (which needs to be estimated with a proxy variable) on the other.[1] I include levels of social spending as a control variable because a larger welfare state is likely to imply higher levels of public spending on education.

Mirroring previous findings in the literature (Ansell 2010; Boix 1997, 1998; Busemeyer 2007, 2009b; Schmidt 2007), I find a positive association between the cabinet share of social democrats and public spending on education (as percentage of GDP; Model 3). The positive association also holds in the case of public spending on VET (Model 9), but is less pronounced in the case of higher education (but see Busemeyer 2009b). In contrast to social democrats, the extensive government participation of conservative parties is associated with lower levels of public spending on education (Model 1), as well as lower public spending on higher education (Model 4). Christian democratic incumbency is also negatively associated with public spending for all levels

---

[1] Unfortunately, the OECD does not provide direct data on public spending on VET. I had to construct a proxy variable instead, which is the share of upper-secondary students in VET multiplied by public spending on all forms of upper-secondary education (as percentage of GDP). In order for the proxy to work, I had to assume that per capita spending for VET and general upper-secondary education is the same (or at least that asymmetries between the two are similar across countries). This measure is far from perfect, but the country values are largely those one would expect given the evidence from the case studies. For the case of the United States, I have inserted a value of zero manually, since the secondary education system does not have a dedicated vocational track. This is done to avoid losing a case. Excluding the case of the United States does not fundamentally affect the results, although the effect of social democracy is somewhat weaker, as could be expected. There is still missing data for New Zealand, such that the number of cases is reduced from 21 to 20 in Models 6 to 9 in Table 3.4.

Table 3.4 Partisan politics and the determinants of different types of education spending, cross-sectional regression analyses

Dependent variable	(1)	(2)	(3)	(4)	(5)	(6)	(7)	(8)	(9)
	Public spending on educational institutions, all levels, % of GDP			Public spending on tertiary education institutions, % of GDP			Public investment in VET (proxy), % of GDP		
Public social spending, % of GDP	−0.00515 (0.0480)	0.135*** (0.0339)	0.0384 (0.0404)	−0.0225 (0.0199)	0.0329 (0.0206)	0.00586 (0.0187)	0.0683*** (0.0148)	0.0680*** (0.0119)	0.0538*** (0.0142)
Cabinet share of conservatives, long-term average	−0.0149* (0.0080)			−0.00694** (0.00252)			0.00107 (0.00238)		
Cabinet share of Christian democrats, long-term average		−0.0179** (0.00793)			−0.00526 (0.00318)			−0.00167 (0.00264)	
Cabinet share of social democrats, long-term average			0.0192** (0.00767)			0.00495 (0.00296)			0.00427** (0.00196)
Constant	5.557*** (0.824)	3.560*** (0.424)	3.969*** (0.563)	1.595*** (0.322)	0.751** (0.270)	0.874*** (0.279)	−0.388 (0.239)	−0.329* (0.175)	−0.299* (0.157)
Observations	21	21	21	21	21	21	20	20	20
R^2	0.242	0.255	0.307	0.276	0.142	0.146	0.548	0.553	0.620

Robust standard errors in parentheses
*** $p < 0.01$, ** $p < 0.05$, * $p < 0.1$

of education (Model 2), but there is no statistically significant effect for public spending on higher education or VET (Models 5 and 8).

The strong left–right difference confirms the notion that partisan power is important not only for the division of labor between public and private financing (see above) but also with regard to the overall levels of public resources devoted to education (Busemeyer 2007; Castles 1989; Schmidt 2007). The absence of a significant association between Christian democracy and spending on VET and the presence of such an effect for social democracy should be interpreted with caution. First of all, the dependent variable is a proxy that is strongly influenced by overall levels of public spending on secondary education, which in turn is likely to reflect social democratic priorities on increasing spending. Second, Christian democrats are not necessarily in favor of increasing spending on VET as such, because any overreaching involvement by the state will risk marginalizing employers. Instead, the Christian democratic approach to VET is to promote employer involvement, which involves employers taking over a significant share of the costs (see the case study of Germany in Chapter 2).

I will now turn from the analysis of (de-)commodification and spending to an analysis of educational stratification, the second dimension identified in Figure 3.1.[2] Educational stratification is strongly related to differences in enrollment patterns at the upper-secondary and post-secondary level. Not surprisingly (since the OECD measure of educational stratification is based on students' expectations of completing higher education), there is a strong negative association between the OECD measure and the share of an age cohort that enters academic higher education (the entry rate, see Model 1 in Table 3.5). There is also a positive association between the share of upper-secondary

---

[2] The number of cases is reduced due to missing data on the entry rate into tertiary type-A education (missing for Canada, France) and the share of upper-secondary students in apprenticeships (missing for Australia, Italy, Japan, New Zealand, Portugal, and the United Kingdom). Data are also missing on the share of upper-secondary students in VET (for both school-based VET and apprenticeship) in New Zealand and the United States. Given the well-known properties of the secondary education systems in these countries, I have manually inserted a value of 0 for some of the quantitative analyses below, but not for the cross-sectional regressions. The Hall–Gingerich indicator of economic coordination is not available for Greece, which leads to a further reduction of cases in some analyses.

Table 3.5 *Educational stratification and enrollment patterns in upper- and post-secondary education, average values 1997–2008*

Dependent variable	(1)	(2)	(3)	(4)	(5)
	\multicolumn{5}{c}{Educational stratification (OECD measure)}
Entry rate into tertiary type-A education	−0.0203***	−0.0225***	−0.0236***		
	(0.00357)	(0.00369)	(0.00535)		
Share of upper-secondary students in VET		0.00592*			
		(0.00307)			
Apprenticeship training share			0.00423	0.0101*	
			(0.00388)	(0.00553)	
Ratio of VET to tertiary education					0.505***
					(0.0847)
Constant	3.559***	3.382***	3.632***	2.316***	1.991***
	(0.213)	(0.256)	(0.309)	(0.134)	(0.122)
Observations	19	17	13	15	17
R^2	0.662	0.736	0.722	0.210	0.502

Robust standard errors in parentheses
*** $p < 0.01$, ** $p < 0.05$, * $p < 0.1$

students in VET and educational stratification (Model 2) in a cross-sectional regression, but the association is weaker than in the previous case (see the negative and significant coefficient estimate of entry rate into tertiary type A in Models 1, 2, and 3). Furthermore, there is no statistical association between the share of upper-secondary students in VET and the entry rate into higher education (the bivariate correlation between the two is merely 0.06). The simple reason for this surprising nonassociation is that in some countries, notably the Scandinavian countries, vocational tracks at the upper-secondary level do not preclude students from moving on to academic higher education at the post-secondary level. In these countries, both the share of students in VET and entry rates into higher education are high. In continental European countries, by contrast, the possibilities that students on the vocational track have of moving into higher education are very restricted, because of the limitations of segmented secondary school systems (Ebner & Nikolai 2010; Nikolai & Ebner 2012). It follows that we could expect a high share of students in apprenticeship-type schemes to be associated with high levels of educational stratification. Model 4 in Table 3.5 confirms this negative bivariate association, but the coefficient is not statistically significant once the entry rate into higher education is included as an additional control (Model 3). This might be because of the reduced number of country cases as a consequence of missing data. The positive effect of the share of upper-secondary education in VET remains significant, however, even when controlling for the entry rate into higher education.

A simple summary measure for cross-country differences in enrollment patterns is the ratio of upper-secondary students in VET to the entry rate into tertiary type-A education (or tertiary enrollment rates). This variable indicates the importance of VET as a final stage in educational careers relative to higher education, taking into account the ease of transition from the vocational tracks at the upper-secondary level into higher education. As expected, this variable is a very strong predictor of differences in educational stratification (the t value is 5.96 and the share of explained variance (R^2) is 0.5; see Model 5 in Table 3.5). As can be seen in Figure 3.6, educational stratification is particularly high in countries where transitions from vocational to higher education face high institutional barriers (e.g., in Germany or Switzerland). In contrast, levels of educational stratification are lower when access to higher education is very open (the liberal skill regime) or when

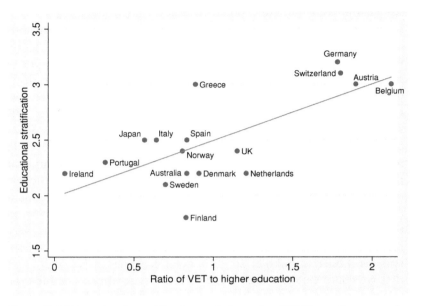

Figure 3.6 Educational stratification and the ratio of VET enrollment to the entry rate into higher education

transitions from vocational to academic higher education do not face institutional barriers or are even actively encouraged (the Scandinavian countries).

Table 3.6 confirms the importance of partisan legacies for enrollment patterns at the upper- and post-secondary level. In Models 1 through 3, I include only partisan variables; in Models 3 through 6, I add economic coordination as a control variable. The importance of VET relative to academic higher education is lower in countries with a strong legacy of conservative partisan government (Models 1 and 4). Above-average government participation by Christian democrats, by contrast, is associated with VET playing a larger role in the education system relative to higher education (Models 2 and 5). These findings resonate well with the case studies by confirming a critical difference between Christian democrats and conservatives in their support for expanding VET as an alternative to academic higher education. Social democratic legacies do not have any significant effect (Models 3 and 6), because social democrats attempt to expand both educational opportunities in VET and higher education. When looking at the association

Table 3.6 *Partisan politics and enrollment patterns in upper- and post-secondary education (I)*

	(1)	(2)	(3)	(4)	(5)	(6)
Dependent variable	\multicolumn{6}{c}{Ratio between share of upper-secondary students in VET and entry rate into tertiary type-A education}
Cabinet share of conservatives, long-term average	−0.00764* (0.00373)			−0.00755* (0.00362)		
Cabinet share of Christian democrats, long-term average		0.0130* (0.00610)			0.0131* (0.00659)	
Cabinet share of social democrats, long-term average			0.00227 (0.00645)			0.00183 (0.00673)
Economic coordination in labor relations				0.0758 (0.527)	0.0514 (0.570)	0.386 (0.587)
Constant	1.200*** (0.189)	0.777*** (0.100)	0.938*** (0.306)	1.149** (0.391)	0.737* (0.374)	0.731 (0.503)
Observations	17	17	17	16	16	16
R^2	0.167	0.283	0.007	0.166	0.283	0.034

Robust standard errors in parentheses
*** $p < 0.01$, ** $p < 0.05$, * $p < 0.1$

148   Part I Determinants of education policy

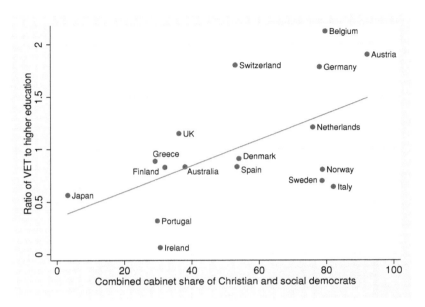

Figure 3.7 Importance of VET relative to higher education and combined cabinet share of Christian and social democrats

between the combined cabinet share of Christian and social democrats on the one hand and the ratio measure on the other (Figure 3.7), we find a significant positive association. The privilege of VET over other forms of upper- and post-secondary education thus seems to depend not only on the presence of Christian democrats in government, but also on their ability to form formal or informal coalitions with social democrats in order to build sustainable cross-class coalitions.

Table 3.7 presents the results from cross-sectional regression analyses of enrollment levels in various types of upper- and post-secondary education. Differences in enrollment are, of course, important determinants of public spending on education, since education is a personnel-intensive social service (Ansell 2010; Busemeyer 2007; Castles 1989, 1998; Nikolai 2007; Wolf 2006; Schmidt 2007). Conversely, it can be argued that when increasing education spending, policy-makers will eventually aim to expand access to higher levels of education, here referring to enrollment. As in the case of spending, there is a positive association between the long-term average cabinet share of social

Table 3.7 *Partisan politics and enrollment patterns in upper- and post-secondary education (II)*

Dependent variable	(1)	(2)	(3)	(4)	(5)	(6)	(7)	(8)	(9)
	Entry-rate tertiary type-A			Share of upper-secondary students in VET			Apprenticeship training share		
Cabinet share of conservatives, long-term average	0.00499 (0.107)			−0.249 (0.168)			−0.0665 (0.216)		
Cabinet share of Christian democrats, long-term average		−0.370** (0.159)			0.231 (0.224)			0.235 (0.252)	
Cabinet share of social democrats, long-term average			0.310** (0.115)			0.429** (0.198)			−0.290 (0.204)
Economic coordination in labor relations	−17.16 (10.85)	−6.419 (12.83)	−22.85* (11.87)	11.25 (22.16)	13.75 (24.64)	12.63 (16.92)	33.22* (15.66)	29.69** (11.67)	53.28*** (11.49)
Constant	63.96*** (8.413)	64.88*** (7.589)	56.65*** (7.873)	46.61** (16.11)	35.38** (16.02)	26.03* (14.13)	1.670 (14.70)	−1.888 (6.044)	−0.561 (6.104)
Observations	18	18	18	18	18	18	14	14	14
R^2	0.104	0.340	0.264	0.164	0.118	0.247	0.249	0.301	0.321

Robust standard errors in parentheses
*** $p < 0.01$, ** $p < 0.05$, * $p < 0.1$

democrats and tertiary enrollment (Model 3 in Table 3.6; see Ansell 2010: 184; Busemeyer 2009b: 119, 121 for similar findings).

Perhaps more interesting than the impact of social democracy are the effects of the various types of right-wing parties. As Ansell (2008, 2010) has argued, the redistributive politics of public investments in higher education are complex. When access to higher levels of education is limited and class bias is prevalent, conservative right-wing parties may actually have an interest in increasing public spending on higher education, since in such a case this type of spending will have a regressive impact, favoring children from the upper-income strata (Ansell 2010: 194). Moving beyond the simple left–right dichotomy reveals important differences between Christian democratic and conservative education policy. First of all, there is no apparent relationship between the cabinet share of secular conservatives and tertiary enrollment (Model 1 in Table 3.7). This indicates that, unlike social democrats, conservative parties have not been actively promoting the opening up of access to higher education. Neither have they been uniformly opposing it, however, especially when a large share of the funding for higher education comes from private sources (the United States, Australia, New Zealand). Model 3 in Table 3.7, in contrast, documents a clearly negative association between tertiary enrollment and the cabinet share of Christian democrats. This association may admittedly be driven by the particular group of countries in which Christian democrats have been notably influential: Belgium, the Netherlands, Italy, Germany, Austria, and – to a certain extent – Switzerland. Even so, the Christian democratic opposition to the expansion of tertiary enrollment is obviously greater than that of the secular conservatives.

The simple reason for these differences between right-wing parties is that Christian democrats have chosen to channel the rising educational aspirations of the middle classes by expanding VET instead of privately funded higher education (see also Figure 3.8). The notion of a segregated and stratified secondary education system fits very well with the partisan ideology of an "organic society" (Van Kersbergen 1995: 186), in which various strata and societal groups contribute differently to the common good. Christian democrats are a less openly upper-class party than secular conservatives, because they strive to mediate and promote cross-class consensus. Instead of deliberately excluding children of the lower strata from education on principle (e.g., by expanding the private

Worlds of skill formation 151

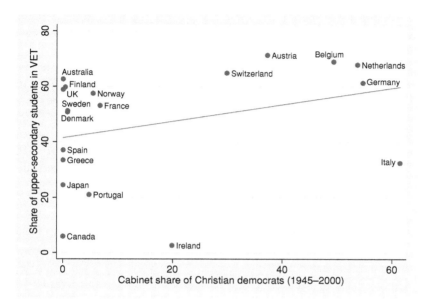

Figure 3.8 Share of upper-secondary students in VET (average 1997–2008) and cabinet share of Christian democrats (1945–2000)

share of education financing), Christian democratic education policy strives to provide the "right" kind of education for future workers at the intermediate skill level. Nevertheless, the Christian democrats are a business-friendly party, especially in countries where they are the dominant right-wing political force, and thus expect VET to be designed in such a way that it meets the skill demands of business most effectively. This differentiates them from social democrats, who may be equally willing to promote VET as the more fitting type of education for their core electoral constituencies, but whose goal remains the promotion of educational opportunities, whereas Christian democrats are more interested in maintaining the supporting role of training for business interests.

Figure 3.8 depicts the association between Christian democracy and the share of upper-secondary students in VET (both school- and workplace-based schemes). As in the case of tertiary enrollment, there is a particular group of countries that is driving this association: Germany, Austria, the Netherlands, Belgium, and Switzerland. Italy is an outlier, because even though Christian democrats were the dominant force there in the postwar decades, its VET share remains very low (as a reminder, tertiary enrollment is also exceptionally low in this country).

The differences within this group of countries can in part be explained by differences in the socioeconomic context with regard to labor-market institutions. Germany, Austria, and Switzerland are characterized by both strong Christian democratic parties and medium-to-high levels of economic coordination, particularly on the side of employers. The case study on Germany revealed that the Christian democrats pushed strongly for the establishment of a collective skill-formation system with dual apprenticeship training at its core.

The case of Denmark is a bit more ambiguous. On the one hand, it too is characterized by high levels of economic coordination, but on the other, the Christian democrats there are politically weak, as in other Scandinavian countries. There are several possible reasons for this. First, as Jensen (2010) has argued, right-wing parties in countries with a strong or even dominant left respond by moving towards the political center and becoming more supportive of the welfare state. Historically, the Danish liberals were a strong driving force behind progressive education reforms (Wiborg 2010). Compared to other countries, the liberals in Denmark were more open to cross-class compromises, primarily with the social democrats; they might in effect have played a role somewhat similar to that of the Christian democrats in other continental European countries. Second, the Danish social democrats were never as strong as their brethren in Sweden. Various attempts by Danish social democrats to introduce comprehensive education of the kind that came into being in Sweden failed because of the opposition of employers' associations (Nelson 2012: 194–5). Third, Denmark's economic structure, rooted in small and medium-sized enterprises, encouraged and enabled collective approaches to the problem of skill formation (Estévez-Abe et al. 2001; Martin & Knudsen 2010; Nelson 2012). Cross-class alliances between employers and strong unions against statist and partisan interventions ensured the stability and survival of the apprenticeship system. Compared to the German system, however, the Danish system is more solidaristic and collective (Busemeyer 2012a,c; Martin & Knudsen 2010; Nelson 2012), because the institutional separation between vocational education and the general schooling and higher education systems is not as pronounced, and the link between initial VET on the one hand and continuing education and active labor-market policies on the other is much more institutionalized.

With regard to the Netherlands and Belgium, policy legacies of apprenticeship training were less entrenched there during the postwar years than in the German-speaking countries. In the case of Belgium, a French-inspired statist approach to education policy likely played a role in expanding school-based forms of VET. VET is still much more entrenched in Belgium than in France, however. In the Netherlands, workplace-based forms of apprenticeship were significantly expanded beginning in the early 1980s under the aegis of governments led by Christian democrats (Anderson & Oude Nijhuis 2012).

The outlier case of Italy can be explained by its complex territorial politics, as well as its conflict-ridden system of industrial relations. If this were about partisan politics in the narrow sense (i.e., without taking into account the institutional context), the long-term dominance of Christian democracy would lead us to expect a strong apprenticeship system and an underdeveloped higher education system. The latter expectation fits empirical reality, since Italy lags behind other European countries with regard to tertiary enrollment. But apprenticeship training and VET in general remain equally underdeveloped in Italy, as can be seen from the data in Figure 3.8. One important explanation for this is the massive differences between northern and southern Italy with regard to economic development and the associated conflicts over cross-regional redistribution (Glassmann 2014). It is telling that in the north, where levels of economic coordination and the potential for cross-class cooperation are generally higher and the business structure is rooted in small and medium-sized enterprises, dual-type apprenticeships are far more widespread than in the south (Crouch *et al.* 1999: 165). A further factor is the relative strength of the Communist Party in the postwar era, which split the left in the areas of politics and the labor market. Conflicts between employers' associations and communist trade unions prevented the formation of the sustainable cross-class coalitions at the national level (although some were feasible at the regional level) that would have been needed in order to establish a comprehensive framework for VET. Interestingly, and in line with theoretical expectations, the Christian democrats passed a law on apprenticeship training in 1955, with provisions for on-the-job training and lower salaries for trainees. The law did not increase employer involvement in VET, however, because the union-dominated labor exchanges meant that employers were severely restricted in their choice of apprentices (Bonoli 2013: 99, 111). Hence, Italian Christian democrats did try to expand apprenticeship training, but failed because the socioeconomic context prevented the formation of lasting cross-class coalitions above the regional level.

I will move next from partisan politics to the socioeconomic context. Labor-market institutions are a particularly important context factor with regard to VET. The VoC literature argues that there are important institutional complementarities between collective wage bargaining and skill formation (Hall & Soskice 2001). Labor-market economists such as Acemoglu & Pischke (1998, 1999) have seconded this claim. Their argument is that because the centralization of wage bargaining leads to lower levels of wage inequality (Wallerstein 1999), firms are more likely to invest in skill formation, since they can later recoup part of what they have invested in training from the skilled workers with firm-specific skills who are willing to remain with them. Collective wage bargaining also forces firms to invest in the skills of the low-skilled in order to increase their productivity (Streeck 1989). As expected, there is a strong and clear positive association between the level of economic coordination and the share of apprenticeship training (Models 7, 8, and 9 in Table 3.7 and Figure 3.9).[3] As levels of coordination increase, employers are more likely to get involved in skill formation, in the form of apprenticeship training. Denmark and Switzerland are outliers because their level of employer involvement is higher than would be expected given their level of coordination. This is most likely due to the structure of their business interests (i.e., a large share of small and medium-sized firms) and policy legacies. What is more, there is a positive association between economic coordination and the general share of students in VET at the upper-secondary education level (Models 4, 5, and 6 in Table 3.7), but this effect is not statistically significant (even when the partisan variables are dropped from the regression). This indicates that coordination is particularly relevant for those types of VET that depend on a high degree of employer involvement. Finally, there is a negative association between economic

---

[3] Unfortunately, the number of cases is reduced significantly in these models because the OECD only provides data on the share of apprenticeship training for a limited number of countries, in part because of the complexity of VET schemes compared to other sectors of the education system (see above for details).

Worlds of skill formation 155

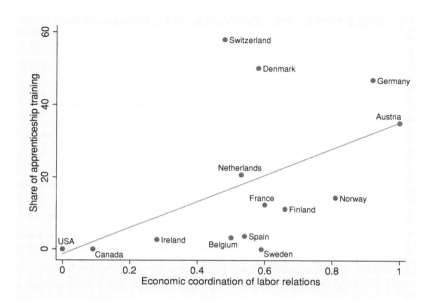

Figure 3.9 Economic coordination and the apprenticeship training share

coordination and levels of enrollment in tertiary education, as could be expected given the demand for vocational skills relative to academic education is higher in CMEs. Again, however, this effect is not statistically significant.

Multivariate regression analyses

The following time-series cross-sectional analyses provide a further robustness test of the central claims developed in this and the previous chapter. The methodological literature has featured much discussion on the benefits and downsides of using this method (Beck & Katz 1995, 1996; Kittel 2006; Kittel & Winner 2005; Plümper *et al*. 2005; Plümper & Troeger 2007). The method gained popularity so quickly because it seemed to show a potential way out of the typical problem in comparative public policy research of having too few cases and too many variables. But there are problems with using panel data that consist of country-year observations. The most common ones are the serial correlation of error terms within countries (what happens in country

X at time t strongly depends on what happened at t − 1), contemporaneous correlation of country cases, and panel heteroskedasticity (differences in over-time variation within countries). Beck & Katz (1995, 1996) proposed calculating "panel-corrected standard errors" to deal with cross-country correlation and panel heteroskedasticity. They also advised including a lagged dependent variable to take care of the problem of serial correlation. This "Beck–Katz standard" was later criticized on various fronts (Plümper *et al.* 2005). The inclusion of a lagged dependent variable typically depresses the explanatory power of the other independent variables (Achen 2000). The inclusion of variables that are largely time-invariant also poses problems (Plümper & Troeger 2007), particularly when they are combined with country dummies (fixed effects) that are supposed to control for country-specific characteristics that are not picked up by the other independent variables (such as "culture" in a very general sense). Finally, some important variables studied by welfare-state scholars, such as social spending, are nonstationary: they trend upwards (or downwards, for that matter) over time, which leads to wrong coefficient estimates (Kittel & Winner 2005). Given these problems, I will use different model specifications in the following section according to which characteristics of the data are to be analyzed. The standard model specification is to calculate panel-corrected standard errors and to model serial correlation in the error term with an AR(1) process. In cases where longer time-series data are available, I run an error-correction model and/or include a lagged dependent variable. The time period in this section can be slightly extended in comparison to the cross-sectional regressions. The OECD does provide data on the public/private division of labor in education financing for a number of countries (e.g., Australia, Canada, Denmark, Japan, the Netherlands, Spain, Sweden, and the United States) for some years before 1997. The same holds for enrollment shares in VET (for which some data for the first half of the 1990s are available for Australia, Austria, Belgium, Denmark, Finland, France, Germany, Italy, Japan, the Netherlands, Norway, Spain, Sweden, and the United Kingdom). I perform linear interpolation for these cases in order to increase the number of observations, but given the limited coverage, it is not advisable to extend the time period to the early 1990s in order to calculate averages. The panel is therefore unbalanced.

The determinants of different types of education spending have by now been analyzed extensively in the literature (Ansell 2008, 2010;

Boix 1997, 1998; Busemeyer 2006, 2007, 2008, 2009b; Castles 1989, 1998; Jensen 2011; Nikolai 2007; Rauh et al. 2011; Schmidt 2002, 2007; Wolf 2006, 2009; Wolf & Zohlnhöfer 2009). For the purpose of the present chapter, the most important finding from this literature is that partisan politics matters – but only to a certain extent. Left partisanship has a positive impact on public education spending, but this effect is most obvious when long-term averages and large cross-national differences are studied (as in the previous section). The short-term effects of left partisanship are less clear-cut, except in the case of higher education, where social democratic government participation does have a positive impact in both the long- and the short-term (Busemeyer 2009b). Ansell (2010) explains this pattern by a shift in partisan preferences once a critical threshold in enrollment has been reached. When higher education systems are elitist, the left does not increase spending on higher education, but this effect reverses when access to higher education opens up.

Because of the focus on spending in the existing literature, in the present chapter I look at the division of labor between public and private sources of funding and at enrollment patterns, since these two elements are most closely related to the two central dimensions of variation identified above. There is, of course, a positive association between spending and enrollment, but it is not as strong as one would expect (see above). There are also other reasons for the focus on enrollment instead of spending; spending data are not available, or, in the case of VET, can only be estimated via proxy. In order to keep the analyses consistent with each other, I therefore focus on enrollment in higher education as well. In the case of higher education, high-quality data on spending are available back to the early 1990s. UNESCO provides data on gross tertiary enrollment extending back to the early 1970s. In this case, then, it *is* possible to study a longer time period.

Before I present the findings, some brief remarks on the operationalization of partisan effects are in order. For the multivariate regressions, I rely on data on the partisan composition of governments provided by Armingeon et al. (2011). Their Comparative Political Data Set includes data on the cabinet share of left, center, and right parties. Center parties are mostly Christian democratic parties, especially in European countries. I nevertheless decided to recode the dataset in a few cases: Armingeon et al. (2011) consider the left-wing parties of Canada and the United States to be centrist parties rather than left parties. I recoded these as left parties. Conversely, the center-right coalition that governed Spain in the late 1970s and then again in the late 1990s was recoded as a right-wing government party. The recoded variable on the cabinet share of centrist parties thus captures the effects of Christian democrats in government more precisely.

I again start with an analysis of the private share in education funding as an indicator of (de-)commodification in education policy (Table 3.8). As was shown in Figure 3.4, I find a robust and statistically significant negative association between levels of public social spending and the private share in education spending. This relationship should be interpreted as an empirical correlation rather than a causal relationship, since the underlying causal mechanisms are not yet clear (but note that Chapter 5 will probe the association between education and the welfare state at the micro-level of attitudes and preferences). Interestingly, there is no such association between the total level of public spending on education and the private share, although it could have been expected that the degree of public investment in the education system would be more important than the size of the welfare state. I also find a negative and significant association between the private share in education spending and the entry rate into tertiary type-A education. Here it is important to remember that the regression analyses also pick up cross-national differences, since in order to be able to include time-invariant variables, such as the degree of coordination, I do not use country fixed effects. Furthermore, the causal relationship between these two variables is more likely to run from private financing to the openness of tertiary education than the other way around. This finding should be interpreted with caution, especially as it vanishes in the case of tertiary education (Models 5 to 8), where it should have been stronger. This could indicate the existence of a tradeoff between the openness of access in higher education and the extensiveness of private financing, at least for the contemporary period. Following Wolf (2009), I include union density as an additional predictor of the private share of spending. As expected, there is a negative association between union density and the private spending share. A more powerful union movement would be likely to push the government to promote public instead of private investment in education, in order to promote educational mobility and maintain the openness of access to education.

With regard to our main variables of interest, I find a positive association between the government participation of conservatives and the private share in education spending, with regard to both spending on all levels of education (Model 1) and spending on tertiary education only (Model 5). The predicted effect of a change in government from one without conservative participation to a completely conservative one amounts to 2.96 percentage points for spending on all levels of education and 8.36 percentage points for spending on higher education (the average in the sample is 11.1 percent in the former case and 23.9 percent in the latter). Comparatively speaking (as a share of a standard deviation), the effect is larger in the case of spending on higher education. Conversely, the government participation of social democrats has a significant and negative effect on the private spending share. In terms of magnitude, the size of the effect is only about half that of the conservative effect in the case of spending on higher education (Model 7), but it remains statistically significant. There is no statistical association between the government participation of Christian democrats and private spending for all levels of education (Model 2). There is a significant negative effect for the case of spending on higher education, however, which in terms of magnitude is much larger than the effect of social democratic participation in government (a decrease of 9.6 percentage points in the case of a complete change in government, as above).

I also find a strong negative association between the degree of economic coordination and the private share of education spending (Models 4 and 8), which was not apparent in the simple cross-sectional regression analyses. But this finding should not be overinterpreted: because the degree of economic coordination does not vary over time, its significance is overestimated in cross-sectional time-series analyses such as these. Most likely the variable has picked up intrinsic differences between countries that are correlated to, but not necessarily conceptually the same as, economic coordination (similar to country fixed effects).

Table 3.9 presents an analysis of enrollment in tertiary education. The dependent variable is the gross level of enrollment in tertiary education, as defined by UNESCO. The definition of this variable covers the number of pupils or students enrolled in a given level of education, without taking into account the age of these students. This figure is then divided by the number of individuals (population) in a

Table 3.8 *Determinants of private share of education spending, 1993–2008, panel-corrected standard errors and panel-specific AR(1) error correction*

Dependent variable	(1)	(2)	(3)	(4)	(5)	(6)	(7)	(8)
	\multicolumn{4}{c}{Private share of education spending, all levels of education (level)}	\multicolumn{4}{c}{Private share of education spending, tertiary education only (level)}
Public social spending, % of GDP	−1.136***	−1.128***	−1.194***	−0.291***	−3.126***	−2.437***	−3.301***	−0.247
	(0.108)	(0.114)	(0.100)	(0.105)	(0.287)	(0.339)	(0.323)	(0.424)
Public education spending, % of GDP	0.635	0.366	0.735	−0.0364	1.258	0.420	1.135	−1.642
	(0.451)	(0.428)	(0.450)	(0.452)	(1.150)	(1.110)	(1.308)	(1.542)
Entry-rate tertiary type-A education	−0.0874***	−0.0555***	−0.0791***	−0.0873***	−0.0930*	−0.0216	−0.0506	−0.0258
	(0.0221)	(0.0180)	(0.0211)	(0.0173)	(0.0481)	(0.0570)	(0.0568)	(0.0751)
Union density	−0.194***	−0.178***	−0.188***	−0.179***	−0.449***	−0.497***	−0.407***	−0.543***
	(0.0169)	(0.0151)	(0.0185)	(0.0135)	(0.0364)	(0.0471)	(0.0829)	(0.0792)
Cabinet share of conservatives, moving average	0.0296*				0.0836***			
	(0.0157)				(0.0165)			
Cabinet share of Christian democrats, moving average		0.00886				−0.0966***		
		(0.0155)				(0.0300)		

Cabinet share of social democrats, moving average			−0.0259** (0.0122)				−0.0327* (0.0168)	
Economic coordination of labor relations				−12.07*** (1.295)				−42.74*** (7.162)
Constant	35.97*** (3.484)	35.62*** (2.812)	37.73*** (3.406)	34.60*** (2.637)	80.20*** (5.902)	78.08*** (6.211)	83.65*** (6.349)	84.01*** (7.817)
Observations	171	171	171	160	168	168	168	159
R^2	0.521	0.668	0.524	0.760	0.781	0.619	0.683	0.537
Number of countries	17	17	17	16	17	17	17	16

Standard errors in parentheses
*** $p < 0.01$, ** $p < 0.05$, * $p < 0.1$

Table 3.9 *Determinants of gross level of enrollment, 1971–2008, error-correction model with country fixed effects*

Dependent variable	(1)	(2)	(3)	(4)
	\multicolumn{4}{c}{Gross enrollment in tertiary education, annual change (first differences)}			
Gross enrollment in tertiary education, lagged level	−0.0592** (0.0315)	−0.0578** (0.0325)	−0.0588** (0.0313)	−0.0598** (0.0325)
Public spending in % of GDP, lagged level (t − 1)	0.0226 (0.0294)	0.0247 (0.0294)	0.0224 (0.0289)	0.0203 (0.0289)
Annual change in public spending	−0.0197 (0.0587)	−0.0253 (0.0576)	−0.0208 (0.0588)	−0.0247 (0.0592)
Share of population aged 65 and above, lagged level (t − 1)	−0.000494 (0.0692)	−0.0377 (0.0738)	−0.00135 (0.0693)	−0.00555 (0.0690)
Annual change in population share of elderly	−0.0883 (0.613)	0.0972 (0.608)	−0.104 (0.620)	−0.0985 (0.626)
Share of employment in services, lagged level (t − 1)	17.21** (7.077)	16.67** (7.159)	16.96** (6.986)	17.34** (7.199)
Annual change in employment share of services	16.56 (12.66)	16.56 (12.39)	16.43 (12.66)	17.02 (12.67)
Cabinet share of conservatives, five-year moving average, lagged level (t − 1)	−0.00232 (0.00549)			
Annual change in moving average of cabinet share of conservatives	0.00881 (0.0132)			

Cabinet share of Christian democrats, five-year moving average, lagged level (t − 1)		−0.0128*** (0.00438)	
Annual change in moving average of cabinet share of Christian democrats		−0.0154 (0.00962)	
Cabinet share of left parties, five-year moving average, lagged level (t − 1)			0.00387 (0.00524)
Annual change in moving average of cabinet share of left parties			−0.00853 (0.0120)
Cabinet share of social democrats, five-year moving average, lagged level (t − 1)			0.00908** (0.00441)
Annual change in moving average of cabinet share of social democrats			0.00612 (0.0111)
Constant	−8.158** (3.408)	−7.688** (3.494)	−8.282** (3.577)	−8.610** (3.626)
Observations	689	696	689	689
R^2	0.083	0.079	0.085	0.090
Number of countries	21	21	21	21

Standard errors in parentheses
*** $p < 0.01$, ** $p < 0.05$, * $p < 0.1$

typical age cohort (five years following the official secondary graduation age). Enrollment levels can therefore be particularly high when a large share of the adult population attends higher education institutions. The measure also does not consider migration flows. Compared to the entry rate into tertiary education used above, this variable is thus less precise, but it has the advantage of being available for a longer period of time.

Because enrollment levels in tertiary education have been going up consistently in recent decades, there is a problem of non-stationarity: an upward trend in the dependent variable that biases the coefficient estimates. I employ an error-correction model (Beck 1991) in order to deal with this problem. In this model specification, the dependent variable is not given in levels, but in first differences (annual change in enrollment from one year to the next). Independent variables are included in two ways: first, as lagged levels whose coefficient estimates capture the long-term trend in the association between this variable and the dependent variable; and second, as first differences (annual changes), which indicate the short-term effects of the particular variable. Error-correction models have become quite popular in comparative welfare state research and political economy (e.g. Busemeyer 2009b; Iversen & Cusack 2000; Kaufman & Segura-Ubiergo 2001) because they are effective in dealing with the problem of nonstationarity and they allow us to differentiate between long- and short-term effects. Their applicability depends on the availability of sufficiently long time series, however, as well as sufficient over-time variation in the dependent variable (otherwise the independent variables would have no variation to explain). I present the findings below, first using an error-correction model with country fixed effects and then with a more conventional model specification.

I include a number of control variables in addition to partisan variables. More specifically, I include public spending as percentage of GDP. This variable captures the overall size of the public sector, given that the size of the welfare state has been identified as an important positive determinant of levels of public education spending (Busemeyer 2007). The share of the population aged 65 and above captures demographic characteristics. I expect these to have a negative impact on levels of enrollment because older societies tend to invest less in education (Cattaneo & Wolter 2007). I also include the share of employment in services relative to other employment sectors. Structural changes of the economy (deindustrialization) have been identified as major driving forces of welfare state expansion (Iversen & Cusack 2000), and it is likely that they are also driving participation levels in higher education. The causality in this particular case could range from the expansion of higher education to the growth of services, but at this point I am less interested in causality than in correlation. From a theoretical perspective, the most important independent variable is the partisan composition of governments. Since there are good reasons to assume that policy-makers' influence on levels of enrollment is less direct than in the case of spending, I use moving averages of the cabinet shares. More specifically, for each country-year, I calculate the five-year average cabinet share of social democrats, applying weights such that the more recent period has a larger influence on the calculation of the average.[4]

Considering the findings in Table 3.9, it is first interesting to note that none of the control variables seems to have a strong impact. This is most likely due to the limited degree of over-time variation in the dependent variable. The preliminary findings of the bivariate analyses with regard to the impact of right-wing government parties are largely confirmed, however: there is no statistical association between the cabinet share of conservative parties and changes in the level of enrollment (Model 1), but there is a significant negative effect from the government participation of Christian democrats. The predicted long-term effect of a change in government from one without any Christian democrats to one made up purely of Christian democrats is a decrease in tertiary enrollment by 22 percentage points.[5] The average in the sample is 42 percent with a standard deviation of 21, meaning that the magnitude of the effect is roughly one standard deviation.

Somewhat surprisingly, there is no statistical association between left-wing government and tertiary enrollment (Model 3), which is at odds with the findings in the literature. As it turns out, however, this non-finding hinges entirely on the classification of North American

---

[4] The most recent year receives a weight of 1, which is reduced by 0.2 for each successive year up until year five.
[5] The long-term effect is calculated by dividing the coefficient of the lagged level variable by the absolute value of the coefficient of the lagged dependent variable; see Iversen & Cusack (2000: 330).

left-wing parties as either centrist or left. When I use a more narrow definition of left partisanship that excludes North American parties (Model 4), I find a significant positive long-term effect, whose statistical significance actually increases when the sample is restricted to the more recent period (results not shown here). Based on Model 4, the predicted long-term effect of a change in government from one without social democrats to one made up purely of social democrats is an increase in tertiary enrollment of 15 percentage points, keeping in mind that these are gross levels of enrollment.

Table 3.10 presents the results of an additional analysis employing a different and perhaps more common model specification (panel-corrected standard errors in combination with a lagged dependent variable; see Beck & Katz 1995, 1996). I also restrict the sample to the more recent period (1993–2008), since both Ansell (2010) and Busemeyer (2009b) have argued that leftist partisan effects on enrollment are more relevant then. Model 1 of Table 3.10 seemingly confirms the non-association between left-wing governments, but when I use the more restrictive definition of left partisanship (Model 2), I find a positive and significant effect of left partisanship on enrollment. Instead of cabinet shares, Model 3 uses a single measure of government partisanship, which goes from 1 for a strong right-wing dominance to 5 for a strong left-wing dominance. The positive (and significant) effect of this variable indicates that government partisanship is indeed an important determinant of levels of tertiary enrollment. Correcting for the depressing impact of the lagged dependent variable, as suggested by Kittel & Winner (2002: 18), the predicted long-term increase in enrollment resulting from a move from a right-wing to a left-wing government is 23 percentage points, which is similar to the estimates from the previous models. We can see from this that above and beyond the association between long-term averages of partisan control of the government and education policy indicators documented in the cross-sectional regressions, it also possible to identify a short-term effect of partisanship, at least in the case of enrollment.

Data on enrollment in different types of VET are much less readily available than enrollment data for tertiary education. UNESCO provides data on upper-secondary students in technical and vocational education that are widely used in the literature (Ansell 2010; Cusack *et al.* 2006; Estévez-Abe *et al.* 2001; Iversen & Soskice 2001). The problem with these data is that they do not distinguish

Worlds of skill formation

Table 3.10 *Regression analysis: left-wing government and gross enrollment levels in tertiary education, 1993–2008, panel-corrected standard errors with lagged dependent variable*

Dependent variable	(1)	(2)	(3)
	\multicolumn{3}{c}{Gross enrollment in tertiary education (level)}		
Gross enrollment in tertiary education, lagged level (t − 1)	0.949*** (0.0194)	0.949*** (0.0182)	0.949*** (0.0195)
Public education spending, % of GDP	0.356** (0.157)	0.276 (0.169)	0.280 (0.185)
Share of population aged 65 and above	0.0748 (0.0798)	0.0393 (0.0824)	0.0436 (0.0874)
Share of employment in services	−5.000** (2.053)	−4.741** (1.998)	−4.582** (2.010)
Cabinet share of leftist parties	−0.000156 (0.00527)		
Cabinet share of social democrats (excluding United States and Canada)		0.00990** (0.00454)	
Government partisanship (1 = right, 5 = left)			0.240** (0.116)
Constant	5.066*** (1.770)	5.417*** (1.904)	5.022*** (1.619)
Observations	298	298	297
R^2	0.953	0.954	0.954
Number of countries	21	21	21

Standard errors in parentheses
*** $p < 0.01$, ** $p < 0.05$, * $p < 0.1$

between the different types of VET: school-based and workplace-based (apprenticeship). This distinction is crucial for our argument. The OECD data, albeit not perfect, are superior to the UNESCO data in this respect. Unfortunately, these are only available for a relatively short time period. Coverage in the early and mid-1990s is spotty, improving only for the late 1990s. Thus, for the case of VET, it will not be possible to use sophisticated model specifications such as the error-correction model. Also, there is very little variation over time; most of the variance is cross-sectional, such that when we include a lagged dependent variable and/or country fixed effects, all other independent variables lose any explanatory power. The following models therefore use levels for both the dependent and the independent variables. Serial autocorrelation in the error term is corrected by employing an AR(1) process. As before, I calculate panel-corrected standard errors and use a similar set of control variables. The only difference is that I pay more attention to measures of economic coordination. I include both the more encompassing measure of economic coordination of labor relations, provided by Hall & Gingerich (2009), and a more narrowly defined measure of the centralization of collective wage bargaining (Visser 2011). The expectation is that high levels of coordination/centralization will be associated with high levels of enrollment in VET, particularly apprenticeship training. I first analyze the determinants of the share of upper-secondary students in VET (both school- and workplace-based; Table 3.11), then look at the share in apprenticeship training (Table 3.12).

Table 3.11 confirms the positive association between economic coordination, centralized collective wage bargaining, and general levels of enrollment in VET. The predictive power of the VoC indicator is much stronger than the narrowly defined measure of wage-bargaining centralization (Models 1, 3, and 5 versus models 2, 4, and 6). Based on these estimates, the predicted difference in the share of upper-secondary students in VET between a pure LME (the United States or the United Kingdom) and a strong CME (Germany, Austria) lies somewhere between 25 and 30 percentage points. Models 1 and 2 also document the positive association between Christian democratic participation in government and levels of enrollment in VET. The government participation of social democrats or conservatives, by contrast, does not seem to have any effect. The predicted change in enrollment resulting from a change of government to Christian democrat is between 6.2 (Model 1) and 9.7 percentage points (Model 2). Compared to the bivariate analyses above, then, the multivariate regressions reveal in a much clearer way the particularly important role of Christian democratic parties as driving forces of the expansion of VET relative to other types of education.

In Table 3.12, I look at the determinants of the share of upper-secondary students in apprenticeships. The size of the sample is

Worlds of skill formation

unfortunately reduced significantly because this variable is only available for a smaller set of countries, and it is even further reduced compared to the cross-sectional analyses above because of missing data for some control variables (e.g., the VoC indicator). The findings should thus be interpreted very carefully. Somewhat surprisingly, the control variables perform better than in the case of total enrollment in VET. Given that school-based VET is an integral part of the universal Nordic model of education, I would have expected a much stronger relationship between the size of the public sector and general levels of enrollment in VET. This positive association is somewhat stronger (and in some cases statistically significant) in the case of apprenticeship training. The fact that GDP growth has a stronger effect on apprenticeship training than on general levels of enrollment in VET is more easily explained, because workplace-based training schemes are more dependent on general economic conditions. The negative effect is again surprising, however, since we could expect enrollment in apprenticeship to increase when economic conditions are favorable.

With regard to partisan politics, the most important thing to note is the difference of effects between rightist and centrist (Christian democratic) government. Whereas conservative government participation has a negative and statistically significant effect on the share of students in apprenticeship training, Christian democratic government participation is positively associated with the share of apprenticeship training (Models 2 and 4). When we simulate changes in government similar to those above, the predicted decrease in the share of apprenticeship training resulting from a change to a conservative government is 2.25 percentage points, whereas Christian democratic government is associated with an increase of 7.5 percentage points.

Economic coordination again has a positive effect on the share of apprenticeship training, but there is no statistical effect for wage-bargaining centralization. When the VoC indicator is included, partisan effects turn insignificant because they are dominated by this variable (the bivariate correlation between the VoC index and Christian democratic government share is 0.38). The predicted difference in the share of apprenticeship training between a pure LME and a pure CME is roughly 40 percentage points, which comes close to the real-world difference between Denmark (47.5 percent) and Ireland (5 percent).

Table 3.11 *Determinants of levels of enrollment in VET, 1993–2008, panel-corrected standard errors and panel-specific AR(1) error correction*

Dependent variable	(1)	(2)	(3)	(4)	(5)	(6)
	\multicolumn{6}{c}{Share of upper-secondary students in VET (school- and workplace-based)}					
Public spending, % of GDP	0.0849	0.188**	0.0369	0.228*	−0.0331	0.103
	(0.0857)	(0.0956)	(0.121)	(0.124)	(0.132)	(0.138)
GDP growth	−0.184	−0.137	−0.238	−0.197	−0.266*	−0.237
	(0.129)	(0.131)	(0.147)	(0.162)	(0.140)	(0.155)
Economic coordination of labor relations	25.81***		29.20***		30.25***	
	(3.626)		(3.610)		(3.961)	
Centralization of collective wage bargaining		0.584**		0.321		0.219
		(0.293)		(0.256)		(0.240)
Cabinet share of Christian democrats	0.0621***	0.0974***				
	(0.0152)	(0.0200)				
Cabinet share of conservatives			−0.0116	−0.0180		
			(0.0119)	(0.0123)		
Cabinet share of social democrats					−0.00278	0.00219
					(0.0111)	(0.0108)

Constant	32.88***	42.19***	34.01***	37.23***	37.00***	40.15***
	(6.279)	(5.198)	(7.905)	(7.033)	(8.092)	(7.176)
Observations	285	268	285	268	285	268
R^2	0.866	0.761	0.812	0.635	0.601	0.487
Number of countries	18	17	18	17	18	17

Standard errors in parentheses
*** $p < 0.01$, ** $p < 0.05$, * $p < 0.1$

Table 3.12 *Determinants of levels of enrollment in apprenticeship training, 1993–2008, panel-corrected standard errors and panel-specific AR(1) error correction*

Dependent variable	(1)	(2)	(3)	(4)	(5)	(6)
	\multicolumn{6}{c}{Share of upper-secondary students in apprenticeship training}
Public spending, % of GDP	−0.0131 (0.0534)	0.109 (0.0714)	−0.0226 (0.0548)	0.358*** (0.0958)	0.0221 (0.0561)	0.256*** (0.0646)
GDP growth	−0.294*** (0.106)	−0.438*** (0.151)	−0.207** (0.101)	−0.515*** (0.187)	−0.264** (0.106)	−0.441*** (0.160)
Economic coordination of labor relations	40.47*** (1.649)		43.95*** (1.737)		41.01*** (1.567)	
Centralization of collective wage bargaining		−0.412 (0.325)		−0.877 (0.592)		−0.399 (0.348)
Cabinet share of conservatives	−0.0114 (0.00778)	−0.0225** (0.0112)				
Cabinet share of Christian democrats			−0.00168 (0.00847)	0.0752*** (0.0197)		
Cabinet share of social democrats					0.0110 (0.00746)	0.00547 (0.00849)

Constant	−1.685	15.35***	−5.062*	4.452	−4.400	6.302**
	(2.798)	(3.721)	(2.602)	(4.753)	(2.798)	(3.056)
Observations	142	128	142	128	142	128
R^2	0.881	0.412	0.824	0.657	0.844	0.549
Number of countries	11	10	11	10	11	10

Standard errors in parentheses
*** $p < 0.01$, ** $p < 0.05$, * $p < 0.1$

Summary and conclusion

This chapter has continued to explore the variation of education and training systems. Like welfare state regimes, education and training systems can be grouped roughly into three clusters: the liberal, the statist, and the collective skill regime. Southern European countries might form a distinct fourth cluster of their own, but the evidence is not conclusive in that respect. Partisan politics and economic coordination have been identified as important determinants of the variation of education systems, both in cross-sectional regressions using long-term averages and in cross-sectional time-series analyses. Conservative government parties are more likely to increase the private share of education financing and decrease the share of apprenticeship training in upper-secondary education. Christian democrats in government, by contrast, are more likely to expand apprenticeship training and to lower enrollment in tertiary education. Finally, social democratic governments are associated with a lower share of private spending in education and a higher share of enrollment in tertiary education. Economic coordination matters most in determining the relative importance of VET – and especially apprenticeship training – as an alternative educational pathway to academic higher education.

PART II

The impact of educational institutions on outcomes and popular attitudes

4 Educational institutions and socioeconomic inequality

Introducing the puzzle

At first sight, the importance of educational institutions in the distribution of skills, life chances, and ultimately income appears obvious. To many policy-makers, investing in skills and education promises to contribute to lowering socioeconomic inequality (e.g., Tony Blair's mantra of "education, education, education"). It seems very plausible to expect that giving children from low-income or otherwise disadvantaged backgrounds access to higher levels of education will contribute to a more equal distribution of skills and therefore lead to a strong compression of incomes. Indeed, investing in human capital has become a popular tool in the hands of leftist government to counter the rising trend of inequality (Boix 1998; Busemeyer 2008, 2009b), especially in times of economic globalization, when governments cannot resort to demand-side-oriented redistributive policies as easily as they could in the postwar decades (Busemeyer 2009b).

The redistributive implications of educational institutions and investments are inherently more complex (Ansell 2008, 2010; Jensen 2011) than those of other social policies, however. There are several reasons for this. First, investing in human capital always creates both public and private benefits. Private benefits materialize in the form of individual wage increases as a result of educational investment. If a student obtains a degree in medicine, for example, her wages will be significantly higher than they would be without such a university degree. Public benefits are more vague and harder to pin down. A well-educated populace may be more active and more engaged in politics. Higher average levels of education might also make economies more competitive on world markets, promoting overall economic well-being.

The total effect of educational investment on social inequality depends very much on the relative distribution of public and private benefits. If private benefits outweigh public benefits, educational investment increases the income of some groups (the well-educated), but not necessarily overall economic well-being. Most importantly, if private benefits are mostly concentrated in the upper half of the income distribution, higher levels of educational investment may actually increase social inequality in terms of income and wealth. This redistributive logic lies behind the formal model developed by Ansell (2008, 2010). When public educational investments are concentrated on an elitist higher education sector, these investments increase the private benefits of those in that sector to the detriment of those outside it. Conversely, if educational investments are more evenly distributed across educational sectors, the private benefits of educational investments are also more equally distributed. When governments invest heavily in VET instead of higher education, the private benefits of educational investments will be more concentrated in the lower half of the skills distribution, potentially contributing to a compression of incomes on the labor market.

Thus the relationship between education and socioeconomic inequality would seem to be quite straightforward. Governments that aim to limit social inequality should invest in VET or general secondary education, whereas governments that aim to maximize wage premiums for the upper half of the skills distribution should focus on higher education (which is effectively the argument of Boix 1998). This perspective is very much rooted in political economy, however, and neglects more sociological arguments that highlight the role of education in contributing to social stratification by exacerbating class divisions and limiting intergenerational social mobility. From the latter perspective, maintaining or even expanding VET as an alternative to higher education contributes to a stratification of educational opportunities, which are very much influenced by individual social background. Large-scale provision of VET might increase the private payoffs for those in the lower half of the skills distribution, but it also diverts the same group from pursuing the more rewarding academic track. Because educational choices are very much conditioned by social background (Boudon 1974; Breen & Goldthorpe 1997), children from households with a nonacademic background are then also more likely to choose a nonacademic career, which stifles intergenerational social mobility and consolidates existing patterns of social stratification. This is why in some countries, VET can be a "safety net" for those with weak academic skills, even as in other cases it can be a "diversion,"

Educational institutions and socioeconomic inequality 179

discouraging youths from nonacademic backgrounds from pursuing an academic career (Shavit & Müller 2000).

In sum, we end up with very different expectations/predictions about the role of VET in social inequality. On the one hand, it increases labor-market returns for the low-skilled; on the other, it helps to maintain existing patterns of occupational and social stratification. An important reason for this confusion is that the pertinent literatures in comparative political economy and welfare state research and in educational sociology have often talked past each other, because of their different conceptions of the concept of inequality itself. Scholars in educational sociology (e.g., Allmendinger 1989; Blossfeld & Shavit 1993; Breen *et al.* 2009; Müller & Shavit 1998; Pfeffer 2008) associate inequality with class-related biases in access to higher levels of education; that is, an unequal distribution of educational opportunities. A well-known finding from this literature is that inequality of educational opportunities is driven by institutional stratification: education systems with segmented secondary school systems and early tracking are associated with higher levels of inequality, often expressed in terms of the influence of parental background on educational attainment (Pfeffer 2008). What is more, this literature argues that inequalities in access to education are "persistent" (Blossfeld & Shavit 1993) in the sense that the decades-long process of educational expansion has not yet eliminated class bias in access to education (Raftery & Hout 1993), although the situation might be different for the most recent period (Breen *et al.* 2009). An important insight from this literature is therefore that the continued survival of VET very much depends on, or is at least associated with, institutionally segregated and stratified secondary education systems, especially in the case of firm-based dual apprenticeships (Pfeffer 2008). What is not studied in this field of research, however, is the association between educational stratification and actual labor-market inequalities in terms of the distribution of income and wealth (an exception is Solga 2012).

The opposite holds for literature in comparative political economy, which for the most part has neglected the influence of educational institutions on socioeconomic inequality. Instead, scholars have emphasized the importance of partisan politics and power resources (Bradley *et al.* 2003; Pontusson *et al.* 2002; Rueda 2008), electoral institutions (Iversen & Soskice 2006, 2009), and the institutional setup of the economy, in particular the centralization of collective wage bargaining

(Rueda & Pontusson 2000; Wallerstein 1999). Recent contributions to the field have focused on the implications of inequality for political participation and party competition (Anderson & Beramendi 2012; Pontusson & Rueda 2010) and the structure of inequality itself (Lupu & Pontusson 2011). Educational institutions, and VET opportunities in particular, are included among the control variables in some studies (Bradley *et al.* 2003; Lupu & Pontusson 2011), but usually fail to produce significant effects. The motivation for including VET as an independent variable is given in Estévez-Abe *et al.* (2001), who essentially put forward the aforementioned argument that a well-established VET regime should be associated with lower levels of socioeconomic inequality because VET opens up opportunities for the low-skilled to get access to high-quality training and subsequent employment that is well paid and secure. In countries with a focus on academic education, by contrast, educational institutions likely reinforce the polarization of skills and labor-market outcomes between the high-skilled and college-educated on the one hand and the low-skilled without any post-compulsory education on the other (Estévez-Abe *et al.* 2001: 176–80). Estevez-Abe *et al.* (2001) do not look at the degree of educational stratification in terms of class-related biases in access to different kinds of education related to the provision of VET, but instead focus solely on labor-market outcomes.

In this chapter, I would like to bring the two different perspectives of political economy and educational sociology together in order to disentangle the complex relationship between educational institutions and socioeconomic inequality. The link to the overall argument of the book is to show that the politically motivated choices concerning the design of educational institutions made during the critical period of the postwar years have important consequences for the contemporary distribution of income and wealth in Western democracies. This supports the notion that education needs to be considered as an integral part of the welfare state because it *does* have redistributive implications. It is a different and much more challenging argument to say that policy-makers were fully aware of these distributive implications when they made their choices. To be sure, as the case studies in Chapter 2 showed, political actors had an intuitive understanding of the broad implications, or at least developed some plausible expectations in that regard. Left parties, for example, attempted to expand access and increase public involvement in the financing and provision of education

Educational institutions and socioeconomic inequality 181

with the aim of lowering inequality. But these actions also had unintended effects, such as the tradeoff between inequality and youth unemployment, which will be revealed in this chapter. Policy-makers may or may not have been aware of such tradeoffs when deciding about the institutional design of their education system. This chapter does not and cannot decide this issue. The far more modest goal here is to analyze how the choices in education policy studied in the previous chapters have had consequences for inequality, rather than to argue that policy-makers were fully aware of all potential effects at the time they made these choices.

The structure of this chapter is similar to the previous ones. I start with a description of the empirical association between educational and socioeconomic inequality and the distribution of country cases on these two dimensions. The subsequent section will develop a theoretical argument for why and how educational institutions matter for socioeconomic inequality. Because there is a dearth of high-quality comparative data on important aspects of education systems, I will present and discuss empirical evidence in the form of bivariate scatterplots and simple cross-sectional regressions. In the final section, I engage in multivariate regression analysis to further substantiate the core claims.

The relationship between educational and socioeconomic inequality

The following section contains a slightly paradoxical argument about the complex relationship between education and socioeconomic inequality: there is no direct association between educational and socioeconomic inequality, but the institutional setup of the education system *does* affect the distribution of income and wealth, as well as labor-market risks. The first part of this argument is substantiated in Figure 4.1, which displays the bivariate association between different measures of educational inequality and wage dispersion – that is, the distribution of market income – without taking into account the impact of taxes and transfers. This is commonly measured as the ratio of the person with an income at the 9th decile in the income distribution to the person with an income at the 1st decile (D9–D1 ratio, taken from the OECD Earnings Inequality Dataset and averaged over the period 1997–2008). We could expect educational institutions to be

Panel A: PISA measure of inequality

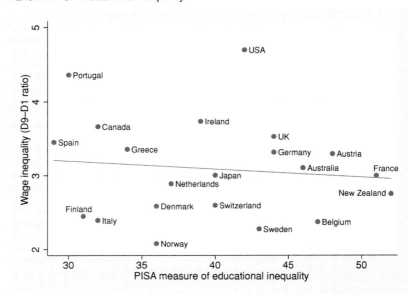

Panel B: Educational inequality (OECD Education at a Glance measure).

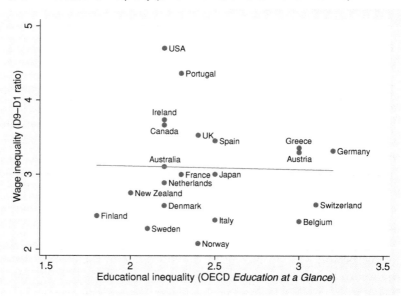

Figure 4.1 Wage dispersion and educational inequality

mostly relevant for the distribution of wages, since educational institutions shape the distribution of skills and therefore market income.[1] But as Figure 4.1 reveals, there is *no* strong association between different measures of educational inequality and wage dispersion. In Panel A of Figure 4.1, I use a measure of educational inequality calculated from the PISA 2009 data (OECD 2010: 34). This measure captures the impact of parental background on educational attainment in reading for 15-year-old students. Higher values indicate a stronger impact of socioeconomic background on educational performance – that is, higher levels of inequality – in the sense that educational disadvantages are transmitted from one generation to the next and the education system is less able to effectively counter existing inequalities. Panel B uses a different measure of educational stratification, also provided by the OECD (OECD 2007: 87). This measure (already used in Chapter 3) captures the difference in expectation of completing higher education (ISCED Levels 5A or 6) between a student with high socioeconomic status and one with low socioeconomic status. The first measure therefore directly captures the association between socioeconomic background and educational attainment, while in the case of the latter, student expectations might also reflect differences in the institutional setup of the education system. In countries where access to university education is more restricted, students are also less likely to expect to complete higher education, even after taking into account socioeconomic background factors. Interestingly, these two measures are only weakly correlated (0.15), indicating that educational inequality is hard to measure and pin down.

The most interesting finding for the purposes of this chapter is that in both cases, there is no apparent relationship with socioeconomic inequality. This means there is no evidence that educational inequality, as conventionally defined, immediately translates into socioeconomic inequality on the labor market. Countries are distributed across the whole range of the two dimensions. Looking at Panel B of Figure 4.1, however, it is possible to identify a number of by-now familiar country groupings and clusters that correspond to a certain extent to welfare state regimes. The Scandinavian countries plus the Netherlands and

---

[1] Using a measure of income inequality after taxes and transfers (net Gini index, Solt 2009) instead of the measure of wage dispersion leads to similar results (not shown here).

France are located in the lower-left quadrant, combining low levels of educational inequality with low levels of socioeconomic inequality. They can also be found in a similar cluster in Panel A, although Sweden exhibits a higher-than-expected level of educational inequality in this case.

A second cluster is formed by the continental European countries with an extensive VET system (Switzerland, Germany, Austria, and Belgium). Belgium is an outlier here because its VET is largely school-based, while the other countries have a workplace-based training system. These countries are also located quite close to each other in Panel A, joined by the outlier France. This country grouping is characterized by medium levels of socioeconomic inequality combined with above-average levels of educational inequality. Germany has been known for its extraordinarily high levels of educational inequality for a long time, a fact usually attributed to the segmented nature of its secondary school system (Pfeffer 2008). The twist in the argument that I develop below is that if Germany's segmented school system does indeed ensure the long-term sustainability of apprenticeship training, it might in the end contribute to mitigating labor-market inequalities.

The liberal Anglo-Saxon countries form a loose cluster in both figures. In these cases, above-average levels of socioeconomic inequality are combined with medium levels of educational inequality. Japan can to a certain extent be considered a member of this group (see Chapter 3, as well as Busemeyer & Nikolai 2010), but it exhibits lower levels of socioeconomic inequality. The interesting characteristic of this group is that in terms of formal institutional stratification, the countries included are much more egalitarian than the continental European countries. In the Northern American countries, as well as in the United Kingdom, comprehensive schools dominate secondary education. What is more, access to higher levels of education is much less restricted in these cases. The data on socioeconomic inequality show, however, that comprehensive secondary schools and relatively open and inclusive systems of higher education are not sufficient conditions for low levels of socioeconomic inequality.

Finally, the southern European countries are clustered in the upper-left corner of Panel A, although they are more spread out in Panel B. These countries suffer from a generally low level of educational attainment (Allmendinger & Leibfried 2003), which might explain the low degree of educational inequality: when the majority of the population

Educational institutions and socioeconomic inequality 185

has few educational qualifications, parental background matters less (although it will probably matter a lot for the few who obtain higher education credentials). The levels of socioeconomic inequality are above average in these countries, associated with dualized labor-market structures and high levels of youth unemployment.

Explaining the complex association between skills and inequality

Should the evidence presented in the previous section be taken as proof that there is no link between the design of educational institutions and socioeconomic inequality? The answer is no, because as I will argue in this section, the association between skills and inequality is complex and the redistributive implications of educational investment depend very much upon the distribution of costs in the financing of education (our first dimension of (de-)commodification of education) and the distribution of resources across educational sectors (related to our second dimension of educational stratification). A second contribution of this chapter is its study of the implications of educational institutions for different dimensions of inequality. A broader conceptualization of labor-market stratification that looks at labor-market risk (in particular youth unemployment) in addition to wage inequality brings to light the existence of tradeoffs between these different dimensions. For instance, statist skill-formation regimes with an emphasis on school-based VET are associated with lower levels of wage inequality than are workplace-based systems, but exhibit much higher levels of youth unemployment.

As a starting point for our discussion, one can imagine a unimodal distribution of academic skills in a given age cohort. The institutions of the education system can exacerbate or mitigate the shape of the distribution as this age cohort moves through the stages of the education system. The existence of a well-established VET system lowers the relative cost of acquiring post-compulsory education for students in the lower half of the academic skills distribution (Breen & Goldthorpe 1997; Hilmert & Jacob 2002; Stocké 2007). On the one hand, this might distract those in the middle segment of the skills distribution from pursuing academic higher education, which they would (have to) do in a different institutional context where VET was not a viable option; on the other, the availability of VET creates incentives for those in the lower third of the skills distribution to work hard in school and opens up pathways to well-paid and secure employment for them (Estévez-Abe *et al.* 2001; Soskice 1994).

In countries without a well-established VET system but with a strong focus on academic post-secondary education, those in the middle segment of the skills distribution opt for higher education (and are willing to pay a significant amount of private resources for it, as in the United States). Those at the lower tail of the skills distribution who fail to gain admission to a university or college, however, are likely to be relegated to low-paid employment. This does not by itself imply that levels of inequality are always higher in countries with a strong focus on higher education, since the total effect very much depends on the openness of access, the financing mechanisms, and the informal stratification of educational institutions within the system (Allmendinger 1989). When access to academic education is very open and/or the system is differentiated (in the sense that it provides access routes for students on the vocational track), expanding higher education might lower socioeconomic inequality. In contrast, when access is limited institutionally or *de facto* by strong mechanisms of stratification between educational institutions within the system in conjunction with high tuition fees, it is likely to exacerbate inequality.

This line of thought can be linked to our first dimension: the division of labor between public and private sources of funding. A core finding of the previous chapters is that the long-term balance between different political parties is a crucial explanatory factor of this variable. Furthermore, the analysis revealed a straightforward left–right cleavage in this case, with leftist parties being more in favor of public involvement in the financing and provision of education and parties of the right more opposed to state involvement. These partisan differences are reflected in the distributive consequences of the division of labor in financing education. Higher levels of state involvement are expected to be associated with a more equalized distribution of private payoffs to education, meaning less income inequality. A high share of private financing, by contrast, is likely to be associated with a more unequal distribution of payoffs. Chapter 5 will explore the microfoundations of this mechanism in terms of attitudes and preferences, showing that high levels of private financing also lower the support for redistribution, as individuals strive to recoup their significant private educational investment on the labor market.

The situation is more complex for the second dimension, educational stratification. Figure 4.1 showed that low levels of educational stratification are not a sufficient condition by themselves for low levels of social inequality. Formally comprehensive secondary school systems and high levels of tertiary enrollment can be associated with higher levels of socioeconomic inequality when the private share in financing is high (e.g., the Anglo-Saxon countries, especially North America). This is because private financing signifies a secondary layer of stratification within a formally unstratified education system. A stronger relative focus on VET holds the potential to reduce socioeconomic inequalities, because it promotes the labor-market integration of those in the lower half of the skills distribution.

This effect needs to be considered in relation to the degree of state involvement, however. In countries where extensive provision of VET is associated with a strong degree of state involvement in the financing and provision of education (the statist skill regimes), levels of socioeconomic inequality are likely to be lower. These are the countries where VET is fully integrated into the upper-secondary school system, as in Sweden. This has two consequences: first, it promotes educational mobility for students on the VET tracks, in the sense that they can easily continue their educational careers at the tertiary level, and second, it marginalizes the role of employers in the provision of initial VET. The opposite can be expected for countries where there is a strict differentiation between VET and general secondary education; that is, in countries with well-developed apprenticeship training schemes (collective skill regimes). Levels of educational stratification are high in such countries, and moving from the VET sector to higher education is still difficult in practice (Nikolai & Ebner 2012; Powell & Solga 2011). The strong separation between academic and vocational education nonetheless helps to maintain high levels of employer involvement in initial VET, because employers are more willing to invest in intermediate-level skills when they can be sure that employees/apprentices will stay with the firm that has trained them, instead of moving on to higher education. In sum, apprenticeship systems may be less effective than school-based VET in lowering income inequality and promoting educational mobility because they have a higher degree of private (employer) involvement.

Employer involvement is crucial, however, when it comes to the second dimension of labor-market stratification after income inequality:

youth unemployment. Since unemployment rates for university graduates are generally low in most countries, the institutional setup of the VET system is an important factor in explaining differences in youth unemployment. A standard finding in the pertinent literature is that transitions from education to employment are much less frictional in countries with a well-developed apprenticeship training system (Allmendinger 1989; Breen 2005; Gangl 2003; Ebner 2013; Müller & Gangl 2003; Wolbers 2007), because apprentices there are already employed in a workplace-based setting and acquire a specific combination of general and occupational skills during the training period. School-based forms of VET are not as effective in lowering youth unemployment as workplace-based forms because their curricula do not necessarily reflect the skill demands of employers, although Scandinavian countries do try to include business representatives in the process of designing and reforming VET curricula. School-based VET systems struggle with establishing direct links between schools and employers. Liberal skill-formation regimes, which privilege academic education over VET, also lack systematic linkages between schools and employers for low-skilled youths. Because labor markets are more flexible and deregulated in these regimes, however, the barriers that youths must overcome to get access to employment are not as high as in other countries. We know this because high levels of employment protection (as well as certain characteristics of the VET system) are associated with above-average levels of youth unemployment (Breen 2005; Wolbers 2007).

Bringing together the various pieces of the puzzle, we can identify a number of interesting tradeoffs between different dimensions of inequality, rooted in the complex nature of the redistributive politics of education. Expanding state involvement in both VET and higher education might help to equalize the distribution of private payoffs on educational investment and increase the educational mobility between VET and higher education. But a high degree of state involvement also leads to the crowding out of employers in the provision of initial VET, which in turn is expected to be associated with higher levels of youth unemployment. Maintaining a high degree of employer involvement therefore entails higher levels of educational stratification, in the form of a more differentiated secondary education system that maintains the separation between vocational and academic education in order to signal to employers that investments in skill formation pay off in the long term.

The different partisan approaches and preferences studied in the previous chapters are related to the question of whether partisan actors will strive to maximize state involvement and educational mobility, or employer and other private involvement. Representatives of the political left who wish to maximize the opportunities for educational advancement by individuals in the lower half of the distribution of skills and income will support the expansion of access to higher levels of education. In the Scandinavian countries, the leftist representatives promoted the integration of VET into the general school system because they did not trust employers to provide sufficiently general skills in firm-based settings (see Chapter 2). This may have contributed to lowering overall levels of social inequality (as will be shown below), but it also led to above-average levels of youth unemployment, because school-based VET is less effective in ensuring smooth transitions from training to employment, particularly in conjunction with medium to high levels of employment protection, as in Sweden.

In the collective skill-formation regimes studied, the dominant position of the Christian democrats in cross-class coalitions ensured that the voice of business representatives remained influential, which was crucial to the survival of the dual-apprenticeship training system. Although these cross-class coalition were less universal than the Scandinavian type, the institutional characteristics of the firm-based training systems ensured smooth transitions and low levels of youth unemployment for those at the lower end of the skills distribution. Conservative welfare states such as Germany are less redistributive than their Scandinavian counterparts (Bradley *et al.* 2003), but the overall level of socioeconomic inequality is still significantly below that of the Anglo-Saxon cluster. The German education system remained segmented and stratified, however, because the welfare state regime did not aim for redistribution *per se*, but rather for status maintenance. The ensuing high level of educational inequality did not directly spill over into socioeconomic inequality, but we can see that there is an important link between the long-term sustainability of the apprenticeship training system and the segmented nature of secondary schooling, as discussed above.

In the liberal skill-formation regimes, the tradeoff was that the expansion of access to higher education and the abolition of credible alternatives in VET led to the emergence of new mechanisms of stratification (or reinforced old ones). Ironically, comprehensive and universal education policies ("academic education for all") are in fact associated with above-average levels of socioeconomic inequality, because the broadening of access to higher education happened alongside a process of differentiation *within* the higher education sector. Access to the higher strata of these differentiated systems is limited, because of either high tuition fees or other barriers of access (selectivity).

Cross-sectional evidence

In order to substantiate the claims made in the previous section, I now present empirical data in the form of bivariate scatterplots and simple cross-sectional regressions. As in the previous chapter, I rely on data from the OECD Education Statistics Database. Because I am interested in explaining broad cross-country differences, the values are all averages for the time period 1997–2008, unless otherwise stated. See the technical appendix at the end of the book for details on sources.

I start out by replicating the scatterplot provided in Estévez-Abe *et al.* (2001: 178). The share of upper-secondary students in VET programs versus general academic programs is given on the x axis of the panels in Figure 4.2. This measure does not distinguish between school-based and workplace-based (apprenticeship) types of VET. Because the data availability is much better in this case than in the case of the more detailed indicators, it is the one most commonly used in the VoC literature (Bradley *et al.* 2003; Cusack *et al.* 2006; Estévez-Abe *et al.* 2001; Iversen & Soskice 2001; Lupu & Pontusson 2011). By and large, the figures confirm the expected negative association between VET and inequality. In Panel A, I display levels of inequality based on household data (the net Gini index) on the y axis, while I use a more narrow definition of wage inequality (the ratio between the person at the 9th decile and the person at the 1st decile) in Panel B. Again, we could expect the institutional setup of the education and training system to be more directly related to the distribution of wages, because educational institutions affect the distribution of skills and, in turn, incomes. The net Gini index of the distribution of household income takes into account the inequality-reducing impact of taxes and transfers, as well as the household structure. In the following section, this will be the more important measure of inequality: first, because it is more encompassing than the wage-dispersion measure, taking

Educational institutions and socioeconomic inequality   191

Panel A: Socioeconomic inequality (Gini index)

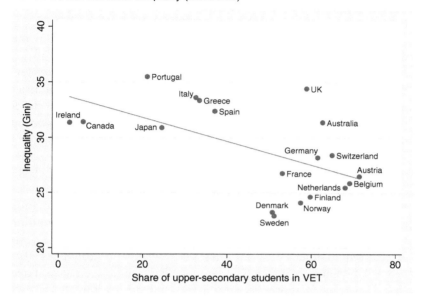

Panel B: Wage inequality (D9–D1 ratio)

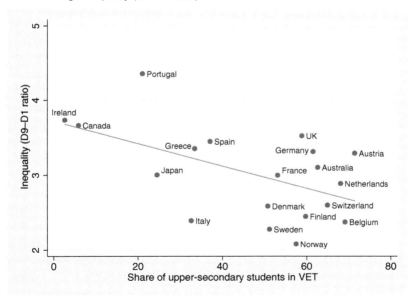

Figure 4.2 VET share and inequality

the household composition into account, and second, because it makes it possible to assess whether education has an inequality-reducing impact above and beyond the impact of taxes and transfers.

Figure 4.2 shows that the negative association between VET and inequality holds in both cases. Furthermore, we see a rather strong clustering of European countries in the lower-right quadrant (high levels of VET and low levels of inequality) and of Anglo-Saxon countries in the upper-left quadrant. The United Kingdom is actually much closer to the European cluster than to the Anglo-Saxon. This is an important difference from the figure in Estévez-Abe *et al.* (2001), according to which the share of VET in the United Kingdom is 10 percent, rather than the 60 percent given in the OECD data. The difficulty of classifying the complex British VET system (see Chapter 2) is obvious. The NVQ system is clearly an important component of the skill-formation regime in terms of sheer numbers, but it remains an open question whether the NVQ should be regarded as a form of VET at the same level as that in other European countries or whether it should be classified as labor-market policy. For example, Payne and Keep have stated that 75 percent of apprenticeships in the United Kingdom are at Level 2 of the NVQ framework, "which would not be recognised as an apprenticeship in countries such as Germany, Denmark and Norway" (Payne & Keep 2011: 12). Classifying the United States is equally difficult. The OECD data do not provide any information on the share of upper-secondary students in VET in the United States. Given the institutional characteristics of the American comprehensive high school, one could easily imagine putting the United States at the same (low) level as Canada and Ireland (as was in fact done in some analyses in the previous chapter). The clustering of countries and the negative association between the incidence of VET and inequality would be even more pronounced if we were to adjust for these country-specific anomalies.

Considerable evidence exists that the provision of VET in general is negatively associated with different measures of socioeconomic inequality, but how much does the type of VET matter? In Figure 4.3, I present data on the share of students going through apprenticeship programs at the secondary level (as a percentage of all upper-secondary students). Unfortunately, this measure is only available for a limited number of countries (see discussion in Chapter 3). Even with these data limitations, however, Figure 4.3 shows that the association between

Educational institutions and socioeconomic inequality 193

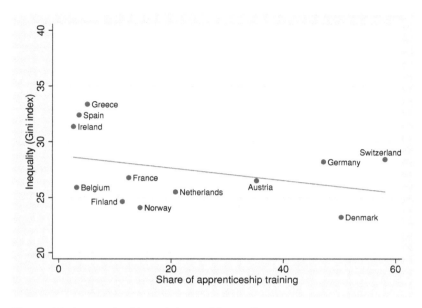

Figure 4.3 Apprenticeship training and inequality

apprenticeship training and inequality is much weaker than in the case of VET in general. This is not surprising, because in contrast to school-based VET, apprenticeship training is not primarily intended to maximize educational opportunities and mobility. In contrast, existing differences between occupations on the labor market are mirrored in training occupations with regard to apprenticeship pay and employment conditions during and after the completion of training.

Turning from VET to higher education, I also find little support for a statistically significant association between enrollment in tertiary education and levels of socioeconomic inequality (Figure 4.4, Panel A). Expanding access to higher education is not a sufficient measure by which to mitigate social inequality, because investments in higher education also create significant private benefits in terms of higher wages for the high-skilled. The overall effect of expanding access to higher education therefore depends on the interaction between the higher education system and the prevailing division of labor between public and private sources of funding. Levels of socioeconomic inequality are significantly higher in countries where a significant share of spending

Panel A: Tertiary enrollment

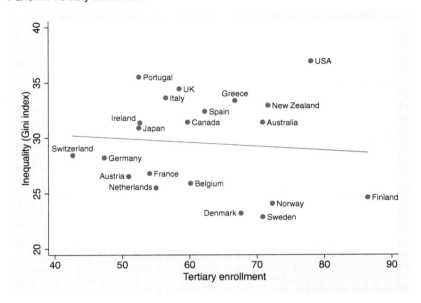

Panel B: The public/private division of labor in the financing of higher education

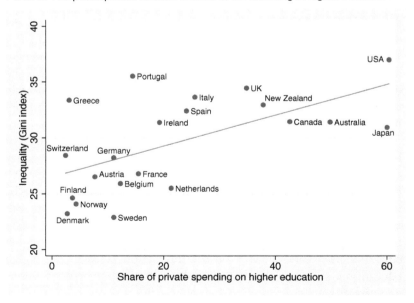

Figure 4.4 Higher education and inequality

Educational institutions and socioeconomic inequality 195

on higher education is financed from private sources, mostly households (Figure 4.4, Panel B). The underlying causal mechanism might be related to self-interest or to differences in welfare state culture (see Chapter 5, as well as Busemeyer 2013). Individuals who have had to pay for a large share of their human capital stock out of their own pocket are less likely to support redistribution and an expansive welfare state, because they want to recoup a part of their private investment via higher wage premiums. In terms of welfare-state culture, the popular support for residual welfare states might go along with a higher willingness to pay for education. Conversely, individuals who have experienced the benefits of a universal, comprehensive, and publicly financed education system might be more likely to support redistribution and the expansion of the welfare state. Although it is hard to pin down the relative importance of these different causal mechanisms, the overall conclusion is straightforward: when it comes to levels of socioeconomic inequality, differences in the way higher education is financed matter more than enrollment levels as such.

I have now presented evidence of a negative association between VET and socioeconomic inequality, but how is VET related to *educational* inequality? From the perspective of educational sociology, we could expect that well-established VET systems would go along with higher levels of educational inequality, since the segmentation of education systems into different academic and vocational tracks is an indication of institutional stratification. And indeed, looking at Panel A of Figure 4.5, which employs the same measure of educational inequality as above, we find a positive association between educational inequality and the share of students in VET. The association also holds when we use the measure of educational inequality based on the PISA study (not shown here). Furthermore, we could expect the association between apprenticeship training and educational inequality to be even more pronounced than in the case of school-based training; countries with extensive school-based VET, such as the Netherlands and some Scandinavian countries, ensure a certain degree of educational mobility by integrating vocational tracks into the general school system. In contrast, options to move from the apprenticeship track to higher education are very limited in the German-speaking countries, which have strong apprenticeship systems, although in recent years all these countries have been slowly moving towards improving the linkage between academic and vocational education (Nikolai & Ebner 2012;

Panel A: Share of upper-secondary students in VET and educational inequality

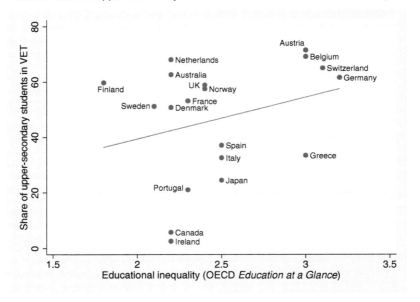

Panel B: Apprenticeship training and educational inequality

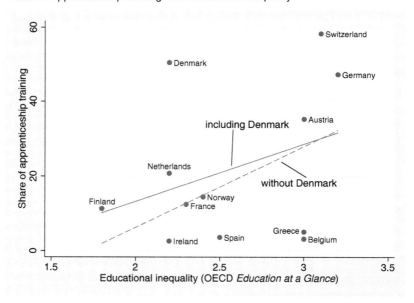

Figure 4.5 VET and educational inequality

Educational institutions and socioeconomic inequality 197

Powell & Solga 2011). The data displayed in Panel B of Figure 4.5 show that there is indeed a positive association between educational inequality and the share of apprenticeship training, although this finding needs to be interpreted cautiously because of the low number of cases. Denmark constitutes an interesting outlier: as in the German-speaking countries, apprenticeship training is the dominant form of VET at the level of secondary education. Unlike in Germany, however, youths who fail to get access to regular training in Denmark can continue their training in school-based or out-of-firm training courses, resulting in a more inclusive training system that is also better connected to the sectors of higher and continuing education (Busemeyer 2012c; Nelson 2012). Excluding the outlier of Denmark (dashed line) increases the slope of the regression line.

When we move from income inequality to youth unemployment as the dependent variable, the simple bivariate scatterplots (Figure 4.6) largely confirm previous findings on the role of VET institutions as determinants of youth unemployment. There *is* a negative association between the share of upper-secondary students in VET as a whole and levels of youth unemployment, but it is very weak (Panel A). The reason is that in this case, the *kind* of VET matters enormously. When VET is provided in the form of combined school- and workplace-based programs (apprenticeships), we find a strong negative association (Panel B). Conversely, when VET is provided mostly in schools, levels of youth unemployment are significantly higher (not shown here, since it is basically the mirror image of Panel B), because the transition from education to employment is less smooth than in the case of apprenticeship training.

Before I move on to multivariate cross-sectional time-series analyses in the following section, I would like to present some findings from simple cross-sectional regression analyses in order to back up the main claims. Unfortunately, the number of cases varies between fifteen and twenty-one in the regressions because of data limitations, particularly with regard to the share of apprenticeship training. What is more, the number of independent variables that can be included in this kind of analysis is necessarily limited because of the small number of cases. Despite these limitations, several findings stand out. First, educational inequality is not statistically associated with socioeconomic inequality. Even controlling for other variables, the coefficient estimate of this variable remains statistically insignificant, and its sign varies across

Panel A: All upper-secondary students in VET

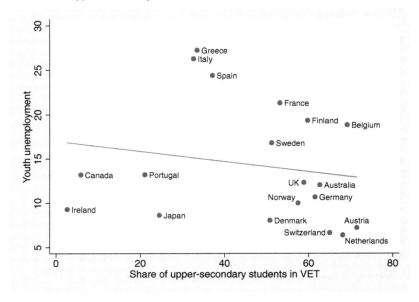

Panel B: Only apprenticeship training

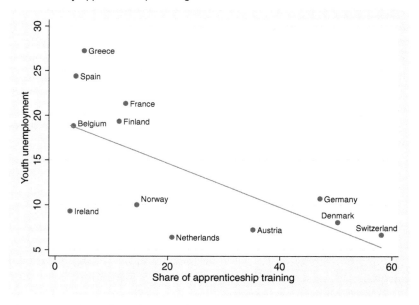

Figure 4.6 VET and youth unemployment

model specifications. Second, the share of upper-secondary students in VET has a statistically significant and negative impact on socioeconomic inequality, even when controlling for educational inequality and social transfers. Based on Model 2, an increase in the enrollment share by 50 percentage points (roughly the difference between Canada and Germany) is predicted to be associated with a reduction in the Gini index of 4.5 points, which is slightly more than one standard deviation (SD = 4.3, mean = 29.5) in the sample. In contrast, there is no statistically significant association between the share of apprenticeship training and socioeconomic inequality, confirming the bivariate observation from above. Third, I also find that in the case of higher education, it matters greatly whether education is financed by public or private sources. Public spending on higher education is negatively and significantly associated with socioeconomic inequality, whereas the opposite can be observed in the case of private education spending (Models 5 and 6 versus Models 7 and 8 in Table 4.1). If we simulate a similar change in the independent variable "public higher education spending" from the level of Germany (0.97 percent of GDP for the time period under observation) to the level of Canada (1.46 percent of GDP), the predicted effect on inequality is a decrease of 4.1 points in the Gini index. Conversely, increasing private spending on higher education from the level of Denmark (0.08 percent of GDP) to that of Australia (0.74 percent) is associated with an increase in the Gini index of 3.3 points. These cases are chosen in order to make the coefficient estimates more tangible. They are not at the extreme points in the distribution of cases, but represent typical cases at the upper and lower ends of the distribution. Finally, the amount of social transfer spending does not have a particularly strong impact on socioeconomic inequality, most likely because the dependent variable is post-tax and post-transfer inequality. The effect is negative, as could be expected, but given that this variable captures the influence of traditional social insurance and assistance schemes, it could have been much stronger. In any case, these regressions show that the institutional setup of the education system matters a lot with regard to inequality, above and beyond the impact of traditional social policies.

Cross-sectional time-series analyses

I have already commented briefly in Chapter 3 on the advantages and disadvantages of cross-sectional time-series analysis in cross-country

Table 4.1 *Educational institutions as determinants of socioeconomic inequality, cross-sectional regressions*

Dependent variable	(1)	(2)	(3)	(4)	(5)	(6)	(7)	(8)
	\multicolumn{8}{c}{Socioeconomic inequality (Gini index)}							
Educational inequality (PISA measure)	−0.00882 (0.123)	−0.00615 (0.120)	−0.0875 (0.137)	0.0423 (0.159)	−0.155* (0.0846)	−0.132 (0.0772)	−0.117 (0.114)	−0.0972 (0.115)
Share of upper-secondary students in VET	−0.105*** (0.0321)	−0.0881** (0.0391)						
Social transfers (% of GDP)		−0.285 (0.237)		−0.615 (0.353)		−0.338* (0.162)		−0.288 (0.250)
Share of apprenticeship training			−0.0656 (0.0547)	−0.0464 (0.0441)				
Public spending on higher education (% of GDP)					−9.554*** (2.239)	−8.296*** (2.248)		
Private spending on higher education (% of GDP)							6.408*** (1.184)	4.989*** (1.473)
Constant	34.23*** (4.393)	37.32*** (4.105)	32.71*** (5.156)	36.14*** (4.713)	46.28*** (4.428)	48.59*** (4.638)	31.95*** (5.062)	35.66*** (5.353)
Observations	19	19	15	15	21	21	20	20
R^2	0.316	0.361	0.137	0.299	0.465	0.522	0.341	0.371

Robust standard errors in parentheses
*** $p < 0.01$, ** $p < 0.05$, * $p < 0.1$

comparative research. Since data for a number of crucial independent variables are available only for the years since the mid-to-late 1990s, the time period of observation (as well as the size of the panel) is restricted. Including a lagged dependent variable, which is advised as a remedy against the problem of serial autocorrelation (Beck & Katz 1995, 1996), would further reduce the length of the time series. Furthermore, including a lagged dependent variable drains the explanatory power of other independent variables (Achen 2000), especially when the time series is short and these other variables change little over time, as in our case. Because of the short time series and the limited variation of both the core independent variables and the dependent variable over time, it is also not possible to apply the more advanced error-correction model that has recently become quite popular. In short, data limitations impose certain restrictions on the methods that can be used. The panel analysis allows us to include more independent variables as controls, but in all honesty, the added value compared to simple cross-sectional regressions is limited in the present case. Nevertheless, robust findings can emerge when we combine different methods. For the panel analyses, the preferred method is to calculate panel-corrected standard errors in order to correct for panel heteroskedasticity and contemporaneous correlation across countries (Beck & Katz 1995) and model serial correlation in the residuals with an autoregressive (AR1) process instead of including a lagged dependent variable. I refrain from using fixed effects (country dummies) because these would be correlated with institutional variables.

Table 4.2 shows the findings of an analysis of the determinants of inequality in terms of the (net) Gini index, which measures the inequality of income distribution at the household level. The control variables perform largely as expected. Economic growth is associated with lower levels of inequality (even though the coefficient estimate usually fails to reach conventional levels of statistical significance), whereas the opposite holds when unemployment increases. The centralization of collective wage bargaining is also associated with lower levels of inequality, confirming one of the central findings in the comparative political economy literature, but again, the effect is not statistically significant. Government partisanship does have an effect, but the direction is surprising. This variable is taken from the Comparative Political Data Set (Armingeon *et al.* 2011) and ranges from 1 (dominance of rightist parties in government) to 5 (dominance of leftist parties). Higher values

Table 4.2 *Socioeconomic inequality and VET share, 1997–2008*

Dependent variable	(1)	(2)	(3)	(4)	(5)	(6)
	\multicolumn{6}{c}{Socioeconomic inequality (Gini index)}					
GDP growth	−0.00667	−0.0229	0.0159	−0.0701	−0.0449	−0.0734**
	(0.0534)	(0.0438)	(0.0778)	(0.0493)	(0.0447)	(0.0306)
Unemployment	0.0196	0.136***	−0.0801	0.177***	0.120***	0.353***
	(0.0489)	(0.0307)	(0.0520)	(0.0505)	(0.0398)	(0.0449)
Wage-bargaining centralization	−0.131	−0.264	−0.0601	−0.160	−0.158	−0.182
	(0.102)	(0.178)	(0.0777)	(0.123)	(0.106)	(0.130)
Government partisanship	−0.266**	−0.0330	−0.252**	−0.0375	−0.221**	0.0195
	(0.106)	(0.0611)	(0.110)	(0.0730)	(0.0954)	(0.0581)
Share of apprenticeship training	−0.0150		−0.0361		−0.0306	
	(0.0208)		(0.0305)		(0.0241)	
Share of upper-secondary students in VET		−0.0562***		−0.0479***		−0.0410***
		(0.00873)		(0.0135)		(0.00840)
Public social spending (% of GDP)			0.233***	−0.186*		
			(0.0630)	(0.0984)		
Social-transfer spending (% of GDP)					−0.177***	−0.545***
					(0.0533)	(0.0465)
Constant	26.95***	30.40***	24.15***	32.20***	29.70***	35.95***
	(0.758)	(0.897)	(1.041)	(0.686)	(0.894)	(0.502)
Observations	95	172	85	156	95	172
R^2	0.985	0.984	0.990	0.981	0.985	0.984
Number of countries	10	17	10	17	10	17

Standard errors in parentheses
*** $p < 0.01$, ** $p < 0.05$, * $p < 0.1$

Educational institutions and socioeconomic inequality 203

indicate more "leftwardness." The negative sign of the coefficient estimates (in some cases statistically significant) indicates that inequality is higher under leftist governments, which runs counter to the expectations of power resources theory (Bradley *et al.* 2003). This finding should not be overinterpreted, however: it could simply be picking up cross-national differences that coincide with changes in government, or it could be related to the reduced number of countries in the sample. More comprehensive tests of the power resources theory must adopt a long-term perspective (see Chapter 3).

The most important finding here is that a higher share of upper-secondary students in VET is associated with a lower level of socioeconomic inequality. This coefficient estimate is statistically significant across all model specifications (Models 2, 4, and 6) and performs much better than the other control variables. As in the bivariate analysis, the share of apprenticeship training is not associated with levels of inequality (Models 1, 3, and 5), meaning that workplace-based types of VET are less effective at reducing inequality than VET as a whole. The negative and significant association holds even after controlling for public social spending and social transfer spending (Models 4 and 6, respectively), which themselves are expected to have a depressing effect on inequality. In contrast to the latter two variables, the magnitude (size of the effect) of the VET variable varies less across model specifications. Compared to the bivariate regressions, the magnitude of the effect of the VET variable is smaller in the case of multivariate regression due to the inclusion of additional control variables. An increase in VET enrollment of 50 percent (the same as above) is predicted to be associated with a decrease in the Gini index of 2.5 points.

Table 4.3 presents my findings on the association between the public/private division of labor in education financing and socioeconomic inequality. In Chapter 3, this variable was shown to be statistically correlated with long-term averages in the distribution of power across different party families. The findings in Table 4.3 corroborate the expectation of a significant and positive (i.e., inequality-enhancing) association between the private share of education financing and socioeconomic inequality, independent of whether I include the private share for all levels of education (Models 1 and 2) or for higher education only (Models 3 and 4). The magnitude of the effect is comparatively large (see Figure 4.7). A change of one standard deviation in the private spending share for all levels of education is predicted to be associated

Table 4.3 *Socioeconomic inequality and the public/private division of labor in education financing, 1997–2008*

Dependent variable	(1)	(2)	(3)	(4)
	\multicolumn{4}{c}{Socioeconomic inequality (Gini index)}			
GDP growth	0.0223	−0.0235	0.0485*	0.00213
	(0.0275)	(0.0202)	(0.0264)	(0.0283)
Unemployment	−0.113***	0.154***	0.0404	0.208***
	(0.0414)	(0.0245)	(0.0413)	(0.0471)
Wage-bargaining centralization	−0.139**	0.0267	−0.115	0.00181
	(0.0675)	(0.0469)	(0.0754)	(0.0575)
Government partisanship	−0.142***	−0.00189	−0.118**	−0.0938
	(0.0537)	(0.0452)	(0.0593)	(0.0614)
Social-transfer spending (% of GDP)		−0.540***		−0.565***
		(0.0317)		(0.0690)
Private share of education spending, all levels of education	0.179***	0.0950***		
	(0.0196)	(0.0194)		
Private share of education spending, tertiary education			0.118***	0.0660***
			(0.00904)	(0.00974)
Constant	27.16***	34.12***	25.84***	33.42***
	(0.557)	(0.793)	(0.418)	(0.990)
Observations	188	188	200	200
R^2	0.968	0.977	0.971	0.967
Number of countries	18	18	19	19

Standard errors in parentheses
*** $p < 0.01$, ** $p < 0.05$, * $p < 0.1$

with an increase in inequality of 1.5 points on the Gini index (Model 1). For the private spending share in higher education only, the size of the predicted effect is an increase of 2.1 points (Model 3).[2] The magnitude of the effects diminishes somewhat when social transfer spending is

---

[2] The standard deviation of the private spending share for all levels of education in the sample is 8.21; for the private spending share for tertiary education, it is 18.17. This is why the effect of the latter variable is larger even though the coefficient estimate is smaller in magnitude.

Educational institutions and socioeconomic inequality 205

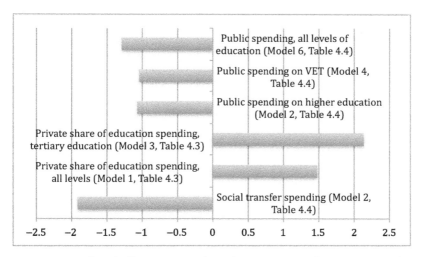

Figure 4.7 Predicted effect on inequality of an increase in the respective independent variable by one standard deviation

included as a control variable (Models 2 and 4), but the coefficient estimate remains statistically significant and positive.

In Table 4.4, I analyze the association between different kinds of education spending and socioeconomic inequality. This provides a further robustness test of the association between education and socioeconomic inequality. Here I focus on education spending as a percentage of GDP, in contrast to the previous analysis, which looked at the private share of education spending and disregarded differences in spending levels. The results confirm that higher levels of public investment in any kind of education (higher education, VET, or all levels of education) are associated with lower levels of socioeconomic inequality. These effects remain highly significant even when controlling for social transfer spending (Models 2, 4, and 6 in Table 4.4), although the magnitude of the coefficient estimate is reduced, as could be expected.

What is the magnitude of the effects, comparatively speaking? Figure 4.7 presents the estimated effects resulting from an increase of one standard deviation in the respective variable. Clearly, social transfer spending is an important negative determinant of inequality. An increase in social transfer spending of one standard deviation is predicted to be associated with a reduction in inequality of 1.91 points. The effects of a similar increase in public investment (as percentage

Table 4.4 *Education spending and socioeconomic inequality (Gini index), 1997–2008*

Dependent variable	(1)	(2)	(3)	(4)	(5)	(6)
	\multicolumn{6}{c}{Socioeconomic inequality (Gini index)}					
GDP growth	0.101	−0.0359	−0.0542	−0.0989**	0.00195	−0.0413
	(0.0732)	(0.0676)	(0.0524)	(0.0410)	(0.0491)	(0.0490)
Unemployment	−0.0564	0.161***	0.312***	0.393***	0.0633	0.110***
	(0.0658)	(0.0377)	(0.0536)	(0.0712)	(0.0521)	(0.0377)
Wage-bargaining centralization	−0.644***	−0.418**	−0.352*	−0.354	−0.428**	−0.204
	(0.212)	(0.187)	(0.205)	(0.227)	(0.168)	(0.157)
Government partisanship	−0.0950	−0.0841	−0.0582	0.0384	−0.226***	−0.119*
	(0.117)	(0.0673)	(0.0741)	(0.0908)	(0.0877)	(0.0685)
Public spending on higher education (% of GDP)	−4.496***	−3.451***				
	(0.847)	(0.680)				
Social transfer spending (% of GDP)		−0.531***		−0.425***		−0.371***
		(0.0402)		(0.0571)		(0.0504)
Public spending on VET (% of GDP, proxy)			−5.444***	−3.849***		
			(0.702)	(0.878)		
Public spending on education, all levels (% of GDP)					−2.036***	−1.370***
					(0.267)	(0.222)
Constant	34.95***	40.86***	30.11***	34.90***	39.31***	40.63***
	(1.206)	(1.047)	(0.860)	(0.621)	(1.662)	(1.475)
Observations	207	207	163	163	207	207
R^2	0.970	0.992	0.980	0.985	0.979	0.984
Number of countries	19	19	17	17	19	19

Standard errors in parentheses

Educational institutions and socioeconomic inequality 207

of GDP) in higher education and VET are quite similar: a predicted reduction in the Gini index of 1.07 and 1.04 points, respectively. The overall effect of a one-standard-deviation increase in public education spending (for all levels of education) is slightly larger (1.29 points), which could indicate that other sectors of the education system, such as primary and early childhood education, might further contribute to reducing inequality. Further research that lies beyond the scope of the present chapter would certainly be welcome here. Finally, the public/private division of labor emerges as a very strong positive predictor of levels of inequality, particularly in the case of higher education. As I said above, the predicted effect at the tertiary level of a one-standard-deviation increase in the private spending share is an increase of 2.14 points in the Gini index.

Table 4.5 looks at the interaction between the private spending share and patterns of enrollment. The theoretical expectation presented above is that higher levels of private involvement in the financing of education should negate the inequality-reducing effects of an expansion in enrollment, especially at the level of higher education. This expectation is largely confirmed by the findings. In Models 2 and 3, I look at the association between enrollment in higher education and private spending share. Model 2 employs a measure of gross tertiary enrollment supplied by UNESCO, which most likely overestimates the size of the higher education sector (see discussion in Chapter 3). Model 3 uses a more narrowly defined measure supplied by the OECD: the entry rate into tertiary type-A higher education (academic higher education). In both cases, I find a significant and negative association with levels of inequality, but this must be interpreted as the effect of enrollment on inequality *when private involvement is zero*, since the models include an interaction term. The positive coefficient estimate of the interaction term indicates that the negative coefficient becomes positive for high levels of private spending. The predicted *positive* effect of tertiary enrollment on inequality for the maximum value of the private spending share variable in the sample is 0.045 for the entry-rate measure and an even larger 0.12 for the gross enrollment measure.

At first sight, the pattern appears to be similar in the case of VET (Model 1). This model confirms the negative association between the share of upper-secondary students in VET and inequality, but again this effect needs to be interpreted as the effect of the VET share when

Table 4.5 *Interactions between private involvement and enrollment patterns*

	(1)	(2)	(3)
Dependent variable	Socioeconomic inequality (Gini index)		
GDP growth	−0.0899*	0.0750***	0.0562**
	(0.0459)	(0.0194)	(0.0274)
Unemployment	0.0467	−0.0384	0.157**
	(0.0584)	(0.0301)	(0.0643)
Wage-bargaining centralization	−0.0412	−0.162**	−0.0692
	(0.0569)	(0.0673)	(0.0879)
Government partisanship	−0.0932	−0.201***	−0.0471
	(0.0847)	(0.0541)	(0.0723)
Private share of education spending, all levels of education	−0.0168		
	(0.0452)		
Share of upper-secondary students in VET	−0.0945***		
	(0.0211)		
Interaction: private share × VET	0.00287***		
	(0.000891)		
Private share of education spending, tertiary education		−0.0429	0.0401
		(0.0442)	(0.0276)
Gross enrollment in tertiary education		−0.0605**	
		(0.0263)	
Interaction: private share (tertiary) × gross tertiary enrollment		0.00267***	
		(0.000810)	
Entry rate to tertiary education			−0.0630***
			(0.0133)
Interaction: private share (tertiary) × entry rate			0.00158***
			(0.000349)
Constant	31.82***	29.56***	27.54***
	(1.268)	(1.406)	(0.711)
Observations	167	185	147
R^2	0.968	0.977	0.981
Number of countries	16	18	17

Standard errors in parentheses
*** $p < 0.01$, ** $p < 0.05$, * $p < 0.1$

the private spending share is zero. In the case of Model 1, I use the private spending share for all levels of education instead of focusing on higher education. As in Models 2 and 3, the sign of the interaction term is positive and the term is statistically significant, indicating that higher levels of private involvement negate the inequality-reducing impact of VET enrollment. In contrast to higher education, however, the positive effect of the interaction is merely equal to the negative effect of enrollment. The joint impact of VET enrollment and private spending share, when the latter reaches its maximum value, is a meager 0.0028 point increase in the Gini index, which statistically speaking is indistinguishable from zero. This nicely corresponds to the finding of a nonassociation between the apprenticeship training share and socioeconomic inequality in Table 4.2, although the private spending share should not be interpreted as a direct indicator of employer involvement in initial VET. To put it simply, private involvement in the financing of education negates the inequality-reducing effect of enrollment expansion. This effect is much stronger in the case of higher education, in the sense that higher levels of enrollment are associated with lower/higher levels of inequality when the private spending share is low/high. In the case of VET, by contrast, high levels of private spending merely negate the inequality-reducing effect of VET enrollment; they do not contribute to higher inequality themselves.

In Table 4.6, I use a different dependent variable as a further check on the robustness of the findings. Until now I have looked at the Gini index as a measure of net household income inequality. The measure used in Table 4.6, by contrast, measures wage inequality, the inequality of market incomes before taxes and transfers. Besides allowing for more robustness checks, this new dependent variable makes it possible to look at the differentiated impact of educational institutions in the upper and lower half of the income distribution, respectively. Models 1 and 4 look at wage inequality across the whole distribution (ratio between incomes at the 9th and 1st deciles). Models 2 and 5 analyze the upper half of the income distribution (D9–D5 ratio), and Models 3 and 6 the lower half (D5–D1 ratio).

In this setup, the negative effect of centralized wage bargaining is more robust and consistent than in the earlier analyses, which is probably related to the shift from the household to the individual level and from net to market income. Socioeconomic control variables do not perform well, probably because changes in inequality take longer to manifest and do not react to short-term changes in the business

Table 4.6 *Educational institutions and wage inequality, 1997–2008*

Dependent variables	(1) D9–D1 ratio	(2) D9–D5 ratio	(3) D5–D1 ratio	(4) D9–D1 ratio	(5) D9–D5 ratio	(6) D5–D1 ratio
GDP growth	0.00526 (0.00429)	0.000700 (0.00186)	0.000774 (0.00130)	−0.00338 (0.00381)	−0.000481 (0.00194)	−0.00175 (0.00112)
Unemployment	0.0196 (0.0134)	0.00809 (0.00631)	0.00145 (0.00310)	−0.00512 (0.00426)	0.000660 (0.00292)	−0.00479* (0.00263)
Wage-bargaining centralization	−0.0368* (0.0214)	−0.0279** (0.0135)	−0.00376 (0.00786)	−0.0549*** (0.0182)	−0.0127*** (0.00284)	−0.0158* (0.00887)
Government partisanship	0.0154 (0.0178)	−0.00112 (0.00721)	0.00324 (0.00757)	−0.000751 (0.00966)	−0.00199 (0.00269)	0.00140 (0.00507)
Share of apprenticeship training	−0.000966 (0.00194)	−0.00106 (0.000834)	7.15×10^{-5} (0.00123)			
Share of upper-secondary students in VET				−0.00847*** (0.00156)	−0.00332*** (0.000620)	−0.00131*** (0.000279)
Constant	2.620*** (0.227)	1.805*** (0.0780)	1.543*** (0.0712)	3.345*** (0.121)	1.998*** (0.0410)	1.668*** (0.0362)
Observations	79	79	79	150	150	150
R^2	0.938	0.991	0.975	0.941	0.987	0.984
Number of countries	10	10	10	17	17	17

Standard errors in parentheses
*** $p < 0.01$, ** $p < 0.05$, * $p < 0.1$

cycle. As before, there is no association between the share of apprenticeship training and wage inequality, no matter whether we look at the whole distribution of incomes or the upper and lower halves. This non-finding could also be a consequence of the low number of country cases in this specification, but it resonates well with previous findings. On the other hand, there is a statistically significant negative association between the share of upper-secondary students in VET as a whole and wage inequality. The effect is significant across all three dependent variables (Models 4, 5, and 6). Somewhat surprisingly, the magnitude of the effect is larger for the upper half of the income distribution (Model 5) than for the lower half (Model 6), although VET could well have been expected to be associated with a stronger compression of incomes in the lower half of the income distribution. But despite this counterintuitive result, the main finding still holds: a larger share of upper-secondary students in VET is negatively associated with levels of wage inequality.

I will now turn to the analysis of the determinants of youth unemployment (Table 4.7). In addition to the control variables used in previous analyses, I also include an index on the strictness of employment-protection legislation developed by the OECD (EPL index). Higher values indicate a higher level of protection against dismissals. Confirming a main finding in the pertinent literature (Breen 2005; Wolbers 2007), I find a positive association between the EPL index and levels of youth unemployment, although the effect is only statistically significant in Models 1 and 3. When employment protection is strong, employers seem to be more reluctant to hire young people, leading to more difficult transitions from education to employment and higher levels of youth unemployment. As could be expected, economic growth depresses youth unemployment, while the overall level of unemployment in a political economy is positively associated with youth unemployment. Wage-bargaining centralization also has a negative and significant effect, indicating that corporatist institutions might be better able to ensure the integration of young people into the labor market than pluralist and deregulated labor relations.

Coming to the main variables of interest, the findings in Model 1 confirm that there is no statistically significant association between the share of upper-secondary students in VET as a whole and youth unemployment. However, the share of apprenticeship training has a highly significant and negative effect on levels of youth unemployment (Model 2). An increase in the share of apprenticeship training by 45

Table 4.7 *Determinants of youth unemployment, 1997–2008*

Dependent variable	(1)	(2)	(3)
	\multicolumn{3}{c}{Youth unemployment}		
GDP growth	−0.129**	−0.252***	−0.0895
	(0.0645)	(0.0664)	(0.0776)
Unemployment	1.846***	1.628***	1.724***
	(0.144)	(0.0711)	(0.0964)
Wage-bargaining centralization	−0.228*	−0.633***	−0.374**
	(0.131)	(0.185)	(0.171)
Strictness of employment-protection legislation, all employees	1.078**	0.337	0.934***
	(0.522)	(0.548)	(0.361)
Government partisanship	0.0989	0.173	0.129
	(0.0731)	(0.119)	(0.0921)
Share of upper-secondary students in VET	0.0102		
	(0.0124)		
Share of apprenticeship training		−0.175***	
		(0.0159)	
Public spending on education (% of GDP, all levels of education)			0.982***
			(0.315)
Constant	−0.438	7.448***	−3.537***
	(0.757)	(1.826)	(1.076)
Observations	172	95	207
R^2	0.908	0.949	0.930
Number of countries	17	10	19

Standard errors in parentheses
*** $p < 0.01$, ** $p < 0.05$, * $p < 0.1$

percentage points (which is roughly the difference between Norway and Switzerland) is predicted to be associated with a decrease in youth unemployment of 7.9 percentage points. The average in the sample is 13.7 percent with a standard deviation of 6.8, so the magnitude of the effect is larger than one standard deviation. When apprenticeship training is included as a variable, the effect of EPL becomes insignificant. This confirms an important finding of Breen (2005), who has argued that a well-developed apprenticeship training system can compensate for the negative effects of strong employment regulation on youth unemployment. This also resonates well with core claims in the VoC literature on the institutional complementarity between employment protection and skill formation (Estévez-Abe *et al.* 2001). Model 3 shows that public spending on education is not an effective cure against high levels of youth unemployment. In fact, the coefficient is positive and statistically significant. This finding should be treated with caution and needs to be verified by additional analyses, but it nevertheless hints at an important tradeoff: higher levels of public involvement in the financing and administration of VET might be effective in lowering levels of inequality (see above), but a strong degree of state involvement can have negative side effects in the form of higher rates of youth unemployment, because it leads to a marginalization of employers in the provision of initial VET.

Summary and conclusion

This chapter complements the previous ones by moving from politics to outcomes. Addressing a major research gap at the interstices between comparative political economy and educational sociology, I found significant evidence for the claim that educational institutions matter with regard to socioeconomic inequality. Scholarship in comparative political economy tends to underestimate the impact of educational institutions on income inequality, because it is more concerned with labor-market institutions and often fails to take into account the crucial importance of different *types* of education (vocational versus academic higher education), as well as differences in the financing of educational investments. Educational sociology, in turn, concentrates on assessing the impact of institutions on inequality *within* the education system, often neglecting the question of how educational inequalities are translated into labor-market and income inequalities.

This chapter has also revealed that the redistributive politics of education are complex and involve multiple tradeoffs. The core findings can be summarized in the form of several theses. First, public involvement in skill formation is associated with lower levels of socioeconomic inequality. A high share of private spending on education, particularly in the case of higher education, is associated with higher levels of socioeconomic inequality. In contrast, higher levels of public spending – independent of whether it is concentrated on VET or higher education – contribute to lowering income inequality. Second, inequality is also lower in countries with well-established VET systems. Workplace-based types of VET may be less effective in reducing inequality than school-based forms, however (this chapter presents correlations, not a more stringent proof of causality), for the simple reason that the link between VET and higher education is more institutionalized and better developed in countries with extensive school-based VET. Third, there is a tradeoff between lower income inequality and youth unemployment: public involvement in VET reduces income inequality, but has no effect (or maybe even a positive effect) on youth unemployment. Apprenticeship training, by contrast, does not reduce income inequality, but it has a strong negative effect on youth unemployment.

5 | *The impact of educational institutions on popular attitudes and preferences*

In the previous chapter, I analyzed the effects of educational institutions on outcomes in terms of socioeconomic inequality. In this chapter, I study the feedback effects of educational institutions on individual attitudes and preferences. The essential purpose of this chapter is to understand the impact of institutional legacies on public opinion as a critical factor in stabilizing the development paths of education regimes over time. At a very general level, institutions and policies in democratic countries cannot be sustained for long without a certain amount of public support and legitimacy (Brooks & Manza 2006, 2007; Rehm 2012). It follows that patterns of public opinion can become an important mechanism contributing to path dependency, one that delimits the range of politically feasible policy options for policy-makers. This hypothesis is related to the concept of positive feedback effects, which Pierson (1994, 1996, 2000, 2001, 2004) famously applied to comparative welfare state research. According to Pierson (2004: 24), positive feedback effects arise because actors develop an interest in maintaining existing institutions for a number of reasons: the establishment of new institutions (e.g., a particular welfare program) entails large setup costs that would be lost if actors were to switch to a different set of institutions; furthermore, the relative benefits of sticking to an existing institutional path increase over time as actors adapt their strategies and expectations and learn to use institutions more effectively.

In his empirical work on welfare state retrenchment, Pierson (1994, 1996) is more concerned with the feedback effects of institutions on organized interests such as welfare state clientele groups. These groups' political opposition then acts as an important barrier against far-reaching retrenchment efforts. This is typical for most of the scholarship in the tradition of historical institutionalism, where the analytical focus is on how collective actors such as employers' associations and labor unions adapt their strategies and preferences to changes in the institutional environment following critical junctures. Korpi (2006), for example, has argued that employers in Sweden did not promote the expansion of the Swedish welfare state as a first-order preference, but changed their strategy in the 1920s and 1930s, when the enactment of generous welfare state benefits became unavoidable, in order to support the specific elements that were most beneficial to them. Another example is the role of unions in vocational training, as mentioned in Chapter 2. Although unions in Germany were quite critical of apprenticeship training at first (Thelen 2004), they adjusted their preferences and strategies after the failure of social democratic attempts at large-scale reform in the 1970s and became strong supporters of such training.

Feedback effects can also be observed at the micro-level of attitudes: the preferences and dominant value orientations of individuals. Although it is hard to quantify exactly how strong the influence of public opinion is relative to organized interests, there is some evidence that popular policy preferences and attitudes are systematically related to policy output (Brooks & Manza 2006, 2007; Rehm 2012; Wlezien 1995; Soroka & Wlezien 2010). In the present chapter, I am less interested in assessing the role of public opinion as a determinant of policy output than in the question of how far existing institutions shape patterns of public opinion in the first place, in the form of policy and institutional feedback effects.

A sizable literature has studied the effects of welfare state institutions on attitudes. The causal mechanisms (self-interest or norms and values) are not always clearly spelled out, but the general expectation in this literature is that attitudes towards the welfare state should vary in line with Esping-Andersen's (1990) "worlds of welfare capitalism" (Andreß & Heien 2001; Arts & Gelissen 2001; Bean & Papadakis 1998; Blekesaune & Quadagno 2003; Jaeger 2009; Lipsmeyer & Nordstrom 2003; Papadakis 1993; Svallfors 1997, 2004, 2010); in other words, that support for the welfare state should be strongest in the Scandinavian countries and weakest in the liberal welfare states. If this pattern were the dominant one, it would be strong support for the positive feedback theory, as well as the congruence between preferences and policies. So far, however, the evidence has been mixed. A recent and sophisticated example is the work of Jaeger (2009), who has found that the level of support for the welfare state is highest in conservative welfare states and not in the Scandinavian countries as one would expect. In line with expectations, the level of support is lowest in the liberal regimes.

This example hints at the fact that there may be different causal mechanisms at work besides positive feedback effects. Some scholars (Brooks & Manza 2006, 2007; Rehm 2012; Soroka & Wlezien 2010; Wlezien 1995; Wlezien & Soroka 2012) have argued that the causal arrow runs from preferences to institutions and policies, and not the other way around. They claim that individual preferences are largely formed on the basis of individual characteristics and needs. Aggregated preferences then influence the design of policies and institutions. Cross-national variation and changes over time can still occur, since individuals are affected differently in different contexts, but once policy output (e.g., education spending) has reached a critical threshold, public opinion may turn against further increases in spending because of the high levels already attained. Conversely, if spending were perceived to be too low, public opinion would turn to support spending increases until some kind of predefined equilibrium had been met. Wlezien (1995) calls this the "public as thermostat" model (see also Soroka & Wlezien 2010), because the public reacts to changes in policy output and policy-makers react to changes in public mood. This might explain why support for the welfare state is higher in conservative welfare states (which still have room to expand) than in Scandinavian countries, but it would not explain why support is lowest in the liberal countries. In any case, it is plausible to assume that individual attitudes with regard to a certain policy always depend on the prevailing status quo. This is also why studies have found that cutting back existing welfare state programs is unpopular no matter what the type of welfare state (Brooks & Manza 2006, 2007; Fraile & Ferrer 2005; Hasenfeld & Rafferty 1989; Roller 1999).

A different possible explanation for the relative weakness of institutional feedback effects is that most of the literature cited above relies on broad measures of welfare state regimes. Given the complexity of welfare states, however, more specific institutional characteristics of the welfare state could affect attitudes in different and potentially conflicting ways. It would seem advisable to use more narrowly defined indicators of specific characteristics of welfare states, rather than broad, encompassing categories (Busemeyer 2013; Jaeger 2006; Jakobsen 2010). In our case, therefore, I have identified two crucial dimensions of variation in education and training regimes: the public/private division of labor in education financing, and institutional stratification in terms of the relative importance of VET versus higher education.

These two dimensions will be central to the empirical work that follows. I will assess the impact of these institutional variables as macro-level variables on attitudes, but they will also roughly guide our selection of the dependent variables: popular support for increasing or decreasing government involvement in, and public spending on, education and popular support for different kinds of education (VET versus academic education).

Institutional factors can influence popular attitudes in two different ways: they can affect average levels of support for a specific policy (technically, these are random-intercept models), or they can mediate the influence of a specific micro-level variable (cross-level interactions or random-slope models). The most straightforward operationalization of the feedback thesis is to argue that prevailing institutions have an influence on the average level of support for a specific policy. This perspective, however, neglects the fact that the effects of certain individual characteristics (such as being rich or highly educated) might be conditioned by the institutional context. A broader perspective on the impact of institutions on attitudes must take into account both the effects on the average level of support and the cross-level interactions.

In addition to institutional factors, material self-interest has been found in the literature on welfare state attitudes to be an important determinant of preferences (Busemeyer 2012b, 2013; Busemeyer *et al.* 2009; Cusack *et al.* 2006; Corneo & Grüner 2002; Fong 2001; Hasenfeld & Rafferty 1989; Iversen & Soskice 2001; Kangas 1997; Moene & Wallerstein 2001, 2003; Papadakis 1993; Rehm 2009). Self-interest is partly determined by exogenous factors, such as the individual's position in terms of income, age, gender, education, and so on. However, an individual's exposure to labor-market and other risks also partly depends on the institutions of the welfare state, which grant benefits selectively and thus create welfare state constituencies that develop a material interest in maintaining these existing policies. Thus institutions again enter through the back door by influencing the distribution of resources in a given society, which is essentially what Pierson (1993: 624) discussed under the heading of "resource/incentive effects" when talking about feedback. Above and beyond self-interest, welfare state institutions also shape the prevailing norms and values and are themselves a concrete manifestation of these values. As Rothstein (1998) famously argued, universal welfare states of the Scandinavian variety are supported by large majorities of the population because they are perceived as fair and just. In contrast, selective or residual welfare states of the liberal variety constantly fuel debates about the "deservingness" (Van Oorschot 2006) of different groups of welfare beneficiaries, undermining their popular legitimacy.

Besides studying the impact of educational institutions on education policy preferences, this chapter also takes up a more general point raised in the introduction: the connection between education and other social policies. This is one of the guiding themes of the book, since it pertains to the question of whether education should be regarded as an integral part of the welfare state from both a political and an analytical perspective. Chapters 2 and 3 have already demonstrated that in terms of political and historical origins, there is a strong connection between the institutional design of education and training regimes and the prevailing coalitions in welfare-state policies (even though there was insufficient space to go into detail on such welfare state policies as such). In Chapter 4, I presented evidence that educational institutions are important with regard to social inequality because they complement the effects of more narrowly defined social policies. The present chapter will show in turn that educational institutions also influence popular attitudes towards the welfare state and that the prevailing distribution of resources (inequality) affects popular attitudes towards the education system. This chapter also concedes a point to Wilensky (1975: 6), however, finding that education is indeed different from other social policies, at least with regard to patterns of public support.

In the next section, I present some descriptive data on two central dimensions of variation in terms of attitudes: support for increasing education spending and recommendations for VET versus academic education. The subsequent section presents evidence on the distinctiveness of education in terms of patterns of public support compared to other social policies. This is followed by an analysis of the micro- and macro-level determinants of popular attitudes towards education policies and the impact of educational institutions on redistributive preferences.

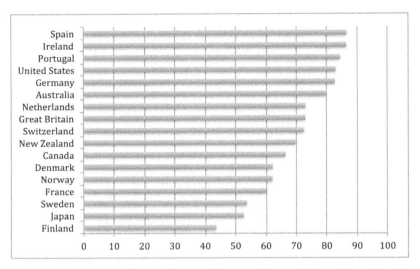

Figure 5.1 Percentage share of respondents in favor of "more" or "much more" government spending on education, ISSP Role of Government IV, 2006

The variation of education policy preferences in OECD countries

This section offers some descriptive statistics on patterns of popular support for our two main dependent variables: public support for increased government spending on education and support for different kinds of education. Increasing public investment in education is a popular issue (Ansell (2010: 136) calls it the "archetypical crowd-pleaser"). Figure 5.1 displays country averages of public support for increases in public educational spending. The data are taken from the 2006 ISSP Role of Government IV survey. Respondents were asked the following question:

Listed below are various areas of government spending. Please show whether you would like to see more or less government spending in each area. Remember that if you say "much more," it might require a tax increase to pay for it.

"Education" is listed as one of several areas where government spending could be increased. Other areas are "pensions," "unemployment," and "health" (care), which I will also include as dependent variables in the next section when I study the peculiarities of education compared to other social policies. The answers of respondents to these questions are coded on a scale from 1 (spend much more) to 5 (spend much less). To simplify the analysis and interpretation of results, I collapse these five categories into two: "more" and "much more" spending are recoded as 1, while the other categories are recoded as 0.

Figure 5.1 documents the high levels of public support for education spending. In almost all countries covered in the survey, the share of respondents in favor of increased spending is significantly above 50 percent. The one notable exception is Finland, which has enjoyed broad international recognition as a role model of education reforms since its top placement in the OECD PISA study (Dobbins & Martens 2011). As we saw in Table 3.1, Finland is also a country with above-average levels of public spending on education: 5.9 percent of GDP on average for the period between 1997 and 2008. The level of public education spending in Japan, by contrast, is only 3.5 percent of GDP for the same period. As in Finland, Japanese popular support for increased levels of government spending on education is low. At the other end of the scale, Portugal and Spain display the highest levels of public support for increased education spending (more than 85 percent). Yet their current levels of public education spending are very different: 4.3 percent of GDP in Spain compared to 5.5 percent of GDP in Portugal (see Table 3.1). These examples show that the feedback mechanisms between the macro-level of policy-making and the micro-level of preferences are much more complex than was initially assumed. It is not automatically the case that high levels of public spending are directly associated with high levels of public support for education spending; if they were, it would indicate some kind of positive feedback mechanism. Neither can we find strong evidence for a dominating negative feedback effect; were this the case, support for more education spending would be much higher in low-spending countries such as Japan. What we can learn from this descriptive evidence, then, is that similar levels of spending (status quo) can be associated with different patterns of popular support.

Citizens vary not only in their attitudes about the level of public investment in education, but also in their preferences concerning the *kind* of education this investment should target. Here it is important to note that I am not concerned with studying actual educational *choices*, as is usually done in educational sociology (Breen & Goldthorpe 1997; Breen & Jonsson 2005; Hillmert & Jacob 2002; Jaeger 2007, 2009; Pfeffer 2008). Individuals (students and their parents) make educational choices under constraints, such as individual academic aptitude and credit limitations. Educational choices are also only relevant for a subset of the population (young persons and, to a certain extent, their parents). Instead, I am interested in what kind of education policy citizens support as a *matter of policy-making*. For instance, a university student might support the expansion of opportunities in VET because she just read Hall & Soskice (2001). Conversely, a construction worker close to retirement might support the expansion of university education because she believed this would be more likely to maximize her retirement income. These examples are fictitious, of course, but the general claim is that there *is* a difference between individual educational choices and individual education policy preferences, and that the latter have not been analyzed sufficiently in the literature.

Unfortunately, there is a shortage of survey data on policy preferences for different kinds of education. Busemeyer *et al.* (2011) use an original dataset for the case of Switzerland, but to my knowledge the only available dataset that covers such issues for cross-national comparisons is the Eurobarometer 62.1 from the year 2004, which contains this question:

Nowadays, which of the following would you recommend to a young person who is finishing compulsory education or secondary education?

1 General or academic studies
2 Vocational training or apprenticeship
3 It depends on the person (SPONTANEOUS)
4 Other (SPONTANEOUS)
5 Don't know

The wording of the question is far from perfect. For one, it does not distinguish between general/academic education at different *levels* of education. Because the question explicitly mentions that it is about post-secondary education, however, most respondents will think of higher (university) education when they hear "general or academic studies." Another weakness is that it asks about "recommendations" for young people, not actual policy preferences. It could well be that individuals would recommend one kind of education while believing

Impact on popular attitudes and preferences 223

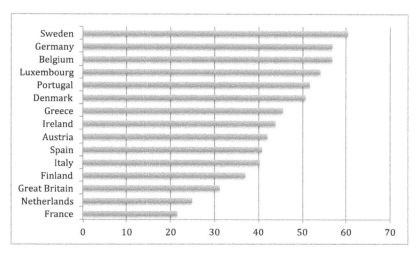

Figure 5.2 Share of respondents recommending general and academic studies rather than VET to school-leavers, Eurobarometer 62.1, 2004

that public policy should be more concerned with the other. For the present purpose, I have to assume that there is a sufficiently close correlation between the given recommendations and actual policy preferences of respondents. I therefore recoded answers to the question by deleting spontaneous and indecisive answers from the sample, so that we are left with a dichotomous variable where 1 equals a preference for general/academic studies and 0 a preference for vocational training.

In Figure 5.2, I plot the share of respondents recommending academic education instead of vocational education to young school-leavers. As in the case of preferences for spending, the ranking of countries is somewhat counterintuitive. For example, Sweden and Germany exhibit the highest shares of citizens recommending academic education. If positive feedback effects were the only causal mechanisms at work, the support for VET should have been much higher in Germany than in Sweden (see, e.g., the case of Austria). Negative feedback effects could again be at work in the case of the United Kingdom, since in this country the support for VET over academic education is strongly above average. The opposite holds in the case of the Netherlands, which combines a well-developed VET system with strong support for VET.

How and why education is different

Before I engage in a more detailed analysis of the impact of prevailing institutions on preferences, I will briefly document how and why education may be different from other social policies. Going back to the model developed by Meltzer & Richard (1981), a core claim in the political economy literature on individual preferences for redistribution is that support for redistribution declines with rising income, as rich individuals have to contribute to the welfare state via higher taxes, whereas the poor benefit from generous social benefits. The redistributive implications of investment in education are less clear-cut than those of other social policies, however (Ansell 2008, 2010; Busemeyer 2012b; Fernandez & Rogerson 1995; Jensen 2011; Levy 2005). For one, educational investment always entails both public and private benefits. Higher levels of education spending might contribute to maintaining the competitiveness of the economy and the general well-being of the population (as education is related to health outcomes), but at the individual level, human capital investment creates significant private benefits: it leads to higher wages. Thus, educational investment is associated with very different outcomes in terms of inequality, depending on which sector of the education system investments are concentrated in, the relative ease of access to higher levels of education, and the impact of labor-market institutions on education-related wage premiums (see Chapter 4).

The distinctiveness of education can also be observed at the micro-level of individual preferences, because in contrast to other social policies, an individual's income position is *not* a strong predictor of their attitudes towards education (Busemeyer 2012b). Table 5.1 presents the results of a regression analysis of individual-level support for increases in public education spending (the dependent variable introduced above). The most important independent variables for the present case are income (given in standardized income deciles) and educational background (years of education). Compared to the inconclusive effect of income, I expect a positive association between educational background and support for education spending. From a very narrow self-interest perspective, it could be argued that highly educated individuals have an incentive to oppose further investment in education in order to limit access to high-skilled labor markets. But highly educated individuals could also support education spending;

Table 5.1 *Individual-level determinants of preferences on education spending*

Dependent variable	(1)	(2)	(3)
	\multicolumn{3}{c}{More government spending on education = 1 / Same or less spending = 0}		
Income	0.00454	0.00694	0.0141
	(0.00882)	(0.00952)	(0.0110)
Gender (female)	0.0793**	0.0708**	0.0363
	(0.0356)	(0.0361)	(0.0426)
Years of education	0.00722***	0.00516***	0.00785***
	(0.00142)	(0.00160)	(0.00213)
Age	−0.00267**		
	(0.00114)		
Retired		−0.131***	−0.0911*
		(0.0474)	(0.0547)
Student, apprentice, trainee		0.305***	0.156
		(0.112)	(0.137)
Labor-market outsider		0.0608	0.0570
		(0.0620)	(0.0760)
Party ID: center			−0.320***
			(0.0566)
Party ID: right			−0.537***
			(0.0480)
Constant	1.261***	1.153***	1.415***
	(0.115)	(0.0976)	(0.117)
Country fixed effects	Yes	Yes	Yes
Observations	18324	18133	13069

Robust standard errors in parentheses
*** $p < 0.01$, ** $p < 0.05$, * $p < 0.1$

given the ubiquitous class bias in access to education, they can expect their children to benefit from such investment. Having spent more time in educational institutions, highly educated individuals may also have been socialized into supporting this kind of social service.

I include a number of control variables at the micro-level besides income and education, such as age, gender, educational background,

Table 5.2 The individual level determinants of preferences for social spending, ISSP Role of Government IV, 2006

	(1)	(2)	(3)	(4)	(5)	(6)	(7)	(8)
Dependent variable	More government spending on pensions	More government spending on pensions	More government spending on health	More government spending on health	More government spending on unemployment	More government spending on unemployment	More government spending on social policy (composite index), linear factor	More government spending on social policy (composite index), linear factor
Income	−0.132***	−0.136***	−0.0986***	−0.0902***	−0.215***	−0.182***	−0.0498***	−0.0466***
	(0.00873)	(0.0101)	(0.0106)	(0.0120)	(0.0130)	(0.0149)	(0.00244)	(0.00279)
Gender (female)	0.0264	−0.0183	0.261***	0.222***	−0.114***	−0.0851*	0.0131	0.00412
	(0.0340)	(0.0398)	(0.0402)	(0.0473)	(0.0391)	(0.0473)	(0.00976)	(0.0114)
Years of education	−0.0117***	−0.0109***	−0.00415**	−0.00350*	−0.00918***	−0.00945***	−0.00344***	−0.00328***
	(0.00151)	(0.00191)	(0.00166)	(0.00207)	(0.00170)	(0.00224)	(0.000427)	(0.000529)
Retired	0.293***	0.308***	0.0707	0.116*	−0.00781	0.0190	0.0542***	0.0657***
	(0.0457)	(0.0524)	(0.0534)	(0.0613)	(0.0509)	(0.0614)	(0.0129)	(0.0148)
Student, apprentice...	−0.471***	−0.578***	0.00809	−0.0121	−0.209*	−0.315**	−0.0955***	−0.127***
	(0.103)	(0.123)	(0.138)	(0.167)	(0.117)	(0.145)	(0.0302)	(0.0364)
Labor market outsider	0.132**	0.141**	0.0957	0.0482	0.551***	0.561***	0.106***	0.103***
	(0.0582)	(0.0704)	(0.0709)	(0.0858)	(0.0609)	(0.0764)	(0.0166)	(0.0200)

Party ID: Center		−0.466*** (0.0536)		−0.453*** (0.0635)		−0.699*** (0.0588)		−0.197*** (0.0150)
Party ID: Right		−0.330*** (0.0442)		−0.562*** (0.0531)		−1.077*** (0.0575)		−0.219*** (0.0129)
Constant	0.781*** (0.0881)	1.086*** (0.105)	2.345*** (0.119)	2.628*** (0.139)	−0.954*** (0.112)	−0.645*** (0.134)	0.123*** (0.0251)	0.242*** (0.0296)
Country fixed effects	Yes	Yes	Yes	Yes	Yes	Yes	Yes	Yes
Observations	18035	13019	18245	13127	17864	12899	17528	12698

Robust standard errors in parentheses
*** $p < 0.01$, ** $p < 0.05$, * $p < 0.1$

labor-market position, and partisan ideology (party ID).[1] Age (or being retired) is expected to have a negative effect, since older people will obviously not benefit from more spending on education (Busemeyer et al. 2009; Cattaneo & Wolter 2007; Plutzer & Berkman 2005). Women are found to be more supportive of welfare state spending in general (Svallfors 1997: 292), so the expected effect on spending support is positive. Being in education likely increases support for more spending on education. Labor-market outsiders could also be expected to support more spending on education, to improve their chances of getting decent employment. They might also prefer to concentrate spending on social benefits, however, especially unemployment spending. Partisanship is hypothesized to contribute above and beyond the effect of self-interest related variables (Hasenfeld & Rafferty 1989). Supporters of the left should be more supportive of increased levels of public spending in general, including education (see Busemeyer et al. 2011). But partisanship is at least partly endogenous, since it also correlates with the other control variables in the regression. I therefore present various model specifications, including and excluding party ID.

Table 5.1 shows that on average, and without taking institutional feedback effects into account, there is *no* statistical association between individual income position and support for public spending on education. The effect of educational background, by contrast, is positive and remains statistically significant across all different model specifications. The control variables perform largely as expected: age or being retired has a negative impact on support for spending; being female has a positive effect. Supporters of the left are more favorable to increasing government spending on education than are supporters of the right. The latter is a nice micro-level confirmation of our central finding in Chapter 3: that parties of the left are more likely to support public involvement in education funding, whereas conservative parties favor private involvement.

In Table 5.2, I run a similar regression model on individual support for other social policies, in particular public spending on pensions (Models 1 and 2), health care (Models 3 and 4), and unemployment

---

[1] Further down, I also include "having children" as an additional control variable related to self-interest. I refrain from doing so here in order to be able to use the same regression model for the different social policy fields.

(Models 5 and 6). In Models 7 and 8, the dependent variable is an indicator of general support for increases in social spending, derived from a factor analysis of the other three dependent variables. As expected, the effect of labor-market position varies across social policy fields. Students are more likely to support spending on education (Table 5.1), but less likely to support spending increases on pensions (Models 1 and 2 in Table 5.2). Labor-market outsiders might not be particularly supportive of education spending, but they support more spending on pensions and unemployment benefits (Table 5.1 versus Models 1, 2, 5, and 6 in Table 5.2). The most important difference, however, is that in all these models, both the individual's income position and their educational background have a significant and *negative* impact on support for social spending. Compared to other social policies, increasing investment in education is a much less contested issue across class lines.

Figure 5.3 is a graphical presentation of the findings in Tables 5.1 and 5.2 and plots predicted probabilities for individual-level support for different social policies in relation to income and educational background.[2] Most importantly, this figure shows that support for education spending increases among well-educated citizens (see the positive slope of the thick black line in Panel A of Figure 5.3) and is independent of differences in income (see the flat black line in Panel B). A second important insight related to the previous finding is that in general, the average public support for increasing spending on education is much higher than that for other social policies. Increasing spending on health and pensions receives more support than increasing spending on unemployment benefits, which could be related to common perceptions about the "deservingness" of benefit recipients (Van Oorschot 2006) or could simply reflect the different sizes of welfare state constituencies. Increasing spending on education is almost as popular as increasing spending on health. But even though spending on health is at least as popular on average as increasing spending on education, because it affects essentially everyone, the figure reveals stronger class-related conflicts over health spending (see the negative effect of income and educational background on support for healthcare spending in Figure 5.3). In sum, this brief analysis confirms that education is indeed different from other social policies with regard to

---

[2] I refrain from plotting confidence intervals in this figure for reasons of presentation and readability.

Panel A: The impact of educational background

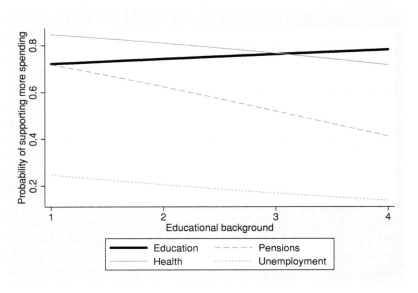

Panel B: The impact of income

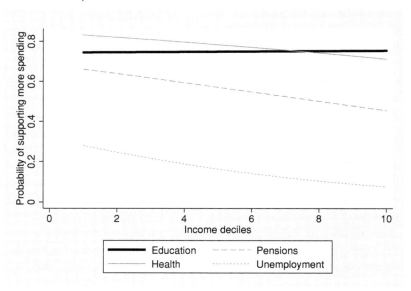

Figure 5.3 Comparison of the impact of income and educational background on spending preferences

patterns of popular support, because it is less contested across the class divide and more popular on average than other social policies.

Institutions and education policy preferences

In this section, I will examine how educational and welfare state institutions affect popular support for increasing levels of public education spending and investment in various kinds of education. A series of multilevel regression models will be used, which combine the micro-level survey data introduced in the previous sections with the macro-level data used in preceding chapters. I first analyze individual support for increasing public spending on education, then look at the preferences for various kinds of education. As stated above, the central hypothesis is that existing institutions create feedback effects at the micro-level of attitudes. Here it is important to distinguish between the effects of macro-level variables on average levels of support for a specific policy (random-intercept models) and the mediating effects of institutions on the impact of micro-level variables (cross-level interactions or random-slope models). In addition to the coefficient estimates, the following tables contain information on the degree of cross-country variance and its statistical significance, as well as the intraclass correlation (correlation of units/individuals within groups/countries). Since partly missing data for the macro-level variables have caused the sample sizes to vary, a straightforward comparative interpretation of these indicators is somewhat futile. I therefore concentrate on the main substantive effects and present the main findings graphically.

First, existing levels of public education spending are likely to have an impact on public support for spending increases. According to the "public as thermostat" model (Wlezien 1995; Soroka & Wlezien 2010), the public will express opposition to further increases in spending when a certain level is reached and demand more spending when it appears too low. Existing levels of public education spending should be negatively associated with the average level of support, so that high levels of spending lower support and vice versa. To operationalize this hypothesis, I include levels of public spending as percentage of GDP for the year 2005 (roughly one year before the field work for the ISSP survey was conducted).

Second, if educational investments have redistributive implications, prevailing levels of inequality should influence the support for spending. A statistical association between these two variables would support the claim that public attitudes on education spending are related to the general conflict over redistribution in the welfare state. As famously argued by Meltzer & Richard (1981), a mean-preserving increase in the level of inequality leads to an increase in the overall demand for redistribution, because the distance between the person with average income and that with median income will increase, as will the share of the population with below-average income. It follows that we should expect a positive association between levels of inequality (the Gini index for the year 2005) and average levels of support for education spending. I again use the net Gini index that measures inequality in household income after taxes and transfers, since I am interested in whether inequality is still associated with support for redistribution even after the impact of the transfer system has been taken into account.[3]

Concerning my main independent variables, the impact of educational stratification on average levels of support is less clear-cut. On the one hand, it could be argued that high levels of educational stratification will depress average levels of support for education spending, as citizens become wary of putting more public resources into an elitist system; on the other, public support for education spending might be particularly strong in stratified education systems, since the expansion of public involvement could be regarded as a means by which to overcome elitism and stratification. Rather than influencing average levels of public support, educational stratification may be more relevant as an institutional variable mediating the impact of other micro-level variables, in particular income and educational background (Ansell 2010; Busemeyer 2012b). When the education system is highly stratified, rich and/or well-educated individuals are more likely to support increasing spending on education. This is because they can be more certain that these investments will benefit them or their children directly: access to higher levels of education is more class-biased in stratified education systems. When institutional stratification is low, increasing spending on education will have a more redistributive impact, so that the preferences of classes are more in line with the classical redistributive struggle between the rich and the poor.

---

[3] A more straightforward application of the Meltzer–Richard model would probably focus on wage dispersion instead of net inequality.

These mediating effects of institutions will be modeled empirically as a cross-level interaction effect between individual income/educational background and educational stratification as a macro-level variable. Educational stratification is operationalized in two different ways. First, I employ the OECD measure of educational stratification used and defined in Chapters 3 and 4. As a reminder, this measure captures the difference in expectations of completing academic higher education between a student with a strong socioeconomic background and one with a weak background. Second, I simply include the share of upper-secondary students in VET as an indicator of the institutional stratification of the education system at the secondary level.

The private share of education spending is also expected to have a negative impact on support for increased public spending. On the one hand, this seems obvious, since a high private spending share should be reflected in strong support for private spending if there is indeed a direct connection between preferences and output; on the other, it might be the case that individuals in countries with high levels of private spending would in fact support an expansion of public spending to complement or supplant private spending (negative feedback). Again, the mediating impact of private spending on micro-level associations might be more important than its effect on the average level. In particular, I expect a negative cross-level interaction effect between individual income and the private spending share. Rich individuals in countries with high levels of private spending should be more opposed to increases in public spending than individuals in countries with less private spending, because the former group benefits from being able to price out low-income individuals from access to high-quality private education.

Table 5.3 presents the findings from multilevel regressions using only micro-level and macro-level variables; Table 5.4 presents additional models that include cross-level interactions. The micro-level control variables perform similarly to the models in Table 5.1. In the present specification, I also include having children as a control variable,[4]

---

[4] More precisely, the variable in the ISSP dataset (HHCYLCE) asks whether respondents live in the same household as their children. Respondents residing with more than one child are coded "1," the remainder "0." This measure does not take into account children who have left the family home, for example to attend university.

Table 5.3 *Multilevel regression of individual support for government spending on education, ISSP 2006*

	(1)	(2)	(3)	(4)	(5)
	\multicolumn{5}{c}{More government spending on education = 1}				
Dependent variable	\multicolumn{5}{c}{Same or less spending = 0}				
Micro-level variables					
Income	6.30×10^{-5}	0.000520	0.000184	−0.00601	−0.00114
	(0.00920)	(0.00920)	(0.00920)	(0.00988)	(0.00977)
Gender (female)	0.0704**	0.0710**	0.0709**	0.0530	0.0652*
	(0.0350)	(0.0350)	(0.0350)	(0.0370)	(0.0362)
Years of education	0.0272***	0.0271***	0.0273***	0.0254***	0.0304***
	(0.00485)	(0.00485)	(0.00485)	(0.00501)	(0.00499)
Has children	0.308***	0.308***	0.309***	0.334***	0.296***
	(0.0376)	(0.0376)	(0.0376)	(0.0396)	(0.0390)
Retired	0.0405	0.0406	0.0429	0.0220	0.0695
	(0.0472)	(0.0472)	(0.0472)	(0.0499)	(0.0488)
Labor-market outsider	0.0516	0.0519	0.0525	0.0272	0.0440
	(0.0824)	(0.0824)	(0.0823)	(0.0861)	(0.0868)
Student or in education	0.392***	0.394***	0.394***	0.372***	0.544***
	(0.129)	(0.129)	(0.129)	(0.130)	(0.141)
Macro-level variables					
Public education spending, % of GDP		−0.329**	−0.138	−0.261	−0.272*
		(0.159)	(0.151)	(0.169)	(0.159)
Socioeconomic inequality (Gini)			0.0851***	0.113***	0.134***
			(0.0303)	(0.0315)	(0.0375)

Private share of education spending				−0.0317** (0.0142)	−0.0332** (0.0149)
Educational stratification				0.491 (0.316)	
Share of upper-secondary students in VET					0.00338 (0.00708)
Constant	0.424*** (0.156)	2.070** (0.810)	−1.431 (1.423)	−2.281 (1.817)	−1.915 (1.821)
Variance components					
Level 2 intercept standard deviation	0.6233 (0.1003)	0.5645 (0.0913)	0.4762 (0.0775)	0.4060 (0.0719)	0.4155 (0.0697)
Intra-class correlation (Rho)	0.1056 (0.0304)	0.0883 (0.0260)	0.0645 (0.0196)	0.0477 (0.0161)	0.0500 (0.0159)
Log-likelihood	−10703.15	−10701.22	−10697.88	−9705.00	−10005.72
Observations	19022	19022	19022	17337	17905
Number of countries	20	20	20	17	19

Standard errors in parentheses
*** $p < 0.01$, ** $p < 0.05$, * $p < 0.1$

Table 5.4 *Multilevel regression (cross-level interactions) of individual support for government spending on education, ISSP 2006*

	(1)	(2)	(3)	(4)	(5)	(6)
Dependent variable	\multicolumn{6}{c}{More government spending on education = 1 / Same or less spending = 0}
Micro-level variables						
Income	−0.00570	−0.192**	−0.000899	−0.0692***	0.00130	0.0532***
	(0.00989)	(0.0829)	(0.000976)	(0.0195)	(0.00922)	(0.0175)
Gender (female)	0.0565	0.0581	0.0651*	0.0722**	0.0713**	0.0738**
	(0.0370)	(0.0371)	(0.0362)	(0.0362)	(0.0350)	(0.0350)
Years of education	−0.0846**	0.0245***	−0.000686	0.0297***	0.0308***	0.0264***
	(0.0363)	(0.00502)	(0.0133)	(0.00499)	(0.00812)	(0.00486)
Has children	0.336***	0.335***	0.295***	0.296***	0.308***	0.306***
	(0.0396)	(0.0396)	(0.0390)	(0.0390)	(0.0376)	(0.0376)
Retired	0.0249	0.0209	0.0709	0.0793	0.0437	0.0491
	(0.0499)	(0.0499)	(0.0488)	(0.0489)	(0.0472)	(0.0473)
Labor-market outsider	0.0337	0.0251	0.0428	0.0564	0.0528	0.0696
	(0.0861)	(0.0860)	(0.0869)	(0.0871)	(0.0823)	(0.0827)
Student or in education	0.380***	0.365***	0.543***	0.582***	0.398***	0.427***
	(0.130)	(0.130)	(0.141)	(0.142)	(0.129)	(0.130)
Macro-level variables						
Public education spending, % of GDP	−0.0864	−0.0931	−0.0954	−0.0940	−0.310**	−0.315**
	(0.170)	(0.170)	(0.152)	(0.153)	(0.146)	(0.148)

Socioeconomic inequality (Gini)	0.0847** (0.0330)	0.0840** (0.0329)	0.120*** (0.0415)	0.121*** (0.0417)	0.121*** (0.0295)	0.123*** (0.0300)
Educational stratification	0.0532 (0.397)	0.376 (0.368)				
Share of upper-secondary students in VET (VET Share)			−0.000445 (0.00829)	0.00266 (0.00769)		
Private share of education spending					−0.0331** (0.0152)	−0.0272* (0.0143)
Cross-level interactions						
Education × educational stratification	0.0479*** (0.0157)					
Income × educational stratification		0.0833** (0.0370)				
Education × VET share			0.000661** (0.000265)			
Income × VET share				0.00162*** (0.000410)		
Education × private share					−0.000250 (0.000506)	
Income × private share						−0.00296*** (0.000837)
Constant	−1.790 (2.070)	−2.477 (2.037)	−2.646 (1.946)	−2.849 (1.950)	−1.173 (1.243)	−1.315 (1.258)

(*cont.*)

Table 5.4 (*cont.*)

	(1)	(2)	(3)	(4)	(5)	(6)
Dependent variable	\multicolumn{6}{c}{More government spending on education = 1}
	\multicolumn{6}{c}{Same or less spending = 0}
Variance components						
Level 2 intercept standard deviation	0.4644	0.4626	0.4663	0.4696	0.4099	0.4161
	(0.0821)	(0.0818)	(0.0781)	(0.0786)	(0.0669)	(0.0679)
Intra-class correlation (Rho)	0.0615	0.0611	0.0620	0.0628	0.0486	0.0500
	(0.0204)	(0.0203)	(0.0195)	(0.0197)	(0.0151)	(0.0155)
Log-likelihood	−9702.44	−9704.61	−10004.81	−10000.20	−10694.78	−10688.65
Observations	17337	17337	17905	17905	19022	19022
Number of countries	17	17	19	19	20	20

Standard errors in parentheses
*** $p < 0.01$, ** $p < 0.05$, * $p < 0.1$

Impact on popular attitudes and preferences

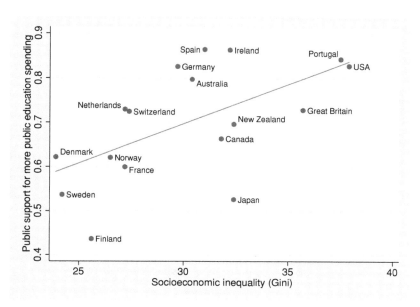

Figure 5.4 Levels of socioeconomic inequality and public support for more government spending on education

which has a strong and positive effect on individual support for education spending. Existing levels of public education spending have a negative effect on average levels of public support for education spending (Model 2), lending some support to Wlezien's (1995) "public as thermostat" argument. The effect is not robust across model specifications, however, and becomes insignificant once I include additional macro-level variables. The prevailing level of socioeconomic inequality, by contrast, has a robust, significant, and positive effect on average levels of support. This association is documented graphically in Figure 5.4. Public support for increasing public spending on education is particularly high in countries with high levels of socioeconomic inequality (the United States and the United Kingdom, but also Portugal). It is low in the Scandinavian countries, which exhibit low levels of inequality. This is evidence that political conflicts over the level of educational investment should be considered part and parcel of the more general conflict over redistribution in Western welfare states.

In contrast to socioeconomic inequality, educational stratification is *not* associated with average levels of public support for education

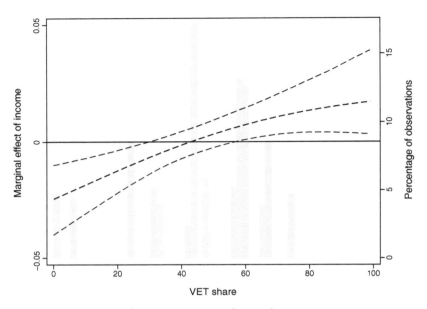

Figure 5.5 Interaction between income and VET share

spending (Models 4 and 5 in Table 5.3), but I did find strong evidence for the fact that educational stratification mediates the impact of income and educational background on support for education spending. As hypothesized, the rich and well-educated are more likely to support education spending in stratified education systems (indicated by the significant coefficient estimates of the cross-level interactions in Models 1 through 4 in Table 5.4). Models 1 and 2 include a cross-level interaction between individual income and educational background on the one hand and the OECD indicator of educational stratification on the other. The same procedure is applied in Models 3 and 4, employing the broader measure of institutional stratification; that is, the share of upper-secondary students in VET. In both cases, the empirical evidence points to the fact that an increase in income at the micro-level is predicted to be associated with higher levels of support for education spending when the system is stratified. Figure 5.5 is a graphical representation of this interaction effect. It shows that the effect of income is negative in countries with a low VET share; increased individual income is associated with lower levels of support for public education spending. When the VET share increases, the income effect becomes positive (richer people are more likely to *support* spending increases). It is likely that the effect would be even more pronounced if we could distinguish support for different educational sectors in the dependent variable (higher education versus vocational education).

Models 4 and 5 in Table 5.3 also indicate a strong and statistically robust association between the private share of education spending and the average levels of support for public spending on education. The coefficient estimate is negative, which means that average support for increasing public spending on education is lower in countries with a high private share of education spending. This evidence supports the feedback argument, in the sense that the existing institutions shape patterns of public support concurrent with the dominant development path. We also need to take into account the associations between macro-level variables themselves, however. Chapter 4 presented evidence that a high private share of spending is associated with higher levels of inequality. We now find that the private share has a significant negative impact on support for spending, whereas inequality has a positive effect. To a certain extent, these two effects cancel each other out. When we include each without the other (not shown here for reasons of space), the private spending share loses statistical significance, whereas inequality remains a highly significant macro-level predictor of support for education spending.

Finally, Model 6 in Table 5.4 reveals a negative interaction effect between individual income and the private share of education spending, but there is no significant interaction effect between educational background and private spending share (Model 5). This interaction is presented graphically in Figure 5.6. On the left-hand side, I plot the interaction between income and the private spending share for all levels of education. On the right-hand side, I use private spending for tertiary education only (this regression is not shown in Table 5.4). The income effect is positive for low levels of private spending, but it turns negative and significant for high levels of private spending. This finding could be interpreted as indicating stronger opposition among rich individuals to increasing public involvement in education systems where the public/private division of labor is already tilted in favor of private investment. Thus the private share in education spending is not only associated with higher levels of social inequality (see Chapter 4) but also increases support among the wealthy for the maintenance of such a private regime.

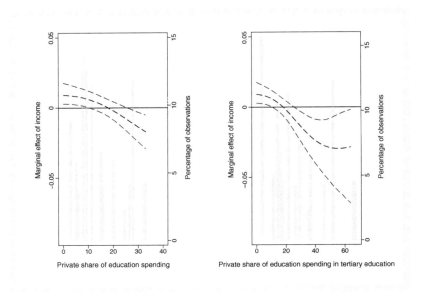

Figure 5.6 Interaction between income and private share of education spending

Table 5.5 presents the determinants of individual preferences for different kinds of education – our second dependent variable of interest. Remember that these are not actual educational choices, but "recommendations" by regular citizens to young school-leavers. The dependent variable is a dummy variable. A value of 1 signifies a recommendation for academic education, while 0 indicates a preference for vocational education. I include a number of common control variables at the micro-level, such as age, years of education, and gender, as well as various indicators of labor-market status. Unfortunately, the Eurobarometer dataset does not contain any information on individual income. The number of countries covered in this set is also limited, because it is restricted to European countries. Missing data on some of the macro-level variables for Greece and Luxembourg means that the number of countries at the macro-level is only thirteen for most models in Table 5.5. For all of these reasons, the findings should be interpreted with great caution.

The analysis reveals that highly educated individuals, as well as students and individuals in other types of education, are more

Table 5.5 *Multilevel regression of preferences for different kinds of education, Eurobarometer 62.1, 2004*

Dependent variable	(1)	(2)	(3)	(4)	(5)
	\multicolumn{5}{l}{Preference for academic education = 1}
	\multicolumn{5}{l}{Preference for vocational education = 0}
Micro-level variables					
Age	0.00294	0.00364	0.00374	0.00365	0.00270
	(0.00228)	(0.00248)	(0.00248)	(0.00248)	(0.00234)
Years of education	0.105***	0.105***	0.106***	0.105***	0.102***
	(0.0100)	(0.0110)	(0.0110)	(0.0110)	(0.0103)
Gender (male)	−0.0706	−0.0689	−0.0688	−0.0691	−0.0639
	(0.0506)	(0.0549)	(0.0549)	(0.0549)	(0.0520)
Retired	−0.366***	−0.354***	−0.350***	−0.353***	−0.373***
	(0.114)	(0.127)	(0.127)	(0.127)	(0.118)
Student	0.500***	0.535***	0.536***	0.535***	0.510***
	(0.130)	(0.143)	(0.143)	(0.143)	(0.133)
Unemployed	−0.289**	−0.255**	−0.251*	−0.254**	−0.284**
	(0.114)	(0.128)	(0.128)	(0.128)	(0.119)
White-collar occupation	0.166*	0.209**	0.214**	0.210**	0.179**
	(0.0891)	(0.0990)	(0.0991)	(0.0990)	(0.0911)
Manual occupation	−0.273***	−0.269***	−0.264***	−0.268***	−0.278***
	(0.0903)	(0.100)	(0.100)	(0.100)	(0.0924)
Self-employed	−0.106	0.00590	0.00738	0.00664	−0.0824
	(0.107)	(0.120)	(0.120)	(0.120)	(0.108)

(*cont.*)

Table 5.5 (cont.)

	(1)	(2)	(3)	(4)	(5)
Dependent variable		Preference for academic education = 1 Preference for vocational education = 0			
Macro-level variables					
Private share of education spending, tertiary education		−0.0284* (0.0148)	−0.0330** (0.0128)	−0.0352** (0.0178)	
Educational stratification		0.620* (0.317)	0.822*** (0.287)	0.684** (0.327)	
Share of upper-secondary students in VET			−0.0121** (0.00556)		
Public social spending, % of GDP				−0.0271 (0.0410)	0.0285 (0.0346)
Constant	−0.896*** (0.181)	−2.084** (0.813)	−1.906*** (0.708)	−1.354 (1.364)	−1.711* (1.010)
Variance components					
Level 2 intercept standard deviation	0.4997 (0.0894)	0.4302 (0.0888)	0.3655 (0.0767)	0.4232 (0.0873)	0.4972 (0.0944)
Intra-class correlation (Rho)	0.0705 (0.0235)	0.0533 (0.0208)	0.0390 (0.0157)	0.0516 (0.0202)	0.0699 (0.0247)
Log-likelihood	−5129.36	−4309.48	−4307.47	−4309.27	−4872.10
Observations	8053	6823	6823	6823	7653
Number of countries	15	13	13	13	15

Standard errors in parentheses
*** $p < 0.01$, ** $p < 0.05$, * $p < 0.1$

likely to recommend academic than vocational education. Retired and unemployed persons, as well as those doing manual labor, are more likely to recommend vocational than academic education. Having a white-collar job has a positive but not robust effect on recommending academic education. Age (probably because of the correlation with the "being retired" dummy) and gender do not have a statistically significant effect. The joint impact of these micro-level variables is considerable. The predicted probability of a highly educated student recommending academic education is 65.9 percent, compared to 21.1 percent for a retired blue-collar worker with little education.

The impact of macro-level variables is of greater interest for the purpose of this chapter. I again include the most important macro-level variables from previous chapters, which turn out to be statistically significant determinants of individual preferences. A high share of private spending on education is associated with a *lower* probability of recommending academic education (Models 2, 3, and 4). This could indicate that high levels of private spending might act as a deterrent to higher levels of participation in tertiary education, although this effect seems to be more relevant at the level of perceptions and preferences than with regard to actual enrollment levels (see Chapter 3). What is more, high levels of educational stratification are associated with a higher probability of recommending academic education instead of VET. When access to higher levels of education is blocked by institutional and other hurdles, the relative value of academic education increases. It is therefore more likely for people to recommend academic over vocational education.

However, there is also evidence for a positive feedback effect: in countries with well-developed VET systems, average levels of support for academic education instead of VET are lower (Model 3). This means that people are more likely to recommend VET over academic education when it is a credible and viable alternative to academic education rather than a dead-end educational track for low achievers. Finally, there is no statistically significant association between levels of public social spending and recommendations for different kinds of education, independent of whether this is included as an individual macro-level variable (Model 5) or in combination with others (Model 4). This finding is at odds with a central thesis of the VoC literature (Estévez-Abe *et al.* 2001), which is that generous welfare states serve an insurance purpose and encourage individuals to invest in vocational

Table 5.6 *Multilevel regressions of preferences for redistribution, ISSP 2006*

Dependent variable	(1)	(2)	(3)	(4)	(5)
	Support for government-induced redistribution (1 = yes, 0 = no)				
Micro-level variables					
Income	−0.170***	−0.169***	−0.167***	−0.179***	−0.166***
	(0.00933)	(0.00929)	(0.00943)	(0.00990)	(0.00962)
Gender (female)	0.166***	0.165***	0.168***	0.157***	0.161***
	(0.0372)	(0.0372)	(0.0380)	(0.0394)	(0.0382)
Years in education	−0.0421***	−0.0417***	−0.0410***	−0.0362***	−0.0429***
	(0.00509)	(0.00509)	(0.00521)	(0.00522)	(0.00519)
Skill specificity	0.0330***	0.0329***	0.0326***	0.0312***	0.0321***
	(0.00605)	(0.00605)	(0.00618)	(0.00644)	(0.00620)
Retired	0.166***	0.168***	0.190***	0.130**	0.173***
	(0.0525)	(0.0525)	(0.0544)	(0.0566)	(0.0527)
Labor-market outsider	0.253***	0.254***	0.265***	0.206**	0.296***
	(0.0974)	(0.0974)	(0.0987)	(0.101)	(0.102)
Student or in education	−0.348**	−0.346**	−0.345**	−0.374**	−0.293**
	(0.145)	(0.145)	(0.146)	(0.147)	(0.148)
Macro-level variables					
Socioeconomic inequality (Gini)		0.111***	0.114***	0.0952***	0.101***
		(0.0285)	(0.0387)	(0.0258)	(0.0329)
Private share of education spending, all levels		−0.0572***		−0.0510***	−0.0577***
		(0.0120)		(0.0106)	(0.0118)

Private share of education spending, tertiary education		−0.0261*** (0.00824)		
Educational stratification			−0.111 (0.247)	
Share of upper-secondary students in VET				−0.00462 (0.00615)
Constant	1.840*** (0.157)	−0.666 (0.771)	−0.873 (1.026)	−0.111 (1.127)
Variance components				
Level 2 intercept standard deviation	0.5957 (0.0973)	0.3946 (0.0656)	0.4806 (0.0812)	0.3354 (0.0612)	0.3775 (0.0645)
Intra-class correlation (Rho)	0.0974 (0.0287)	0.0452 (0.0143)	0.0656 (0.0207)	0.0331 (0.0120)	0.0415 (0.0136)
Log-likelihood	−9613.84	−9605.80	−9189.49	−8673.30	−9127.78
Observations	17315	17315	16606	15414	16588
Number of countries	20	20	19	17	19

Standard errors in parentheses
*** $p < 0.01$, ** $p < 0.05$, * $p < 0.1$

skills. Given the limits of the dataset, however, this finding could be a consequence of the exclusion of important non-European LMEs.

Educational institutions and redistributive preferences

The previous section looked at the effects of educational institutions on preferences for education spending and different kinds of education. In the following, I will instead focus on the implications of educational institutions for individual-level support for redistribution more generally. The purpose of this section is to demonstrate the interconnectedness of the general conflict over redistribution and the design of educational institutions. It is therefore connected to the overall topic of unearthing the linkages between education and the welfare state, at both the micro- and the macro-level.

Unlike in the previous sections, the dependent variable in the following analysis is individual support for redistribution, measured by responses to the following question in the ISSP Role of Government IV survey:

On the whole, do you think it should or should not be the government's responsibility to... reduce income differences between the rich and the poor?[5]

Respondents' answers have been grouped into four categories ("definitely should be," "probably should be," "probably should not be," "definitely should not be"). As before, indecisive answers were deleted from the sample and the four categories have been collapsed into two – support (1) or oppose (0) government-induced redistribution – in order to keep the analyses as simple and accessible as possible.

Table 5.6 presents the findings of multilevel regression analyses of the determinants of support for redistribution. The set of controls at the individual level is similar to the one used in Table 5.2, with one exception: here, I also include an indicator of skill specificity. As is argued in the literature (Cusack *et al.* 2006; Iversen 2005; Iversen & Soskice 2001), having a set of specific vocational skills that is less easily

---

[5] The same question was asked in the more recent 2009 ISSP survey on social inequality, but I decided to use the question from the older survey in order to be able to use the same set of controls at the micro- and macro-level as in the previous analyses.

transferable between different jobs is expected to increase individual demand for social protection in the form of redistribution. The positive and significant coefficient estimate of this variable in Table 5.6 confirms this hypothesis. The other micro-level control variables also perform as expected: high levels of income and education are associated with less support for redistribution, while being female, retired, or a labor-market outsider increases support.

How do macro-level variables affect support for redistribution? Starting with socioeconomic inequality, an important implication of the Meltzer–Richard model (Meltzer & Richard, 1981) is that higher levels of inequality should be associated with stronger popular support for redistribution. This relationship does not seem to hold at the macro-level, since the amount of redistribution as a difference between pre- and post-tax inequality is lower in states with high levels of pre-tax inequality (what Lindert (2004) and Iversen & Soskice (2009) call the "Robin Hood paradox"). Recent research by Finseraas (2009) based on multilevel regression analysis of survey data has largely confirmed the predictions of the Meltzer–Richard model, however: he found that on average, support for redistribution is higher in countries with higher levels of inequality.

The regressions in Table 5.6 confirm the existence of a positive association between existing levels of inequality and average levels of support for redistribution. The coefficient estimate of this variable is statistically significant and robust across all model specifications. However, its significance depends on the inclusion of the private spending share variable (the bivariate correlation between the two is 0.56), making the overall association between inequality and support for redistribution rather weak. This is an interesting contrast to the relatively strong association between inequality and support for education spending (see Figure 5.5). The variation around the mean is particularly large for high levels of inequality. In some countries (Portugal, Spain, and Ireland), high levels of inequality are associated with more support for redistribution, while in others (the United States, the United Kingdom, Australia, and New Zealand), the opposite is the case. Of course, one core distinction between these groups of countries is that in the former, education is largely publicly funded, whereas in the latter private education spending is more important. In other words, high levels of private education spending in most Anglo-Saxon countries may increase the general acceptance of higher levels of inequality in the population and thus lower the popular demand for redistribution.

A simple explanation for this mechanism is rooted in self-interest: as mentioned above, an individual's stock of human capital is an important determinant of redistributive preferences in terms of the total amount of human capital accumulated (income, education), the difference in kinds of skills (Iversen & Soskice 2001), and the associated labor-market risks (Rehm 2009, 2012). To this list, one could add differences with regard to how much individuals had to pay out of pocket to acquire human capital. It could be expected that individuals who had to pay for a significant share of their human capital stock on their own would be less likely to support government-induced redistribution, since this would reduce the return they received on their educational investments. An alternative explanation might focus on the effects of welfare-state institutions more broadly defined in terms of culture (Jo 2011; Pfau-Effinger 2005; Van Oorschot *et al.* 2008). After health care, schools and education are probably the most visible part of the welfare state for children and middle-class parents. Before individuals become unemployed or retire, they come into contact with the education system. This contact is not ephemeral (as it may be in the case of health care), but lasts over a period of several years. Individual experiences in the education system have a long-lasting impact on the formation of personal identities, as well as expectations with regard to the role of the state: when education is largely provided and financed by the state, individuals socialized into a state-run education system are more likely to also support government involvement in the welfare state and redistribution. The concrete hypothesis that can be derived from these considerations is that a high share of private education spending should be associated with lower average levels of support for redistribution.

Indeed, the findings presented in Table 5.6 reveal a statistically significant and negative association between the private spending share in education and average levels of support for redistribution, independent of whether I include the private share for all levels of education (Models 2, 4, and 5) or tertiary education only (Model 3), where the association is expected to be more pronounced, since private spending is more important in that sector (Wolf & Zohlnhöfer 2009). Unlike the effect of inequality, the negative association between private spending share and support for redistribution holds when the other macro-level

Impact on popular attitudes and preferences 251

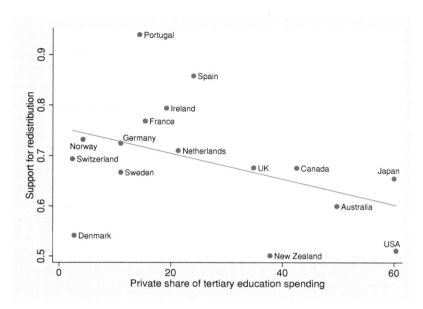

Figure 5.7 Popular support for redistribution and private share of tertiary education spending

variables are dropped from the regression (p-value = 0.022, not shown in Table 5.6). Figure 5.7 is a graphic representation of this association. There are some outliers (Portugal, Spain, Denmark), but overall there is a negative relationship between the private spending share and average levels of support for redistribution.

In contrast to the division of labor in education financing, educational stratification does not matter with regard to redistributive preferences (Models 4 and 5). From a theoretical perspective, the causal connection between matters of education financing and redistribution is more direct than that between institutional stratification and redistribution. This is commensurate with one of the core findings of Chapter 4: there is no direct association between educational stratification and levels of socioeconomic inequality.

Summary and conclusion

This chapter has identified a third important linkage between education and the welfare state, in addition to politics and outcomes:

the effects of educational institutions on individual-level attitudes and preferences for education policies and redistribution more generally. The analysis of feedback effects complements the previous analysis by identifying popular attitudes as important micro-level foundations of path dependency. Crucial decisions about the institutional design of education and training systems in the postwar period manifest themselves as contemporary cross-national differences. These differences have implications for the continued popular support of various policy options.

The chapter started out by reaffirming the distinctiveness of education in comparison to other social policies at the micro-level. Whereas income and educational background are strong negative determinants of individual support for increasing spending on pensions, health care, and unemployment benefits, their effect on support for higher levels of government spending on education is neutral (in the case of income) or even positive (in the case of educational background). Employing multilevel regression analyses, I showed that macro-level institutions mediate the micro-level effects of income and educational background. When the education system is stratified, high-income and well-educated people are more likely to support spending increases on education, because these will benefit them or their children directly.

The analyses also revealed complex feedback mechanisms. In some cases, I found evidence for a positive feedback effect, in the sense that citizens express support for existing institutions. For example, individuals are more likely to recommend vocational education instead of academic education in countries with a well-developed VET system. Average levels of support for redistribution are lower in countries with a high share of private education spending. In other cases, however, negative feedback effects are more important. High levels of inequality are associated with increased support for redistribution. High levels of public education spending are related to lower levels of support for additional government spending. Further research beyond the scope of this chapter should try to entangle these complex feedback mechanisms by identifying conditions under which positive or negative feedback dominates.

6 Conclusion

This book has explored the various political and institutional linkages between education and the welfare state. I found a modicum of support for Wilensky's claim that "education is special" (Wilensky 1975: 3). Education is indeed different from other social policies, because the redistributive implications of educational investment are very complex. However, as this book has shown, education should still be considered (and analyzed) as part and parcel of encompassing welfare state regimes: there are multiple linkages between education and other parts of the welfare state, in terms of politics, outcomes, and popular attitudes.

To recap, the core argument of the book is that political choices about the institutional design of education and training systems made during the critical juncture of the postwar decades have strong implications for the future development paths of skill regimes, as well as for contemporary patterns of inequality and popular attitudes. The politico-economic coalitions that drove the expansion of the welfare state in the postwar decades were also the driving forces behind critical, path-forming education reforms of the time, leading to the creation of three distinct development paths that resemble the established worlds of welfare capitalism (Esping-Andersen 1990). The long-term balance of power between partisan actors was identified as an important determinant of differences in the division of labor between public and private financing of education and the importance of VET relative to academic higher education. The survival of VET as a viable alternative to academic higher education very much depended on the existence of cross-class coalitions in the labor-market arena; that is, on high levels of economic coordination. The partisan balance of power would then decide whether VET was to be integrated into the general secondary school system (the social democratic path) or keep its status as a separate and distinct educational track (the Christian democratic path). Where VET declined, the brunt of post-secondary education was channeled into academic higher education, often leading to increases in the private share of education financing (the liberal-conservative path).

Whether and in which form VET survived had strong implications for contemporary patterns of social inequality. Levels of socioeconomic inequality are significantly lower in countries with well-established VET systems, since VET opens up access to well-paid and secure employment for those in the lower half of the skills distribution. The effect of tertiary education, by contrast, very much depends on its financing: when higher education (as well as other kinds of education) is financed from public sources, investment in education is associated with lower levels of inequality, whereas the opposite holds when private financing dominates. Apprenticeship training was found to be more effective in reducing youth unemployment than in mitigating labor-market inequality.

Finally, the institutional setup of the education and training system creates feedback effects at the micro-level of popular attitudes and preferences. When access to higher levels of education is limited, rich and well-educated people are more likely to support increased public education spending, since this will benefit them and/or their children. Private financing of education is associated with lower levels of support for redistribution, confirming the macro-level association between private financing and wage inequality. The underlying causal mechanism might be that individuals who have paid for a significant share of their human capital stock from their own pockets are less likely to support government policies that will reduce their education-related wage premiums. I also found evidence for negative feedback effects (institutions undermining their own support), which is at odds with the mainstream of comparative welfare state research (Pierson 1994, 1996, 2001; Rothstein 1998), which emphasizes positive feedback effects. For example, individuals are more likely to oppose increases in spending when public spending is already at a high level. The feedback mechanisms between the macro-level of institutions and the micro-level of attitudes thus seem to be more complex than initially assumed. Changes in popular support for policy options might be an important driving force in policy and institutional change more generally (Rehm 2012).

In closing, I want to highlight the contribution of the book's findings to two contemporary debates on the relationship between skills and inequality that have been relevant both in the sphere of academia and in politics more generally: the debate on skill-biased technological change (Goldin & Katz 2008) on the one hand, and the debate on the social investment state on the other. Interestingly, the first is more influential in the US/North American context, while the second is mostly a European affair.

Skill-biased technological change

In a seminal contribution, Goldin & Katz (2008) identified "the race between education and technology" as the crucial factor influencing changes in inequality over time. Their core argument is that these changes in inequality (mostly in the United States, but also in other countries) can largely be explained by changes in the mismatch between the supply and demand for high-skilled employees. When the supply of high-skilled workers increases relative to demand, for example because of a larger number of university graduates, the wages of the high-skilled are reduced due to wage competition, resulting in lower levels of inequality. Conversely, when the supply of the high-skilled decreases relative to demand, their wages will increase, resulting in more inequality. Since Goldin & Katz's (2008) work is based on the assumption of rational choice, individuals have an incentive to pursue higher education as long as it promises higher wages. In the long run, this should lead to a rough balance between the supply and demand of high-skilled workers. Judging from a recent increase in inequality in the United States and elsewhere, however, the balancing-out mechanism does not work as smoothly as it used to, for two reasons: first, skill-biased technological change causes the demand for high-skilled employees to increase, while demand for low-skilled work declines; second, the supply of high-skilled workers has reached an upper limit. At least in the case of the United States, according to Goldin & Katz (2008), the university system cannot produce more graduates than it does already. Not everyone can be turned into a knowledge worker. As limited supply meets an increasing demand for high-skilled workers, there is a relative increase in the wage premium of the high-skilled and thus a higher level of inequality.

Elegant as it may be, there are several fundamental flaws in the story about skills and inequality told by Goldin & Katz (2008), which are revealed by the findings of this book. First of all, Goldin and Katz underestimate the role of politics in shaping the institutional design of the education system; that is, the "supply side" of the labor market (Boix 1998; Busemeyer & Iversen 2012). Even though there might be strong economic incentives to pursue a university education, the question of granting access to higher levels of education is a highly political one, as the country case studies have shown. Those currently enjoying the payoffs of higher education in the form of wage premiums have a strong incentive to maintain this privilege by limiting access to higher education, whereas those left out have an incentive to gain access. This in turn is related to the partisan conflict about opening up access to higher education, as Ansell (2010) has shown. Most importantly, from the perspective of comparative political economy, cross-country differences in the balance of power between partisan and economic actors have had strong implications for the institutional design of education and training systems and for the resulting patterns of socioeconomic inequality. In other words, skill-biased technological change, or socioeconomic changes in the structure of the economy more generally, do not translate automatically into changes in inequality. Instead, socioeconomic changes interact with and are filtered by the existing institutions of the skill-formation regime (Busemeyer & Iversen 2012).

In particular, the quantitative analysis of determinants of inequality in Chapter 4 has demonstrated that the private share of education spending is an important factor in influencing the supply of high-skilled workers. Although the macro-level analysis in Chapter 4 surely needs to be complemented with micro-level studies (for an overview, see Stevens *et al.* 2008), there is ample evidence for large cross-national differences in levels of tertiary enrollment for countries at the same technological level, suggesting that the availability of educational opportunities is not entirely determined by some kind of natural limit defined by the innate distribution of academic skills in the population; instead, countries with a strong public commitment to expanding access to higher levels of education exhibit higher levels of participation in tertiary education than private systems. For example, in the immediate postwar years, the United States was far ahead of European countries in terms of participation and graduation rates in tertiary education (Busemeyer 2006). These days, the United States has been surpassed in this measure by a number of European countries, particularly Nordic countries such as Denmark and Finland (OECD 2012: 67). The limiting of the supply of high-skilled university graduates in the United States cannot be explained by economic factors alone, however, but has been conditioned by political and institutional factors. It is the effect of a particular institutional setup of the skill-formation regime that favors private spending relative to public commitment. This particular division of labor, moreover, is related to differences in the balance of power between partisan actors, as Chapter 3 has shown.

A second major shortcoming of the Goldin–Katz story is that it does not take into account the role of VET. The Goldin–Katz distinction between the high- and low-skilled reflects the institutional design of the US/American skill-formation regime, which draws a stark distinction between university/college graduates on the one hand and high school graduates or dropouts on the other. The category of intermediate-level skills is completely left out of the picture. A core insight of this book, following Estévez-Abe *et al.* (2001), is that well-established VET regimes at the level of upper and post-secondary education contribute to lowering inequality because they enhance the skill levels of those in the lower half of the skills distribution. As the VoC literature (Hall & Soskice 2001) has argued, once a skill-formation regime is in place, firms develop comparative institutional advantages based on the availability of different kinds of human capital in a particular economy. This in turn increases the demand for employees with intermediate-level occupational skills, potentially reducing the wage gap between university and VET graduates.

Complementing the perspective of Goldin & Katz (2008), Brown *et al.* (2011) have emphasized the contribution of economic globalization to increasing labor-market competition, not only in the low-skilled service sector but increasingly also in the high-skilled one. In the "Global Auction" depicted by Brown *et al.* (2011), university graduates in Western countries are now facing competition for white-collar jobs at the intermediate skill level (e.g., back-office operations, accounting, and software programming) from the newly educated in emerging economies such as India and China. Certain kinds of service-sector jobs can be outsourced to other countries more easily than other, low-skilled jobs in the service economy, especially personal services that are tied to a particular place (such as hairdressing or waiting tables). Again, institutional differences in the design of skill-formation regimes are neglected in the account of Brown *et al.* (2011). Countries with a strong focus on VET instead of higher education have often been regarded as being ill-equipped for the transition from the industrial to the service economy (Anderson & Hassel 2013; Wren 2013) because their skill formation regimes are rooted in the declining manufacturing sector. But if joint investments in vocational skills are indeed based on broad cross-class compromise, as is argued in this book and the VoC literature more generally (Iversen 2005), these joint skill investments might prevent, or at least slow down, the outsourcing of jobs at the intermediate skill level. Recent developments in the wake of the global economic and financial crisis suggest that policy-makers in LMEs are increasingly perceiving the strong dependence of the economy on services as a vulnerability instead of a comparative strength. This is exemplified by the recent (re)discovery of the value of apprenticeship training in the United Kingdom, as well as by President Obama's attempt to restore the competitiveness of the manufacturing sector in the United States.

Despite my general critique of them above, both Goldin & Katz (2008) and Brown *et al.* (2011) make an important contribution by highlighting how structural changes in the economy that are common across all advanced democracies affect the association between skills and inequality. This book has emphasized the importance of cross-country differences, but there is a general trend across Western industrialized countries that is often captured in vaguely defined concepts such as skill-biased technological change, globalization, and liberalization. While in previous eras of closed economies and Fordist mass production the socioeconomic developments might have favored or even caused a certain compression of wage inequality, these forces seem to pull in an entirely different direction in the contemporary period. A comprehensive understanding of the complex relationship between skills and inequality should recognize both the importance of this general trend and how it interacts with country- or context-specific institutions (this is why Thelen (2012) refers to different "trajectories of liberalization").

Interpreted from a different angle, the fact that institutions matter with regard to how the ubiquitous forces of structural change are translated into policy output and outcomes suggests that there remains some leeway for political action. One European example of how policy-makers and experts try to make use of the remaining room for maneuver is the recent debate on the merits of the social investment state, which I will discuss next.

Education in the social investment state

The rise of the paradigm of the social investment state started in earnest in the late 1990s and early 2000s, when a number of seminal contributions were published by leading academics such as Giddens (1998) and Esping-Andersen (2002). The central promise of the social investment state, and what made it so appealing to policy-makers of the center-left such as Tony Blair in the United Kingdom and Gerhard Schröder in Germany, was to strike a new compromise between the twin goals of promoting economic growth and maintaining social solidarity in the face of increasing globalization. Unlike the radical left, centrist social democrats have always been concerned about bringing these two goals into balance; Keynesianism provided a postwar rationale for why it should be both economically sound and socially just to increase social benefits. Expanding social transfers boosted demand (and therefore growth) and at the same time contributed to redistribution. The tumultuous 1970s witnessed the decline of Keynesianism in the United Kingdom and the United States, and the rise of neoliberalism as the dominant paradigm of economic policy-making (Hall 1992). After the demise of Keynesianism, policy-makers from the center-left lacked a convincing and credible alternative to neoliberalism that could continue to promote the twin goals of economic growth and social solidarity and be viable in the postindustrial and globalized economy.

The social investment approach holds the promise to be this alternative paradigm. In contrast to Keynesianism, and like neoliberalism, it focuses on the supply side of the economy (Morel *et al.* 2012: 5–10). The shift from the demand to the supply side is explained by the fact that efforts to stimulate economic demand with social transfers will not be effective in an open economy, since beneficiaries might easily spend the money on foreign goods and services (Boix 1998). Globalization also reinforces skill-biased technological change, due to the comparative advantages in high-skilled labor of advanced economies and the transformation from an industrial to a postindustrial service and knowledge economy.

In this situation, human capital investment plays a critical role in minimizing potential tradeoffs; promoting educational opportunities from early childhood education, through VET and higher education, to lifelong learning – together with active labor-market policies – is at the core of the social investment paradigm (Hemerijck 2012; Morel *et al.* 2012). Human capital investment might be regarded as being more effective than social transfers at stimulating growth, because investment boosts productivity levels. Expanding educational opportunities, particularly for the low-skilled, may also contribute to lowering inequality. This focus on human capital goes along with a reorientation of the function and purpose of the welfare state. Instead of compensating individuals for income loss due to unemployment or skill obsolescence *ex post*, the social investment paradigm envisions an activist state that prevents poverty and low-skilled employment by investing in skill formation and education as early as possible in the life course. This has been argued most forcefully by Esping-Andersen (2002), who promotes a "child-centred social investment strategy," claiming that educational and other social inequalities can be prevented most effectively by concentrating on early childhood education. Nevertheless, the investment approach is also feasible for later stages in the life cycle. The second most obvious example of a recalibration of welfare state policies in line with the social investment paradigm is the turn from passive to activist labor-market policies across the OECD world (Bonoli 2012, 2013). Again, the idea here is to move from a passive and *ex post* compensation of social risk to an activist approach, preventing the emergence of social problems by improving the skills of individuals.

The political driving forces behind the rise of the social investment paradigm are varied. As hinted at above, the initial impetus came from policy-makers of the center-left, who regarded the social investment paradigm as a promising instrument by which to appeal to new electoral constituencies in the middle classes (e.g., Schröder's *Neue Mitte*). Some policy instruments in the investment catalogue have always been popular with the right, however; particularly activist labor-market policies with a strong workfare component (King 1995). Expanding childcare, although initially pioneered by the social democratic Nordic welfare states, has become a popular project of both the left and the right in continental European countries that were once lagging behind the Nordic countries because of the latter's increasing female labor-market participation (Flecksenstein *et al.* 2011; Morgan 2012). The social investment paradigm also enjoys considerable support from international organizations such as the OECD, as well as the European Union (Hemerijck 2012: 46).

The empirical analysis of Chapter 4 showed that increasing public investment in education can indeed contribute to lowering inequality, in line with the social investment paradigm. However, I also found that the magnitude of this effect very much depends on the kind of education that is promoted. This book has concentrated on education policy at the upper and post-secondary levels; future research needs to focus more on the contribution of early childhood education to the lowering of socioeconomic inequalities. In contrast to some of the literature (Wren 2013) and regular OECD recommendations to expand access to higher education (OECD 2012: 13–15), I found that promoting opportunities in VET may actually be more effective in mitigating inequalities. School-based forms of VET can help limit wage inequality and promote the educational mobility of low-skilled youths, because VET integrates this group into the general secondary schooling system. Workplace-based forms of VET such as apprenticeship training, on the other hand, are linked to a stronger segmentation and stratification of secondary education, which is associated with higher levels of educational inequality. But apprenticeship training is also much more effective at creating a smooth transition from training to employment, resulting in lower levels of youth unemployment than in school-based VET systems (Gangl 2003; Wolbers 2007). Thus, hybrid cases such as Denmark, which combines elements of the continental European and the Scandinavian models, might be better able to resolve the tradeoffs between different dimensions of inequality than the more frequently discussed models. In the case of higher education, expanding enrollment is not a sufficient condition for lowering inequality. When a large share of spending on higher education stems from private sources, and when labor markets are flexible and deregulated, enabling the high-skilled to reap large wage premiums, expanding higher education most likely does not contribute much to lowering inequality.

In sum, this book has shown that promoting educational opportunities at various stages in the life cycle does have implications for the distribution of income and life chances, but it is certainly not a panacea. I therefore side with Allmendinger (2009), Allmendinger & Nikolai (2010), and Vandenbroucke & Vleminckx (2011: 451), who argue that welfare state policies should be balanced on two pillars: the new social investment pillar and a social protection pillar rooted in more traditional social insurance policies. This balancing-out of activation on the one hand with insurance and redistribution on the other increases the chances that existing welfare states will be sustainable in the long run, from both a political and an economic perspective. If welfare state reforms focus too narrowly on the investment aspect and use it to justify and sugar-coat retrenchment in other parts of the welfare state (Taylor-Gooby 2008), the public could end up opposing the social investment strategy. Furthermore, there is most likely a hard core of low-skilled individuals who are extremely hard to "activate" through labor-market or education policies and who will probably continue to depend on traditional social welfare policies (Allmendinger & Nikolai 2010: 116). Even so, overcoming the traditional focus of many European welfare states on passive social transfers will increase the support for social policies among both employers and the (upper) middle class, whose support is crucial to maintaining the financial and political viability of welfare states.

All in all, the social investment approach holds considerable potential as a policy paradigm, when and if it is based on a balanced approach between investment and social protection. Two caveats must be added, though. First, implementing the social investment paradigm is not a free lunch – at least in the short run. Investing in childcare, VET, lifelong learning, and active labor-market policies requires additional funding if the balanced approach to welfare state restructuring is to be taken seriously. In these times of renewed austerity, coming up with additional funds for social investment will be extremely challenging, but not impossible (Diamond & Little 2012). The examples of former laggards in childcare provision (e.g., Germany and the Netherlands) catching up with pioneers such as France and the Scandinavian countries show that policy change is possible, despite the constraints of globalization and austerity (Fleckenstein *et al.* 2011; Morgan 2012), even though it may proceed in small incremental steps.

The second caveat is more substantial: reforming welfare states along the lines of the social investment paradigm requires a significant redefinition of the function of social and education policy vis-à-vis the market. Esping-Andersen's (1990) concept of de-commodification defines the function of social policy as creating a certain independence of individuals from market forces. The social investment paradigm, by contrast, implies a redefinition of this function. Instead of creating a sphere that is independent of market forces, social policy is believed to contribute to boosting economic performance, for example by maximizing employment for the formerly unemployed or by improving the skill set of low-skilled individuals. From this more critical perspective, the promotion of early childhood education is an attempt to implement the economic goal of making use of all remaining potential for employment, undermining social networks and family structures (Streeck 2008). It is telling that the seemingly obvious policy solution to gender discrimination on the labor market is to expand early childhood education to enable women to participate, although other possibilities, such as reducing working time for both men and women, are imaginable.

The redefinition of education and social policy as instruments for the boosting of economic productivity is gaining momentum at the international level. The expanding involvement of institutions such as the OECD and the EU is associated with the redefinition of the purpose of education from a "decommodified," Humboldtian conception towards a more functionalist one (Walkenhorst 2008). Both the OECD and the EU need to legitimate their involvement in economic terms: the EU in order to promote the establishment of the European Single Market and the OECD because its mission as a think tank is to promote economic cooperation and development. Thus, the involvement of intra- and international institutions in the social investment debate intensifies the refocusing of welfare state policies and institutions from de-commodification towards re-commodification.

But this criticism, however valid, should not be overestimated, especially if the social investment pillar is complemented by a second pillar focusing on redistribution and social insurance, as outlined above. Furthermore, we should recall that the Keynesian paradigm also served the dual purpose of promoting both social equality *and* economic development. Expanding social transfers in the name of Keynesianism may contribute to lowering inequality, but it also boosts economic demand. The Swedish welfare state, often used as a role model in the social investment debate (Morel *et al.* 2012: 3–4), has always been ambiguous about the real extent of de-commodification. On the one hand, the generosity of benefits in Scandinavian welfare states is much higher than that in other countries (Esping-Andersen 1990; Allan & Scruggs 2004); on the other, employment levels are also much higher, and unemployment levels much lower. This means that the real extent of de-commodification in terms of the labor force that does not participate in employment is actually quite limited. The granting of de-commodification on paper depends on, or at least goes along with, a high level of the commodification of labor on labor markets. In this respect, the social investment paradigm is not all that different from previous paradigms or models in trying to wed concerns about social inequality to economic functionalism. In fact, it may well be the case that in order for welfare states to be sustainable in the long run, they need the support of both the general public and significant parts of the business community.

Avenues for future research

In closing, I wish to briefly highlight some possible avenues for future research. Chapter 5 provided a first glimpse of the complexity of the feedback mechanisms between the macro-level of institutions and policies and the micro-level of attitudes and preferences. While many questions remain, the empirical evidence points to the fact that both positive and negative feedback mechanisms are at work, although it is not clear what factors decide which type of feedback will dominate in a particular case. In addition, the case studies, as well as anecdotal evidence, suggest that policy-makers sometimes care about public opinion but that in other cases organized labor-market and elite partisan interests will dominate. The saliency of a particular issue might be an explanation for the changing relative influence of public opinion and organized interests (Culpepper 2010), but the obvious follow-up question is when and how issues become salient, and whether saliency can be manipulated by political actors (Baumgartner & Jones 1993). In general, I believe that more committed interaction between comparative welfare state research and political-science research on public opinion and voter participation could open up a new and fruitful research agenda on these issues.

Finally, this book has focused on post-secondary education. Recent policy developments in many European countries, however, have been mainly concerned with the expansion of early childhood education and lifelong learning. In fact, the current period might become a critical juncture for the expansion of early childhood and continuing education, just as the postwar period was for upper and post-secondary education. Despite a general trend across European and OECD countries, we can observe a large degree of cross-country variation in terms of both the rate of expansion and the particular institutions of financing and provision that are being established (Bonoli 2013; Morgan

2012). Of particular importance is the division of labor between public and private financing and provision – a variable that I found to be of primary importance in the historical development of post-secondary education as well. It is indeed puzzling why voters in one country would be willing to accept, tolerate, and/or support fees of several thousand dollars (United States) or Swiss francs (Switzerland), when voters in another expect free and public provision of education (the Scandinavian countries). Since this is a new policy field, very little is known so far about the factors explaining variation at the macro-level and differences in public attitudes, and much remains to be done.

Appendix
Data sources for quantitative analyses (all chapters)

Variable	Description and source
Private share of education spending, all levels of education	Own calculations based on public share of spending on educational institutions, OECD Education Statistics Database
Private share of education spending, tertiary education	Own calculations based on public share of spending on educational institutions, tertiary education only, OECD Education Statistics Database
Educational stratification	Odds ratios that students expect to complete ISCED levels 5A or 6 by socioeconomic status (2003), OECD (2007: 87)
Share of students in VET	Share of upper-secondary students in vocational programs, OECD Education Statistics Database
Share of students in apprenticeship	Share of upper-secondary students in vocational programs combining school and work-based education, OECD Education Statistics Database
Public spending on education	Public spending on educational institutions as percentage of GDP, OECD Education Statistics Database
Private spending on education	Private spending on educational institutions as percentage of GDP, OECD Education Statistics Database
Population share with upper-secondary education	Share of population (15- to 64-year-olds) with at least upper-secondary education, per cent, OECD Education Statistics Database
Employer involvement in VET	Index of employer involvement in the provision of initial VET, based on expert survey, Busemeyer & Schlicht-Schmälzle (2014)

Variable	Description and source
Public commitment to VET	Index of public commitment to the provision of VET, based on expert survey, Busemeyer & Schlicht-Schmälzle (2014)
Public social spending	Public social expenditure in cash as percentage of GDP, Armingeon *et al.* (2011)
Postwar cabinet share of Christian democrats, conservatives, liberals, and social democrats	Data on partisan composition of postwar government, Schmidt (2003)
Economic coordination in labor relations	Index of coordination in labor relations, Hall & Gingerich (2009: 458)
Public spending on tertiary education	Public spending on educational institutions as percentage of GDP, tertiary education only, OECD Education Statistics
Public spending on VET (proxy)	Own calculations: spending on upper-secondary education (all sources) as percentage of GDP, multiplied by share of upper-secondary students in vocational programs, based on data from OECD Education Statistics Database
Entry-rate tertiary education	Entry rate into tertiary type-A (academic) education, OECD Education Statistics Database
Union density	Net union membership as proportion of wage and salary earners in employment, Armingeon *et al.* (2011)
Employment share in services	Civilian employment in services, Armingeon *et al.* (2011)
GDP growth	Growth of real GDP, percentage change from previous year, Armingeon *et al.* (2011)
Government partisanship	Cabinet composition (Schmidt index): (1) hegemony of right-wing (and center) parties, (2) dominance of right-wing (and center) parties, (3) balance of power between left and right, (4) dominance of social democratic and other left parties, (5) hegemony of social democratic and other left parties, Armingeon *et al.* (2011)

Variable	Description and source
Cabinet share of right-wing/center/left-wing parties	Before performing the changes as documented in the main text: cabinet composition: right-wing/center/left-wing parties in percentage of total cabinet posts, Armingeon et al. (2011)
Socioeconomic inequality (Gini)	Estimate of Gini index of inequality in equivalized (square root scale) household disposable income, using Luxembourg Income Study data as the standard, Solt (2009)
PISA measure of educational inequality	Slope of socioeconomic gradient (impact of social background on PISA reading score), OECD (2010: 34).
Wage inequality, various measures	Ratio of wages at 9th to 1st decile (D9–D1 ratio), at 9th to 5th decile, (D9–D5 ratio), and at 5th to 1st decile (D5–D1 ratio) in distribution of wage income, OECD Earnings Inequality Dataset (accessed via OECD.stats)
Tertiary enrollment	Gross enrollment in tertiary education, UNESCO Education Statistics Database
Youth unemployment	Unemployment rate, ages 15–24, all persons (male and female), OECD Short-Term Labour Market Statistics Dataset (accessed via OECD.stats)
Social transfers	Social security transfers as a percentage of GDP, social assistance grants, and welfare benefits paid by general government (benefits for sickness, old age, family allowances, etc.), Armingeon et al. (2011)
Wage-bargaining centralization	Dominant level(s) at which wage bargaining takes place: 5 = national or central level; 4 = national or central level, with additional sectoral/local or company bargaining; 3 = sectoral or industry level; 2 = sectoral or industry level, with additional local or company bargaining; 1 = local or company bargaining, Country Data ICTWSS (Visser 2011)

Additional note: linear interpolation was used to smooth over short breaks in time-series data for selected variables.

Bibliography

Aasen, P. (2003). What happened to Social-Democratic Progressivism in Scandinavia? Restructuring Education in Sweden and Norway in the 1990s. In M. W. Apple (ed.), *The State and the Politics of Knowledge* (pp. 109–47). London and New York, NY: Routledge.

Acemoglu, D. & Pischke, J.-S. (1998). Why Do Firms Train? Theory and Evidence. *Quarterly Journal of Economics*, 113(1), 79–119.

Acemoglu, D. & Pischke, J.-S. (1999). Beyond Becker: Training in Imperfect Labour Markets. *Economic Journal*, 109(453), F112–42.

Achen, C. (2000). Why Lagged Dependent Variables Can Suppress the Explanatory Power of Other Independent Variables. Paper prepared for the Annual Meeting of the Political Methodology Section of the American Political Science Association. Ann Arbor, MI: University of Michigan.

Ainley, P. (2001). From a National System Locally Administered to a National System Nationally Administered: The New Leviathan in Education and Training in England. *Journal of Social Policy*, 30(3), 457–76.

Allan, J. P. & Scruggs, L. (2004). Political Partisanship and Welfare State Reform in Advanced Industrial Societies. *American Journal of Political Science*, 48, 496–512.

Allmendinger, J. (1989). Educational Systems and Labour Market Outcomes. *European Sociological Review*, 5(3), 231–50.

Allmendinger, J. (2009). Der Sozialstaat des 21. Jahrhunderts braucht zwei Beine. *Aus Politik und Zeitgeschichte*, 45/2009, 3–5.

Allmendinger, J. & Leibfried, S. (2003). Education and the Welfare State: Germany's Poverty and Plenty and the Many Worlds of "Competence Distribution" in the EC and the OECD. *Journal of European Social Policy*, 13(1), 63–81.

Allmendinger, J. & Nikolai, R. (2010). Bildungs- und Sozialpolitik: Die zwei Seiten des Sozialstaats im internationalen Vergleich. *Soziale Welt*, 61(2), 105–19.

Anderson, C. J. & Beramendi, P. (2012). Left Parties, Poor Voters, and Electoral Participation in Advanced Industrial Societies. *Comparative Political Studies*, 45(6), 714–46.

Anderson, K. M. (2009). The Church as Nation? The Role of Religion in the Development of the Swedish Welfare State. In K. Van Kersbergen & P. Manow (eds), *Religion, Class Coalitions, and Welfare States* (pp. 210–35). Cambridge and New York, NY: Cambridge University Press.

Anderson, K. M. & Hassel, A. (2013) Pathways of Change in CMEs: Training Regimes in Germany and the Netherlands. In: Wren, A. (ed.), *The Political Economy of the Service Transition* (pp. 171–94). Oxford and New York, NY: Oxford University Press.

Anderson, K. M. & Oude Nijhuis, D. (2012). The Long Road to Collective Skill Formation in the Netherlands. In M. R. Busemeyer & C. Trampusch (eds), *The Political Economy of Collective Skill Formation* (pp. 101–25). Oxford and New York, NY: Oxford University Press.

Andreß, H.-J. & Heien, T. (2001). Four Worlds of Welfare State Attitudes? A Comparison of Germany, Norway, and the United States. *European Sociological Review*, 17(4), 337–56.

Ansell, B. W. (2008). University Challenges: Explaining Institutional Change in Higher Education. *World Politics*, 60(January 2008), 189–230.

Ansell, B. W. (2010). *From the Ballot to the Blackboard: The Redistributive Political Economy of Education*. Cambridge: Cambridge University Press.

Antikainen, A. (2006). In Search of the Nordic Model in Education. *Scandinavian Journal of Educational Research*, 50(3), 229–43.

Armingeon, K., Engler, S., Potolidis, P., Gerber, M., & Leimgruber, P. (2011). Comparative Political Data Set 1960–2008. Institute of Political Science, University of Berne.

Arnesen, A.-L. & Lundahl, L. (2006). Still Social and Democratic? Inclusive Education Policies in the Nordic Welfare States. *Scandinavian Journal of Educational Research*, 50(3), 285–300.

Arreman, I. E. & Holm, A.-S. (2011). Privatisation of Public Education? The Emergence of Independent Upper Secondary Schools in Sweden. *Journal of Education Policy*, 26(2), 225–43.

Arts, W. & Gelissen, J. (2001). Welfare States, Solidarity and Justice Principles: Does the Type Really Matter? *Acta Sociologica*, 44(4), 283–99.

Bache, I. (2003). Governing through Governance: Education Policy Control under New Labour. *Political Studies*, 51, 300–314.

Baethge, M. (1970). *Ausbildung und Herrschaft: Unternehmerinteressen in der Bildungspolitik*. Frankfurt a.M.: Europäische Verlagsanstalt.

Baethge, M. (1983). Berufsbildungspolitik in den siebziger Jahren: Eine Lektion in ökonomischer Macht und politischer Ohnmacht. In A. Lipsmeier (ed.), *Berufsbildungspolitik in den 70er Jahren: Eine kritische Bestandsaufnahme für die 80er Jahre* (pp. 145–57). Wiesbaden: Franz Steiner Verlag.

Baldi, G. (2012). Schools with a Difference: Policy Discourses and Education Reform in Britain and Germany. *West European Politics*, 35(5), 999–1023.
Ball, S. J. & Larsson, S. (1989). Education, Politics and Society in Sweden: an Introduction. In S. J. Ball & S. Larsson (eds), *The Struggle for Democratic Education: Equality and Participation in Sweden* (pp. 1–17). New York, NY, Philadelphia, PA, and London: The Falmer Press.
Baumgartner, F. R. & Jones, B. D. (1993). *Agendas and Instabiliy in American Politics*. Chicago, IL: University of Chicago Press.
Bean, C. & Papadakis, E. (1998). A Comparison of Mass Attitudes towards the Welfare State in Different Institutional Regimes, 1985–1990. *International Journal of Public Opinion Research*, 10(3), 211–36.
Beck, N. (1991). Comparing Dynamic Specifications: The Case of Presidential Approval. *Political Analysis*, III, 51–87.
Beck, N. & Katz, J. (1995). What to Do (and Not to Do) with Time-Series Cross-Section Data. *American Political Science Review*, 89(3), 634–47.
Beck, N. & Katz, J. (1996). Nuisance vs. Substance: Specifiying and Estimating Time-Series-Cross-Section Models. *Political Analysis*, 6, 1–36.
Becker, G. S. (1993). *Human Capital: A Theoretical and Empirical Analysis with Special Reference to Education* (3rd edn). Chicago, IL and London: University of Chicago Press.
Becker, U. (2007). Open Systemness and Constested Reference Frames and Change: A Reformulation of the Varieties of Capitalism Theory. *Socio-Economic Review*, 5, 261–86.
Björklund, A., Clark, M. A., Edin, P.-A., Fredriksson, P., & Krueger, A. B. (2005). *The Market Comes to Education in Sweden: An Evaluation of Sweden's Surprising School Reforms*. New York, NY: Russell Sage Foundation.
Blekesaune, M. & Quadagno, J. (2003). Public Attitudes toward Welfare State Policies: A Comparative Analysis of 24 Countries. *European Sociological Review*, 19(5), 415–27.
Blossfeld, H.-P. & Shavit, Y. (1993). *Persistent Inequality: Changing Educational Attainment in Thirteen Countries*. Boulder, CO: Westview Press.
Boeri, T., Börsch-Supan, A., Tabellini, G., Moene, K. O., & Lockwood, B. (2001). Would You Like To Shrink the Welfare State? A Survey of European Citizens. *Economic Policy*, 16(32), 9–50.
Boix, C. (1997). Political Parties and the Supply Side of the Economy: The Provision of Physical and Human Capital in Advanced Economies, 1960–1990. *American Journal of Political Science*, 41(3), 814–45.
Boix, C. (1998). *Political Parties, Growth and Equality: Conservative and Social Democratic Economic Strategies in the World Economy*. Cambridge: Cambridge University Press.

Bonoli, G. (2012). Active Labour Market Policy and Social Investment: A Changing Relationship. In N. Morel, B. Palier, & J. Palme (eds), *Towards a Social Investment Welfare State? Ideas, Policies and Challenges* (pp. 181–204). Bristol and Chicago, IL: Policy Press.

Bonoli, G. (2013). *The Origins of Active Social Policy: Labour Market and Childcare Policies in a Comparative Perspective.* Oxford and New York, NY: Oxford University Press.

Bosch, G. (2010). Zur Zukunft der dualen Berufsausbildung in Deutschland. In G. Bosch, S. Krone, & D. Langer (eds), *Das Berufsbildungssystem in Deutschland: Aktuelle Entwicklungen und Standpunkte* (pp. 37–61). Wiesbaden: VS Verlag für Sozialwissenschaften.

Boudon, R. (1974). *Education, Oportunity, and Social Inequality.* New York, NY: John Wiley & Sons.

Bradley, D., Huber, E., Moller, S., Nielsen, F., & Stephens, J. D. (2003). Distribution and Redistribution in Postindustrial Democracies. *World Politics*, 55(January 2003), 193–228.

Breen, R. (2005). Explaining Cross-National Variation in Youth Unemployment. *European Sociological Review*, 21(2), 125–34.

Breen, R. & Goldthorpe, J. H. (1997). Explaining Educational Differentials: Towards a Formal Rational Action Theory. *Rationality and Society*, 9, 275–305.

Breen, R. & Jonsson, J. O. (2005). Inequality of Opportunity in Comparative Perspective: Recent Research on Educational Attainment and Social Mobility. *Annual Review of Sociology*, 31, 223–43.

Breen, R., Luijkx, R., Müller, W., & Pollak, R. (2009). Nonpersistent Inequality in Educational Attainment: Evidence from Eight European Countries. *American Journal of Sociology*, 114(5), 1475–521.

Brooks, C. & Manza, J. (2006). Why Do Welfare States Persist? *Journal of Politics*, 68(4), 816–27.

Brooks, C. & Manza, J. (2007). *Why Welfare States Persist: The Importance of Public Opinion in Democracies.* Chicago, IL: University of Chicago.

Brown, P., Lauder, H., & Ashton, D. (2011). *The Global Auction: The Broken Promises of Education, Jobs, and Incomes.* Oxford and New York, NY: Oxford University Press.

Bunar, N. (2010a). The Controlled School Market and Urban Schools in Sweden. *Journal of School Choice*, 4, 47–73.

Bunar, N. (2010b). Choosing for Quality or Inequality: Current Perspectives on the Implementation of School Choice Policy in Sweden. *Journal of Education Policy*, 25(1), 1–18.

Bundesregierung (1974a). Aktionsprogramm "Berufliche Bildung" des Bundesministers für Arbeit und Sozialordnung, Bonn 1970, (Auszug) [1970]. In P. Pulte & K.-H. Vorbrücken (eds), *Berufliche Bildung:*

39 Modelle, Meinungen und Entwürfe zu einem Reformvorhaben (pp. 24–33). Opladen: Heggen-Verlag.

Bundesregierung (1974b). Sozialbericht 1972, Teil II, 2. Berufliche Bildung vom Mai 1972 [1972]. In P. Pulte & K.-H. Vorbrücken (eds), *Berufliche Bildung: 39 Modelle, Meinungen und Entwürfe zu einem Reformvorhaben* (pp. 16–23). Opladen: Heggen-Verlag.

Busemeyer, M. R. (2006). Der Kampf um knappe Mittel: Die Bestimmunsfaktoren der öffentlichen, privaten und sektoralen Bildungsausgaben im OECD-Länder Vergleich. *Politische Vierteljahresschrift*, 47(3), 393–418.

Busemeyer, M. R. (2007). The Determinants of Public Education Spending in 21 OECD Democracies, 1980–2001. *Journal of European Public Policy*, 14(4), 582–610.

Busemeyer, M. R. (2008). Bildung und die "neue" Sozialdemokratie: Eine Analyse aus der Sicht der vergleichenden Staatsausgabenforschung. *Politische Vierteljahresschrift*, 49(2), 283–308.

Busemeyer, M. R. (2009a). Asset Specificity, Institutional Complementarities and the Variety of Skill Regimes in Coordinated Market Economies. *Socio-Economic Review*, 7(3), 375–406.

Busemeyer, M. R. (2009b). Social Democrats and the New Partisan Politics of Public Investment in Education. *Journal of European Public Policy*, 16(1), 107–26.

Busemeyer, M. R. (2009c). *Wandel trotz Reformstau: Die Politik der beruflichen Bildung seit 1970*. Frankfurt and New York, NY: Campus.

Busemeyer, M. R. (2012a). Business as a Pivotal Actor in the Politics of Training Reform: Insights from the Case of Germany. *British Journal of Industrial Relations*, 50(4), 690–713.

Busemeyer, M. R. (2012b). Inequality and the Political Economy of Education: An Analysis of Individual Preferences in OECD Countries. *Journal of European Social Policy*, 22(3), 219–40.

Busemeyer, M. R. (2012c). *Reformperspektiven der beruflichen Bildung: Erkenntnisse aus dem internationalen Vergleich*. Bonn and Berlin: Friedrich-Ebert Stiftung.

Busemeyer, M. R. (2013). Education Funding and Individual Preferences for Redistribution. *European Sociological Review*, 29(6), 1122–33.

Busemeyer, M. R. & Iversen, T. (2012). Collective Skill Systems, Wage Bargaining, and Labor Market Stratification. In M. R. Busemeyer & C. Trampusch (eds), *The Political Economy of Collective Skill Formation* (pp. 205–33). Oxford and New York, NY: Oxford University Press.

Busemeyer, M. R. & Nikolai, R. (2010). Education. In H. Obinger, C. Pierson, F. G. Castles, S. Leibfried, & J. Lewis (eds), *The Oxford Handbook of the Welfare State* (pp. 494–508). Oxford and New York, NY: Oxford University Press.

Busemeyer, M. R. & Schlicht-Schmälzle, R. (2014). Partisan Power, Economic Coordination and Variations in Vocational Training Systems in Europe. *European Journal of Industrial Relations*, 20(1), 55–71.

Busemeyer, M. R. & Trampusch, C. (2011). Review Article: Comparative Political Science and the Study of Education. *British Journal of Political Science*, 41(2), 413–43.

Busemeyer, M. R. & Trampusch, C. (2012). Introduction: The Comparative Political Economy of Collective Skill Formation. In M. R. Busemeyer & C. Trampusch (eds), *The Political Economy of Collective Skill Formation* (pp. 3–38). Oxford and New York, NY: Oxford University Press.

Busemeyer, M. R., Goerres, A., & Weschle, S. (2009). Attitudes towards Redistributive Spending in an Era of Demographic Ageing: The Rival Pressures from Age and Income in 14 OECD Countries. *Journal of European Social Policy*, 19(3), 195–212.

Busemeyer, M. R., Cattaneo, M. A., & Wolter, S. C. (2011). Individual Preferences for Vocational vs. Academic Education: Microlevel Evidence for the Case of Switzerland. *Journal of European Social Policy*, 21(3), 253–73.

Campbell, A. (2002). Self-Interest, Social Security, and the Distinctive Participation Patterns of Senior Citizens. *American Political Science Review*, 96(3), 565–74.

Campbell, J. L. & Pedersen, O. K. (2007). The Varieties of Capitalism and Hybrid Success: Denmark in the Global Economy. *Comparative Political Studies*, 40(3), 307–32.

Castles, F. G. (1982). The Impact of Parties on Public Expenditure. In F. G. Castles (ed.), *The Impact of Parties: Politics and Policies in Democratic Capitalist States* (pp. 21–96). London: Sage.

Castles, F. G. (1989). Explaining Public Education Expenditure in OECD Nations. *European Journal of Political Research*, 17, 431–48.

Castles, F. G. (1998). *Comparative Public Policy: Patterns of Post-War Transformation*. Cheltenham: Edward Elgar.

Castles, F. G. (2013). The Real Issue for Future Comparative Policy Research: Does Government Matter? In K. Armingeon (ed.), *Staatstätigkeiten, Parteien und Demokratie: Festschrift für Manfred G. Schmidt* (pp. 185–204). Wiesbaden: VS Verlag für Sozialwissenschaften.

Cattaneo, M. A. & Wolter, S. C. (2007). Are the Elderly a Threat to Educational Expenditures? CESifo Working Paper, 2089.

Cheung, S. Y. & Egerton, M. (2007). Great Britain: Higher Education Expansion and Reform – Changing Educational Inequalities. In Y. Shavit, R. Arum, A. Gamoran & G. Menahem (eds), *Stratification in Higher Education: A Comparative Study* (pp. 195–219). Standford, CA: Standford University Press.

Chitty, C. (2004). *Education Policy in Britain*. Houndmills, Basingstoke, Hampshire, and New York, NY: Palgrave Macmillan.

Clark, B. R. (1983). *The Higher Education System: Academic Organization in Cross-National Perspective*. Berkeley, CA: University of California Press.

Coffield, F. (1992). Training and Enterprise Councils: The Last Throw of Voluntarism? *Policy Studies*, 13(4), 11–32.

Corina, J. (1975). Planning and the British Labour Market: Incomes and Manpower Policy, 1965–70. In J. Hayward & M. Watson (eds), *Planning, Politics and Public Policy: The British, French and Italian Experience* (pp. 177–201). London and New York, NY: Cambridge University Press.

Corneo, G. & Grüner, H. P. (2002). Individual Preferences for Political Redistribution. *Journal of Public Economics*, 83, 83–107.

Crouch, C. (1992). The Dilemmas of Vocational Training Policy: Some Comparative Lessons. *Policy Studies*, 13(4), 33–48.

Crouch, C. (1993). *Industrial Relations and European State Traditions*. Oxford: Clarendon Press.

Crouch, C., Finegold, D., & Sako, M. (1999). *Are Skills the Answer? The Political Economy of Skill Creation in Advanced Industrial Countries*. Oxford and New York, NY: Oxford University Press.

Culpepper, P. D. (2003). *Creating Cooperation: How States Develop Human Capital in Europe*. Ithaca, NY and London: Cornell University Press.

Culpepper, P. D. (2007). Small States and Skill Specificity: Austria, Switzerland, and Interemployer Cleavages in Coordinated Capitalism. *Comparative Political Studies*, 40(6), 611–37.

Culpepper, P. D. (2010). *Quiet Politics and Business Power: Corporate Control in Europe and Japan*. Cambridge and New York, NY: Cambridge University Press.

Cusack, T., Iversen, T., & Rehm, P. (2006). Risks at Work: The Demand and Supply Sides of Government Redistribution. *Oxford Review of Economic Policy*, 22(3), 365–89.

Cusack, T. R., Iversen, T., & Soskice, D. (2007). Economic Interests and the Origins of Electoral Systems. *American Political Science Review*, 101(3), 373–91.

Deeg, R. & Jackson, G. (2006). How Many Varieties of Capitalism? Comparing the Comparative Institutonal Analyses of Capitalist Diversity. MPIfG Discussion Paper 06(2).

Deissinger, T. & Hellwig, S. (2005). Apprenticeships in Germany: Modernising the Dual System. *Education + Training*, 47(4/5), 312–24.

Deutscher Bildungsrat. (1991). Empfehlungen der Bildungskommission: Zur Verbesserung der Lehrlingsausbildung [1969]. In G. Pätzold (ed.), *Quellen und Dokumente zur betrieblichen Berufsbildung 1945–1990, 2. Halbband* (pp. 487–92). Köln and Wien: Böhlau Verlag.

Deutscher Bundestag. (1989). Unterrichtung durch die Bundesregierung: Berufsbildungsbericht 1989, BT-Drucksache 11/4442.

Diamond, P. & Liddle, R. (2012). Aftershock: The post-crisis social investment welfare state in Europe. In N. Morel, B. Palier & J. Palme (eds), *Towards a Social Investment Welfare State? Ideas, Policies and Challenges* (pp. 285–308). Bristol and Chicago, IL: Policy Press.

DIHT and DIuH (1958). *Keine Experimente in der Berufsbildung: Eine Äußerung des Deutschen Industrie- und Handelstages zu wichtigen Gegenwartsfragen*. Bonn: DIHT.

Dingeldey, I. (1996). Wandel gewerkschaftlicher Strategien in der britischen Berufsbildungspolitik der 1980er und 1990er Jahre. *Politische Vierteljahresschrift*, 37(4), 687–712.

Dobbins, M. & Martens, K. (2011). Towards an Education Approach à la Finlandaise? French Education Policy after PISA. *Journal of Education Policy*, 27(1), 23–43.

Dore, R. & Sako, M. (1998). *How the Japanese Learn to Work* (2nd edn). London and New York, NY: Routledge.

Easton, D. (1965). *A Systems Analysis of Political Life*. New York, NY: John Wiley & Sons.

Ebner, C. (2013). *Erfolgreich in den Arbeitsmarkt? Die duale Berufsausbildung im internationalen Vergleich*. Frankfurt and New York, NY: Campus.

Ebner, C. & Nikolai, R. (2010). Duale oder schulische Berufsausbildung? Entwicklungen und Weichenstellungen in Deutschland, Österreich und der Schweiz. *Swiss Political Science Review*, 16(4), 617–48.

Edelstein, B. & Nikolai, R. (2013). Strukturwandel im Sekundarbereich. Determinanten schulpolitischer Reformprozesse in Sachsen und Hamburg. *Zeitschrift für Pädagogik*, 59(4), 482–94.

Ellwein, T. (1998). Die deutsche Gesellschaft und ihr Bildungswesen: Interessenartikulation und Bildungsdiskussion. In C. Führ & C.-L. Furck (eds), *Handbuch der deutschen Bildungsgeschichte: Band VI, 1945 bis zur Gegenwart, Erster Teilband: Bundesrepublik Deutschland* (pp. 87–109). München: Verlag C.H. Beck.

Elzinga, A. (1993). Universities, research and the transformation of the State in Sweden. In S. Rothblatt & B. Wittrock (eds), *The European and American university since 1800: Historical and sociological essays* (pp. 191–233). Cambridge and New York, NY: Cambridge University Press.

Emmenegger, P. (2009). Specificity vs. Replaceability: The Relationship between Skills and Preferences for Job Security Regulations. *Socio-Economic Review*, 7(3), 407–30.

Erk, J. (2003). Federal Germany and Its Non-Federal Society: Emergence of an All-German Educational Policy in a System of Exclusive Provincial Jurisdiction. *Canadian Journal of Political Science*, 36(2), 295–317.

Esping-Andersen, G. (1990). *The Three Worlds of Welfare Capitalism*. Cambridge: Polity Press.

Esping-Andersen, G. (1999). *Social Foundations of Postindustrial Economies*. Oxford and New York, NY: Oxford University Press.

Esping-Andersen, G. (2002). *Why We Need a New Welfare State*. Oxford and New York, NY: Oxford University Press.

Estevez-Abe, M., Iversen, T., & Soskice, D. (2001). Social Protection and the Formation of Skills: A Reinterpretation of the Welfare State. In P. A. Hall & D. Soskice (eds), *Varieties of Capitalism: The Institutional Foundations of Comparative Advantage* (pp. 145–83). Oxford and New York, NY: Oxford University Press.

Evans, B. (1992). *The Politics of the Training Market: From Manpower Services Commission to Training and Enterprise Councils*. London and New York, NY: Routledge.

Faulstich, P. (1977). *Interessenkonflikte um die Berufsbildung: Das Verhältnis von gesellschaftlichen Interessenstrukturen und staatlicher Bildungspolitik*. Weinheim and Basel: Beltz Verlag.

Fenwick, I. G. K. (1976). *The Comprehensive School 1944–1970: The Politics of Secondary School Reorganisation*. London: Methuen.

Fernandez, R. & Rogerson, R. (1995). On the Political Economy of Education Subsidies. *Review of Economic Studies*, 62(2), 249–62.

Ferrera, M. (1996). The "Southern Model" of Welfare in Social Europe. *Journal of European Social Policy*, 6(1), 17–37.

Finegold, D. & Soskice, D. (1988). The Failure of Training in Britain: Analysis and Prescription. *Oxford Review of Economic Policy*, 4(3), 21–53.

Finn, D. (1987). *Training Without Jobs: New Deals and Broken Promises: From Raising the School Leaving Age to the Youth Training Scheme*. Houndmills, Basingstoke, Hampshire, and London: Macmillan Education.

Finseraas, H. (2009). Income Inequality and Demand for Redistribution: A Multilevel Analysis of European Public Opinion. *Scandinavian Political Studies*, 32(1), 94–119.

Fleckenstein, T., Saunders, A. M., & Seeleib-Kaiser, M. (2011). The Dual Transformation of Social Protection and Human Capital: Comparing Britain and Germany. *Comparative Political Studies*, 44(12), 1622–50.

Fong, C. (2001). Social Preferences, Self-Interest, and the Demand for Redistribution. *Journal of Public Economics*, 82, 225–46.

Fraile, M. & Ferrer, M. (2005). Explaining the Determinants of Public Supports for Cuts in Unemployment Benefits Spending across OECD countries. *Internatonal Sociology*, 20(4), 459–81.

Fuller, A. & Unwin, L. (2003). Creating a "Modern Apprenticeship": A Critique of the UK's Multi-Sector, Social Inclusion Approach. *Journal of Education and Work*, 16(1), 5–25.

Fuller, A. & Unwin, L. (2009). Change and Continuity in Apprenticeship: The Resilience of a Model of Learning. *Journal of Education and Work*, 22(5), 405–16.

Fuller, A. & Unwin, L. (2011). Vocational Education and Training in the Spotlight: Back to the Future for the UK's Coalition Government? *London Review of Education*, 9(2), 191–204.

Gangl, M. (2003). The Structure of Labour Market Entry in Europe: A Typological Analysis. In W. Müller & M. Gangl (eds), *Transitions from Education to Work in Europe: The Integration of Youth into EU Labour Markets* (pp. 107–28). Oxford: Oxford University Press.

Giddens, A. (1998). *The Third Way: The Revival of Social Democracy*. Cambridge: Polity Press.

Gingrich, J. R. (2011). *Making Markets in the Welfare State: The Politics of Varying Market Reforms*. Cambridge and New York, NY: Cambridge University Press.

Glassmann, U. (2014). Social Rights, Family Networks and Regional Varieties of Capitalism in Mediterranean Countries. *Regional Studies*, available from http://www.tandfonline.com/doi/abs/10.1080/00343404.2013.871629?queryID=%24%7BresultBean.queryID%7D#.U7WYMPldWSo (last accessed April 30, 2014).

Gleeson, D. & Keep, E. (2004). Voice without Accountability: The Changing Relationship between Employers, the State and Education in England. *Oxford Review of Education*, 30(1), 37–63.

Goldin, C. & Katz, L. F. (2008). *The Race between Education and Technology*. Cambridge: Belknap Press.

Gordon, P., Aldrich, R., & Dean, D. (1991). *Education and Policy in England in the Twentieth Century*. London: Woburn Press.

Gospel, H. F. (1994). The Survival of Apprenticeship Training: A British, American, Australian Comparison. *British Journal of Industrial Relations*, 32(4), 505–22.

Gospel, H. F. (1995). The Decline of Apprenticeship Training in Britain. *Industrial Relations Journal*, 26(1), 32–44.
Gospel, H. F. & Fuller, A. (1998). The Modern Apprenticeship: New Wine in Old Bottles? *Human Resource Management Journal*, 8(1), 5–22.
Graf, L., Lassnigg, L., & Powell, J. J. W. (2012). Austrian Corporatism and Institutional Change in the Relationship between Apprenticeship Training and School-based VET. In M. R. Busemeyer & C. Trampusch (eds), *The Political Economy of Collective Skill Formation* (pp. 150–78). Oxford and New York, NY: Oxford University Press.
Graham, A. (1997). The UK 1979–95: Myths and Realities of Conservative Capitalism. In C. Crouch & W. Streeck (eds), *Political Economy of Modern Capitalism: Mapping Convergence and Diversity* (pp. 117–32). London, Thousand Oaks, CA, and New Delhi: Sage Publications.
Greinert, W.-D. (1998). *Das "deutsche System" der Berufsausbildung: Tradition, Organisation, Funktion* (3rd edn). Baden-Baden: Nomos.
Greinert, W.-D. (2006). Geschichte der Berufsausbildung in Deutschland. In R. Arnold & A. Lipsmeier (eds), *Handbuch der Berufsbildung* (pp. 499–508). Wiesbaden: VS Verlag für Sozialwissenschaften.
Hacker, J. S. (2004). Privatizing Risk without Privatizing the Welfare State: The Hidden Politics of Social Policy Retrenchment in the United States. *American Political Science Review*, 98(2), 243–60.
Hall, P. A. (1992). The Movement from Keynesianism to Monetarism: Instituitonal Analysis and British Economic Policy in the 1970s. In S. Steinmo, K. Thelen & F. Longstreth (eds), *Structuring Politics: Historical Institutionalism in Comparative Perspective* (pp. 90–113). Cambridge and New York, NY: Cambridge University Press.
Hall, P. A. & Gingerich, D. W. (2004). "Spielarten des Kapitalismus" und institutionelle Komplementaritäten in der Makroökonomie – Eine empirische Analyse. *Berliner Journal für Soziologie*, 14(1), 5–32.
Hall, P. A. & Gingerich, D. W. (2009). Varieties of Capitalism and Institutional Complementarities in the Political Economy: An Empirical Analysis. *British Journal of Political Science*, 39, 449–82.
Hall, P. A. & Soskice, D. (2001). An Introduction to Varieties of Capitalism. In P. A. Hall & D. Soskice (eds), *Varieties of Capitalism: The Institutional Foundations of Comparative Advantage* (pp. 1–68). Oxford and New York, NY: Oxford University Press.
Hall, P. A. & Taylor, R. C. R. (1996). Political Science and the Three New Institutionalisms. *Political Studies*, 44(5), 936–57.
Hall, P. A. & Thelen, K. (2009). Institutional Change in Varieties of Capitalism. *Socio-Economic Review*, 7(1), 7–34.

Hancké, B. (2009). *Debating Varieties of Capitalism: A Reader*. Oxford and New York, NY: Oxford University Press.

Härnqvist, K. (1989). Comprehensiveness and Social Equality. In S. J. Ball & S. Larsson (eds), *The Struggle for Democratic Education: Equality and Participation in Sweden* (pp. 18–31). New York, NY, Philadelphia, PA, and London: The Falmer Press.

Harrison, N. (2011). Have the Changes Introduced by the 2004 Higher Education Act Made Higher Education Admissions in England Wider and Fairer? *Journal of Education Policy*, 26(3), 449–68.

Hasenfeld, Y. & Rafferty, J. A. (1989). The Determinants of Public Attitudes Toward the Welfare State. *Social Forces*, 67(4), 1027–48.

Hassel, A. (2007). What Does Business Want? Labour Market Reforms in CMEs and Its Problems. In B. Hancké, M. Rhodes & M. Thatcher (eds), *Beyond Varieties of Capitalism: Conflict, Contradictions, and Complementarities in the European Economy* (pp. 253–77). Oxford and New York, NY: Oxford University Press.

Hatcher, R. (2011). The Conservative-Liberal Democrat Coalition Government's "Free Schools" in England. *Educational Review*, 63(4), 485–503.

Häusermann, S. (2010). *The Politics of Welfare State Reform in Continental Europe: Modernization in Hard Times*. Cambridge and New York, NY: Cambridge University Press.

Häusermann, S., Picot, G., & Geering, D. (2013). Review Article: Rethinking Party Politics and the Welfare State – Recent Advances in the Literature. *British Journal of Political Science*, 43(1), 221–40.

Hega, G. M. & Hokenmaier, K. G. (2002). The Welfare State and Education: A Comparison of Social and Educational Policy in Advanced Industrial Societies. *German Policy Studies*, 2(1), 143–73.

Heidenheimer, A. J. (1973). The Politics of Public Education, Health and Welfare in the USA and Western Europe: How Growth and Reform Potentials Have Differed. *British Journal of Political Science*, 3(3), 315–40.

Heidenheimer, A. J. (1981). Education and Social Security Entitlements in Europe and America. In P. Flora & A. J. Heidenheimer (eds), *The Development of Welfare States in Europe and America* (pp. 269–304). New Brunswick, NJ and London: Transaction Books.

Heidenheimer, A. J. (1996). Throwing Money and Heaving Bodies: Heuristic Callisthenics for Comparative Policy Buffs. In L. M. Imbeau & R. D. McKinlay (eds), *Comparing Government Activity* (pp. 13–25). Houndmills, London: Macmillan.

Heidenheimer, A. J. (1997). *Disparate Ladders: Why School and University Policies Differ in Germany, Japan, and Switzerland*. New Brunswick, NJ and London: Transaction Publishers.

Heidenheimer, A. J., Heclo, H., & Adams, C. T. (1990). *Comparative Public Policy: The Politics of Social Choice in America, Europe, and Japan* (3rd edn). New York, NY: St. Martin's Press.

Hemerijck, A. (2012). Two or Three Waves of Welfare State Transformation? In N. Morel, B. Palier & J. Palme (eds), *Towards a Social Investment Welfare State? Ideas, Policies and Challenges* (pp. 33–60). Bristol and Chicago, IL: Policy Press.

Hepp, G. F. (2011). *Bildungspolitik in Deutschland: Eine Einführung*. Wiesbaden: VS Verlag für Sozialwissenschaften.

Herrlitz, H.-G., Hopf, W., & Titze, H. (1998). *Deutsche Schulgeschichte von 1800 bis zur Gegenwart: Eine Einführung, mit einem Kapitel über die DDR von Ernst Cloer*. Weinheim and München: Juventa Verlag.

Hibbs, D. A. (1977). Political Parties and Macroeconomic Policy. *American Political Science Review*, 71(4), 1467–87.

Hickox, M. & Lyon, E. S. (1998). Vocationalism and Schooling: The British and Swedish Experiences Compared. *British Journal of Sociology of Education*, 19(1), 25–37.

Hilbert, J., Südmersen, H., & Weber, H. (1990). *Berufsbildungspolitik: Geschichte – Organisation – Neuordnung*. Opladen: Leske + Budrich.

Hillmert, S. & Jacob, M. (2002). Social Inequality in Higher Education: Is Vocational Training a Pathway Leading to or Away from University? *European Sociological Review*, 19(3), 319–34.

Hudson, C. & Lidström, A. (2002). National School Policy Changes in Britain and Sweden. In C. Hudson & A. Lidström (eds), *Local Education Policies: Comparing Sweden and Britain* (pp. 27–64). Houndmills, Basingstoke, Hampshire, and New York, NY: Palgrave.

Husén, T. (1965). Educational Change in Sweden. *Comparative Education*, 1(3), 181–91.

Iversen, T. (2005). *Capitalism, Democracy, and Welfare*. Cambridge: Cambridge University Press.

Iversen, T. & Cusack, T. R. (2000). The Causes of Welfare State Expansion: Deindustrialization or Globalization? *World Politics*, 52, 313–49.

Iversen, T. & Soskice, D. (2001). An Asset Theory of Social Policy Preferences. *American Political Science Review*, 95(4), 875–93.

Iversen, T. & Soskice, D. (2006). Electoral Institutions and the Politics of Coalitions: Why Some Democracies Redistribute More Than Others. *American Political Science Review*, 100(2), 165–81.

Iversen, T. & Soskice, D. (2009). Distribution and Redistribution: The Shadow of the Nineteenth Century. *World Politics*, 61(3), 438–86.

Iversen, T. & Stephens, J. D. (2008). Partisan Politics, the Welfare State, and Three Worlds of Human Capital Formation. *Comparative Political Studies*, 41(4–5), 600–37.

Jacobs, A. M. (2008). The Politics of When: Redistribution, Investment and Policy Making for the Long Term. *British Journal of Political Science*, 38, 193–220.

Jaeger, M. M. (2006). Welfare Regimes and Attitudes Towards Redistribution: The Regime Hypothesis Revisited. *European Sociological Review*, 22, 157–70.

Jaeger, M. M. (2007). Economic and Social Returns to Educational Choices: Extending the Utility Function. *Rationality and Society*, 19(4), 451–83.

Jaeger, M. M. (2009). United but Divided: Welfare Regimes and the Level and Variance in Public Support for Redistribution. *European Sociological Review*, 25(6), 723–37.

Jakobi, A. P., Martens, K., & Wolf, K. D. (2010). Introduction: A Governance Perspective on Education Policy. In A. P. Jakobi, K. Martens & K. D. Wolf (eds), *Education in Political Science: Discovering a Neglected Field* (pp. 1–20). London and New York, NY: Routledge.

Jakobsen, T. G. (2010). Public versus Private: The Conditional Effect of State Policy and Institutional Trust on Mass Opinion. *European Sociological Review*, 26(3), 307–18.

Jensen, C. (2010). Issue Compensation and Right-Wing Government Social Spending. *European Journal of Political Research*, 49, 282–99.

Jensen, C. (2011). Capitalist Systems, De-industrialization, and the Politics of Public Education. *Comparative Political Studies*, 44(4), 412–35.

Jo, N. K. (2011). Between the Cultural Foundations of Welfare and Welfare Attitudes: The Possibility of an In-Between Level Conception of Culture for the Cultural Analysis of the Welfare. *Journal of European Social Policy*, 21(1), 5–19.

Johnson, C. (1995). Die Rolle intermediärer Organisationen beim Wandel des Berufsbildungssystems. In H. Wiesenthal (ed.), *Einheit als Interessenpolitik: Studien zur sektoralen Transformation Ostdeutschlands* (pp. 126–59). Frankfurt and New York, NY: Campus.

Jonsson, J. O. & Erikson, R. (2007). Sweden: Why Educational Expansion Is Not Such a Great Strategy for Equality – Theory and Evidence. In Y. Shavit, R. Arum, A. Gamoran, & G. Menahem (eds), *Stratification in Higher Education: A Comparative Study* (pp. 113–39). Stanford, CA: Stanford University Press.

Kalyvas, S. N. & Van Kersbergen, K. (2010). Christian Democracy. *Annual Review of Political Science*, 13, 183–209.

Kamm, R. & Köller, M. (2010). Hochschulsteuerung im deutschen Bildungsföderalismus. *Swiss Political Science Review*, 16(4), 649–86.

Kangas, O. (1997). Self-Interest and the Common Good: The Impact of Norms, Selfishness and Context in Social Policy Opinions. *Journal of Socio-Economics*, 26(5), 475–94.

Kauder, B. & Potrafke, N. (2013). Government Ideology and Tuition Fee Policy: Evidence from the German States. CESifo Working Paper 4205.
Kaufman, R. R. & Segura-Ubiergo, A. (2001). Globalization, Domestic Politics, and Social Spending in Latin America: A Time-Series Cross-Section Analysis, 1973–97. *World Politics*, 53(July), 553–87.
Keep, E. (1999). UK's VET Policy and the "Third Way": Following a High Skills Trajectory or Running Up a Dead End Street? *Journal of Education and Work*, 12(3), 323–46.
Keep, E. (2006). State Control of the English Education and Training System – Playing with the Biggest Train Set in the World. *Journal of Vocational Education and Training*, 58(1), 47–64.
Keep, E. & Mayhew, K. (2010). Moving beyond Skills as a Social and Economic Panacea. *Work, Employment and Society*, 24(3), 565–77.
Kenworthy, L. & Pontusson, J. (2005). Rising Inequality and the Politics of Redistribution in Affluent Countries. *Perspectives on Politics*, 3(3), 449–71.
King, D. (1993). The Conservatives and Training Policy 1979–1992: From a Tripartite to a Neoliberal Regime. *Political Studies*, 41(2), 214–35.
King, D. (1995). *Actively Seeking Work? The Politics of Unemployment and Welfare Policy in the United States and Great Britain*. Chicago, IL: University of Chicago Press.
King, D. (1997). Employers, Training Policy, and the Tenacity of Voluntarism in Britain. *Twentieth Century British History*, 8(3), 383–411.
King, D. & Wickham-Jones, M. (1998). Training Without the State? New Labour and Labour Markets. *Policy & Politics*, 26(4), 439–55.
Kittel, B. (2006). A Crazy Methodology? On the Limits of Macro-Quantitative Social Science Research. *International Sociology*, 12(5), 647–77.
Kittel, B. & Obinger, H. (2003). Political Parties, Institutions, and the Dynamics of Social Expenditure in Times of Austerity. *Journal of European Public Policy*, 10, 20–45.
Kittel, B. & Winner, H. (2002). How Reliable is Pooled Analysis in Political Economy? The Globalization-Welfare State Nexus Revisited. MPIfG Discussion Paper 02/3.
Kittel, B. & Winner, H. (2005). How Reliable is Pooled Analysis in Political Economy? The Globalization-Welfare State Nexus Revisited. *European Journal of Political Research*, 44, 269–93.
Klitgaard, M. B. (2008). School Vouchers and the New Politics of the Welfare State. *Governance*, 21(4), 479–98.
Knight, C. (1990). *The Making of Tory Education Policy in Post-War Britain 1950–1986*. London, New York, NY, and Philadelphia, PA: The Falmer Press.

Korpi, W. (1983). *The Democratic Class Struggle*. London and Boston, MA: Routledge.
Korpi, W. (2006). Power Resources and Employer-Centered Approaches in Explanations of Welfare States and Varieties of Capitalism: Protagonists, Consenters, and Antagonists. *World Politics*, 58(2), 167–206.
Kuda, E. & Mignon, U. (1982). *Berufliche Bildung: Situation Konflikte Lösungen*. Köln: Bund-Verlag.
Kwon, H. Y. & Pontusson, J. (2010). Globalization, Labour Power and Partisan Politics Revisited. *Socio-Economic Review*, 8(2), 251–81.
Lawton, D. (1992). *Education and Politics in the 1990s: Conflict or Consensus?* London and Washington, DC: The Falmer Press.
Lawton, D. (2005). *Education and Labour Party Ideologies 1900–2001 and Beyond*. London and New York, NY: RoutledgeFalmer.
Lee, D. (1989). The Transformation of Training and the Transformation of Work in Britain. In S. Wood (ed.), *The Transformation of Work? Skill, Flexibility and the Labour Process* (pp. 156–70). London, Boston, MA, Sydney, and Wellington: Unwin Hyman.
Lehmbruch, G. (1979). Liberal Coporatism and Party Government. In P. C. Schmitter & G. Lehmbruch (eds), *Trends Toward Corporatist Intermediation* (pp. 147–83). Beverly Hils, CA and London: Sage.
Lehmbruch, G. (2000). *Parteienwettbewerb im Bundesstaat: Regelsysteme und Spannungslagen im politischen System der Bundesrepublik Deutschland*. Wiesbaden: Westdeutscher Verlag.
Lemke, H. (1969). Zur Verabschiedung des Berufsbildungsgesetzes: Restauration statt Reform. *Blätter für deutsche und internationale Politik*, 14(12).
Levy, G. (2005). The Politics of Public Provision of Education. *Quarterly Journal of Economics*, 120(4), 1507–34.
Lieberman, E. S. (2005). Nested Analysis as a Mixed-Method Strategey for Comparative Research. *American Political Science Review*, 99(3), 435–52.
Lijphart, A. (1999). *Patterns of Democracy*. New Haven, CT: Yale University Press.
Lindblad, S. & Wallin, E. (1993). On Transitions of Power, Democracy and Education in Sweden. *Journal of Curriculum Studies*, 25(1), 77–88.
Lindert, P. H. (2004). *Growing Public: Social Spending and Economic Growth since the Eighteenth Century, Volume I*. Cambridge and New York, NY: Cambridge University Press.
Lipsmeier, A. (1992). Der historische Kontext des Berufsausbildungssystems: wichtige Reformen und berufsbildungspolitische Diskussionen seit dem Berufsbildungsgesetz. In R. Koch & J. Reuling (eds), *Modernisierung, Regulierung und Anpassungsfähigkeit des Berufsausbildungssystems*

der Bundesrepublik Deutschland, Berichte zur beruflichen Bildung, Heft 170 (pp. 13–27). Berlin and Bonn: Bundesinstitut für Berufsbildung.

Lipsmeyer, C. S. & Nordstrom, T. (2003). East versus West: Comparing Political Attitudes and Welfare Preferences across European Societies. *Journal of European Public Policy,* 10(3), 339–64.

Lundahl, L. (1990). New Variations on Old Themes: The Swedish Conservative Party and the Battle over Comprehensive Education 1900–1985. *Journal of Education Policy,* 5(2), 157–66.

Lundahl, L. (1997). A Common Denominator? Swedish Employers, Trade Unions and Vocational Education. *International Journal of Training and Development,* 1(2), 91–103.

Lundahl, L. (1998). Still the Stepchild of Swedish Educational Politics? Vocational Education and Training in Sweden in the 1990s. In L. Lundahl & T. Sander (eds), *Vocational Education and Training in Germany and Sweden: Strategies of Control and Movements of Resistance and Opposition* (pp. 39–53). Umeå: TNTEE Editorial Office.

Lundahl, L. (2002). Sweden: Decentralization, Deregulation, Quasi-Markets – And Then What? *Journal of Education Policy,* 17(6), 687–97.

Lundahl, L., Erixon Arreman, I., Lundström, U., & Rönnberg, L. (2010). Setting Things Right? Swedish Upper Secondary School Reform in a 40-Year Perspective. *European Journal of Education,* 45(1), 46–59.

Lupu, N. & Pontusson, J. (2011). The Structure of Inequality and the Politics of Redistribution. *American Political Science Review,* 105(2), 316–36.

Lynch, L. M. (1994). Payoffs to Alternative Training Strategies at Work. In R. B. Freeman (ed.), *Working under Different Rules* (pp. 63–95). New York, NY: Russell Sage Foundation.

Mäding, H. (1985). Die Finanzkrise und das Scheitern der Fortschreibung des Bildungsgesamtplanes. In G. Brinkmann (ed.), *Probleme der Bildungsfinanzierung* (pp. 209–33). Berlin: Dunckler & Humblot.

Mahoney, J. & Thelen, K. (2010). A Theory of Gradual Institutional Change. In J. Mahoney & K. Thelen (eds), *Explaining Institutional Change: Ambiguity, Agency, and Power* (pp. 1–37). Cambridge and New York, NY: Cambridge University Press.

Manow, P. & Van Kersbergen, K. (2009). Religion and the Western Welfare State – The Theoretical Context. In K. Van Kersbergen & P. Manow (eds), *Religion, Class Coalitions, and Welfare States* (pp. 1–38). Cambridge and New York, NY: Cambridge University Press.

Mares, I. (2001). Firms and the Welfare State: When, Why, and How Does Social Policy Matter to Employers? In P. A. Hall & D. Soskice (eds),

Varieties of Capitalism: The Institutional Foundations of Comparative Advantage (pp. 184–212). Oxford and New York, NY: Oxford University Press.

Mares, I. (2003). *The Politics of Social Risk: Business and Welfare State Development*. Cambridge: Cambridge University Press.

Marsden, D. & Ryan, P. (1990). Institutional Aspects of Youth Employment and Training Policy in Britain. *British Journal of Industrial Relations*, 28(3), 351–69.

Marsden, D. & Ryan, P. (1991). Initial Training, Labour Market Structure and Public Policy: Intermediate Skills in British and German Industry. In P. Ryan (ed.), *International Comparisons of Vocational Education and Training for Intermediate Skills* (pp. 251–285). London, New York, NY, and Philadelphia, PA: The Falmer Press.

Marshall, T. H. (1964). *Class, Citizenship, and Social Development*. Garden City, NY: Doubleday.

Martin, C. J. (2006). Sectional Parties, Divided Business. *Studies in American Political Development*, 20, 160–84.

Martin, C. J. (2012). Political Institutions and the Origins of Collective Skill Formation Systems. In M. R. Busemeyer & C. Trampusch (eds), *The Political Economy of Collective Skill Formation* (pp. 41–67). Oxford and New York, NY: Oxford University Press.

Martin, C. J. & Knudsen, J. S. (2010). Scenes from a Mall: Retail Training and the Social Exclusion of Low-Skilled Workers. *Regulation & Governance*, 2010(4), 345–64.

Martin, C. J. & Swank, D. (2008). The Political Origins of Coordinated Capitalism: Business Organizations, Party Systems and State Structure in the Age of Innocence. *American Political Science Review*, 102(2), 181–98.

Martin, C. J. & Swank, D. (2011). Gonna Party like it's 1899: Party Systems and the Origins of Varieties of Coordination. *World Politics*, 63(1), 78–114.

Martin, C. J. & Swank, D. (2012). *The Political Construction of Business Interests: Coordination, Growth and Equality*. Cambridge and New York, NY: Cambridge University Press.

Martin, C. J. & Thelen, K. (2007). The State and Coordinated Capitalism: Contributions of the Public Sector to Social Solidarity in Postindustrial Societies. *World Politics*, 60(October), 1–36.

Mayhew, K., Deer, C., & Dua, M. (2004). The Move to Mass Higher Education in the UK: Many Questions and Some Answers. *Oxford Review of Education*, 30(1), 65–82.

Mayntz, R. & Scharpf, F. W. (1995). Steuerung und Selbstorganisation in staatsnahen Sektoren. In R. Mayntz & F. W. Scharpf (eds),

Gesellschaftliche Selbstregelung und politische Steuerung (pp. 9–38). Frankfurt and New York, NY: Campus.
Meltzer, A. H. & Richard, S. F. (1981). A Rational Theory of the Size of Government. *Journal of Political Economy*, 89(5), 914–27.
Merkel, W., Petring, A., Henkes, C., & Egle, C. (2006). *Social Democracy in Power: The Capacity to Reform*. Abingdon and New York, NY: Routledge.
Mettler, S. & Soss, J. (2004). The Consequences of Public Policy for Democratic Citizenship: Bridging Policy Studies and Mass Politics. *Perspectives on Politics*, 2(1), 55–73.
Meyer, J. W., Ramirez, F. O., & Soysal, Y. N. (1992). World Expansion of Mass Education, 1870–1980. *Sociology of Education*, 65(2), 128–49.
Mitter, W. (1991). Comprehensive Schools in Germany: Concepts, Developments and Issues. *European Journal of Education*, 26(2), 155–65.
Moene, K. O. & Wallerstein, M. (2001). Inequality, Social Insurance, and Redistribution. *American Political Science Review*, 95(4), 859–74.
Moene, K. O. & Wallerstein, M. (2003). Earnings Inequality and Welfare Spending: A Disaggregated Analysis. *World Politics*, 55(4), 485–516.
Mons, N. (2004). Politiques de decentralisation en éducation: Diversité internationale, legitimations théoriques et justifications empirique. *Revue française de pédagogie*, 146, 41–52.
Morel, N., Palier, B., & Palme, J. (2012). Beyond the Welfare State as We Knew It? In N. Morel, B. Palier & J. Palme (eds), *Towards a Social Investment Welfare State? Ideas, Policies and Challenges* (pp. 1–30). Bristol and Chicago, IL: Policy Press.
Morgan, K. J. (2012). Promoting Social Investment through Work-Family Policies: Which Nations Do It and Why? In N. Morel, B. Palier & J. Palme (eds), *Towards a Social Investment Welfare State? Ideas, Policies and Challenges* (pp. 153–77). Bristol and Chicago, IL: Policy Press.
Müller, W. & Gangl, M. (2003). The Transition from School to Work: A European Perspective. In W. Müller & M. Gangl (eds), *Transitions from Education to Work in Europe: The Integration of Youth into EU Labour Markets* (pp. 1–19). Oxford and New York, NY: Oxford University Press.
Müller, W. & Shavit, Y. (1998). The Institutional Embeddedness of the Stratification Process: A Comparative Study of Qualifications and Occupations in Thirteen Countries. In Y. Shavit & W. Müller (eds), *From School to Work: A Comparative Study of Educational Qualifications and Occupational Destinations* (pp. 1–48). Oxford: Clarendon Press.
Müller, W. C. & Strom, K. (1999). *Policy, Office, or Votes? How Political Parties in Western Europe Make Hard Decisions*. Cambridge and New York, NY: Cambridge University Press.

Nelson, M. (2012). Continued Collectivism: The Role of Trade Self-Management and the Social Democratic Party in Danish Vocational Education and Training. In M. R. Busemeyer & C. Trampusch (eds), *The Political Economy of Collective Skill Formation* (pp. 179–202). Oxford and New York, NY: Oxford University Press.

Nikolai, R. (2007). *Die Bildungsausgaben der Schweiz im intranationalen und internationalen Vergleich*. Berlin: dissertation.de.

Nikolai, R. & Ebner, C. (2012). The Link between Vocational and Higher Education in Switzerland, Austria and Germany. In M. R. Busemeyer & C. Trampusch (eds), *The Political Economy of Collective Skill Formation* (pp. 234–58). Oxford and New York, NY: Oxford University Press.

Nilsson, A. (2011). Apprenticeship in Decay? Sweden 1940–1965. *Bulletin of Institute of Vocational and Technical Education*, 8, 25–31.

Nilsson, L. (1983). Vocational Education in Swedish Secondary Schools: Trends and Reforms. *European Journal of Education*, 18(1), 31–43.

OECD. (2007). *Education at a Glance 2007: OECD Indicators*. Paris: OECD.

OECD. (2010). *PISA 2009 Results: Overcoming Social Background: Equity in Learning Opportunities and Outcomes*, Volume II. Paris: OECD.

OECD. (2012). *Education at a Glance 2012: OECD Indicators*. Paris: OECD.

Offe, C. (1975). *Berufsbildungsreform: Eine Fallstudie über Reformpolitik*. Frankfurt: Suhrkamp.

Opper, S. (1989). Sweden: The "Integrated" Upper Secondary School as Main Provider of Vocational Education. *European Journal of Education*, 24(2), 139–57.

Overesch, A. (2007). *Wie die Schulpolitik ihre Probleme (nicht) löst: Deutschland und Finnland im Vergleich*. Münster, New York, NY Munich, and Berlin: Waxmann.

Palier, B. (ed.). (2010). *A Long Goodbye to Bismarck? The Politics of Welfare Reform in Continental Europe*. Amsterdam: Amsterdam University Press.

Palier, B. & Thelen, K. (2010). Institutionalizing Dualism: Complementarities and Change in France and Germany. *Politics & Society*, 38(1), 119–48.

Papadakis, E. (1993). Class Interests, Class Politics and Welfare State Regimes. *British Journal of Sociology*, 44(2), 249–70.

Paulston, R. G. (1968). *Educational Change in Sweden: Planning and Accepting the Comprehensive School Reforms*. New York, NY: Teachers College Press.

Payne, J. & Keep, E. (2011). One Step Forward, Two Steps Back? Skills Policy in England under Coalition Government. *SKOPE Research Paper*, 102(July).
Perry, P. J. C. (1976). *The Evolution of British Manpower Policy from the Statute of Artificers 1563 to the Industrial Training Act 1964*. London: British Association for Commercial and Industrial Education.
Pfau-Effinger, B. (2005). Culture and Welfare State Policies: Reflections on a Complex Interrelation. *Journal of Social Policy*, 34(1), 3–20.
Pfeffer, F. T. (2008). Persistent Inequality in Educational Attainment and its Institutional Context. *European Sociological Review*, 24(5), 543–65.
Pierson, P. (1993). When Effect becomes Cause: Policy Feedback and Political Change. *World Politics*, 45(4), 595–628.
Pierson, P. (1994). *Dismantling the Welfare State? Reagan, Thatcher, and the Politics of Retrenchment*. Cambridge: Cambridge University Press.
Pierson, P. (1996). The New Politics of the Welfare State. *World Politics*, 48, 143–79.
Pierson, P. (2000). Increasing Returns, Path Dependence, and the Study of Politics. *American Political Science Review*, 94(2), 251–67.
Pierson, P. (ed.). (2001). *The New Politics of the Welfare State*. Oxford and New York, NY: Oxford University Press.
Pierson, P. (2004). *Politics in Time: History, Institutions, and Social Analysis*. Princeton, NJ and Oxford: Princeton University Press.
Pierson, P. (2005). The Study of Policy Development. *Journal of Policy History*, 17(1), 34–51.
Pilz, M. (2009). Initial Vocational Training from a Company Perspective: A Comparison of British and German In-House Training Cultures. *Vocations and Learning*, 2(1), 57–74.
Plümper, T. & Troeger, V. E. (2007). Efficient Estimation of Time-Invariant and Rarely Changing Variables in Finite Sample Panel Analyses with Unit Fixed Effects. *Political Analysis*, 15, 124–39.
Plümper, T., Troeger, V. E., & Manow, P. (2005). Panel Data Analysis in Comparative Politics: Linking Method to Theory. *European Journal of Political Research*, 44, 327–54.
Plutzer, E. & Berkman, M. (2005). The Graying of America and Support for Funding in the Nation's Schools. *Public Opinion Quarterly*, 69(1), 66–86.
Pontusson, J. & Rueda, D. (2010). The Politics of Inequality: Voter Mobilization and Left Parties in Advanced Industrial States. *Comparative Political Studies*, 43(6), 675–705.
Pontusson, J., Rueda, D., & Way, C. R. (2002). Comparative Political Economy of Wage Distribution: The Role of Partisanship and Labour Market Institutions. *British Journal of Political Science*, 32, 281–308.

Powell, J. J. W. & Solga, H. (2011). Why are Higher Education Participation Rates in Germany so Low? Institutional Barriers to Higher Education Expansion. *Journal of Education and Work*, 24(1–2), 49–68.

Raftery, A. E. & Hout, M. (1993). Maximally Maintained Inequality: Expansion, Reform, and Opportunity in Irish Education. *Sociology of Education*, 66(1), 41–62.

Rauh, C., Kirchner, A., & Kappe, R. (2011). Political Parties and Higher Education Spending: Who Favours Redistribution? *West European Politics*, 34(6), 1185–206.

Rehm, P. (2009). Risk and Redistribution: An Individual-Level Analysis. *Comparative Political Studies*, 42(7), 855–81.

Rehm, P. (2012). Social Policy by Popular Demand. *World Politics*, 63(2), 271–99.

Richard, D. (2012). *The Richard Review of Apprenticeships*. London: School for Startups.

Rohlfing, I. (2008). What You See and What You Get: Pitfalls and Principles of Nested Analysis in Comparative Research. *Comparative Political Studies*, 41(11), 1492–514.

Roller, E. (1999). Shrinking the Welfare State: Citizens' Attitudes towards Cuts in Social Spending in Germany in the 1990s. *German Politics*, 8(1), 21–39.

Rose, R. & Davies, P. L. (1994). *Inheritance in Public Policy: Change without Choice in Britain*. New Haven, CT: Yale University Press.

Rothstein, B. (1987). Corporatism and Reformism: The Social Democratic Institutionalization of Class Conflict. *Acta Sociologica*, 30(3–4), 295–311.

Rothstein, B. (1996). *The Social Democratic State: The Swedish Model and the Bureaucratic Problem of Social Reforms*. Pittsburgh, PA and London: University of Pittsburgh Press.

Rothstein, B. (1998). *Just Institutions Matter: The Moral and Political Logic of the Universal Welfare State*. Cambridge: Cambridge University Press.

Rueda, D. (2008). Left Government, Policy, and Corporatism: Explaining the Influence of Partisanship on Inequality. *World Politics*, 60(April), 349–89.

Rueda, D. & Pontusson, J. (2000). Wage Inequality and Varieties of Capitalism. *World Politics*, 52(3), 350–83.

Ryan, P. (2000). The Institutional Requirements of Apprenticeship: Evidence from Smaller EU Countries. *International Journal of Training and Development*, 4(1), 42–65.

Ryan, P. & Unwin, L. (2001). Apprenticeship in the British "Training Market." *National Institute Economic Review*, 178(October), 99–114.

Sabatier, P. (1991). Toward Better Theories of the Policy Process. *PS: Political Science and Politics*, 24(2), 147–56.
Scharpf, F. W. (1988). The Joint Decision Trap: Lessons from German Federalism and European Integration. *Public Administration*, 66, 239–78.
Scharpf, F. W. (1997). *Games Real Actors Play: Actor-Centered Institutionalism in Policy Research.* Boulder, CO: Weastview.
Scharpf, F. W. (2000). *Interaktionsformen: Akteurzentrierter Institutonalismus in der Politikforschung.* Opladen: Leske und Budrich.
Schlicht, R. (2010). *Determinanten der Bildungsungleichheit: Die Leistungsfähigkeit von Bildungssystemen im Vergleich der deutschen Bundesländer.* Wiesbaden: VS Verlag für Sozialwissenschaften.
Schmidt, M. G. (1980). *CDU und SPD an der Regierung: Ein Vergleich ihrer Politik in den Ländern.* Frankfurt and New York, NY: Campus Verlag.
Schmidt, M. G. (1982). *Wohlfahrtsstaatliche Politik unter bürgerlichen und sozialdemokratischen Regierungen: Ein internationaler Vergleich.* Frankfurt and New York, NY: Campus.
Schmidt, M. G. (1996). When Parties Matter: A Review of the Possibilities and Limits of Partisan Influence on Public Policy. *European Journal of Political Research*, 30(2), 155–83.
Schmidt, M. G. (2002). Warum Mittelmaß? Deutschlands Bildungsausgaben im internationalen Vergleich. *Politische Vierteljahresschrift*, 43, 3–19.
Schmidt, M. G. (2003). *The Partisan Composition of Governments in OECD Democracies, Dataset.* Heidelberg: University of Heidelberg, Institute for Political Science.
Schmidt, M. G. (2007). Testing the Retrenchment Hypothesis: Educational Spending, 1960–2002. In F. G. Castles (ed.), *The Disappearing State? Retrenchment Realities in an Age of Globalisation* (pp. 159–83). Cheltenham and Northampton: Edward Elgar.
Schmidt, M. G. (2008). Germany: The Grand Coalition State. In J. M. Colomer (ed.), *Comparative European Politics*, (3rd edn) (pp. 58–93). New York, NY: Milton Park.
Schmitter, P. C. (1979). Still the Century of Corporatism? In P. C. Schmitter & G. Lehmbruch (eds), *Trends Toward Corporatist Intermediation* (pp. 7–52). Beverly Hills, CA and London: Sage.
Seawright, J. & Gerring, J. (2008). Case Selection Techniques in Case Study Research: A Menu of Qualitative and Quantitative Options. *Political Research Quarterly*, 61(2), 294–308.
Shavit, Y. & Müller, W. (2000). Vocational Secondary Education: Where Diversion and Where Safety Net? *European Societies*, 2(1), 29–50.

Skilbeck, M., Connell, H., Lowe, N., & Tait, K. (1994). *The Vocational Quest: New Directions in Education and Training*. London and New York, NY: Routledge.

Skocpol, T. (1979). *States and Social Revolutions*. Cambridge and New York, NY: Cambridge University Press.

Solga, H. (2012). Bildung und materielle Ungleichheiten: Der investive Sozialstaat auf dem Prüfstand. In R. Becker & H. Solga (eds), *Soziologische Bildungsforschung, Sonderheft 52 der Kölner Zeitschrift für Soziologie und Sozialpsychologie* (pp. 459–87). Wiesbaden: VS Verlag für Sozialwissenschaften.

Solt, F. (2009). Standardizing the World Income Inequality Database. *Social Science Quarterly*, 90(2), 231–42.

Soroka, S. N. & Wlezien, C. (2010). *Degrees of Democracy: Politics, Public Opinion, and Policy*. Cambridge and New York, NY: Cambridge University Press.

Soskice, D. (1994). Reconciling Markets and Institutions: The German Apprenticeship System. In L. M. Lynch (ed.), *Training and the Private Sector: International Comparisons* (pp. 25–60). Chicago, IL and London: University of Chicago Press.

Steedman, H. (2011). Apprenticeship Policy in England: Increasing Skills versus Boosting Young People's Job Prospects. CEP Policy Analysis CEPPA013.

Steinmo, S., Thelen, K., & Longstreth, F. (eds). (1992). *Structuring Politics: Historical Institutionalism in Comparative Analysis*. Cambridge: Cambridge University Press.

Stephens, J. D. (1979). *The Transition from Capitalism to Socialism*. London: Macmillan.

Stern, J. (2000). *Programme versus Pragmatik: Parteien und ihre Programme als Einfluß- und Gestaltungsgröße auf bildungspolitische Entscheidungsprozesse*. Frankfurt, Berlin, Bern, Bruxelles, New York, NY, Oxford, and Wien: Lang.

Stocké, V. (2007). Explaining Educational Decision and Effects of Families' Social Class Position: An Empirical Test of the Breen-Goldthorpe Model of Educational Attainment. *European Sociological Review*, 23(4), 505–19.

Stratmann, K. (1990a). Das Ende der Reformillusionen – die erstaunliche Reformresistenz des Dualen Systems bei hoher quantitativer Aufnahmefähigkeit in den 1970er Jahren. In K. Stratmann & M. Schlösser (eds), *Das Duale System der Berufsbildung: Eine historische Analyse seiner Reformdebatten, Gutachten für die Enquete-Kommission "Zukünftige Bildungspolitik – Bildung 2000" des Deutschen Bundestages* (pp. 175–243). Frankfurt: Verlag der Gesellschaft zur Förderung arbeitsorientierter Forschung und Bildung (GFAB).

Stratmann, K. (1990b). "Der Bildungsauftrag der Wirtschaft" als Ausdruck berufsständisch-restaurativer Abwehr von befürchteten Verschulungstendenzen – der berufsbildungstheoretisch begründete Rückzug der Berufspädagogik in den 1950er Jahren. In K. Stratmann & M. Schlösser (eds), *Das duale System der Berufsbildung. Eine historische Analyse seiner Reformdebatten; Gutachten für die Enquete-Kommission "Zukünftige Bildungspolitik – Bildung 2000" des Deutschen Bundestages unter Mitarbeit von Markus Joh. Lier* (pp. 53–108). Frankfurt: GAFB.

Stratmann, K. (1990c). Die Sicherung des Bestandes bei zunehmend schärferer Kritik des Bestehenden – die rechtliche Fundierung des Dualen Systems am Ende der 1960er Jahre. In K. Stratmann & M. Schlösser (eds), *Das duale System der Berufsbildung. Eine historische Analyse seiner Reformdebatten; Gutachten für die Enquete-Kommission "Zukünftige Bildungspolitik – Bildung 2000" des Deutschen Bundestages unter Mitarbeit von Markus Joh. Lier* (pp. 109–74). Frankfurt: GAFB.

Stevens, M. L., Armstrong, E. A., & Arum, R. (2008). Sieve, Incubator, Temple, Hub: Empirical and Theoretical Advances in the Sociology of Higher Education. *Annual Review of Sociology*, 34: 127–51.

Streeck, W. (1989). Skills and the Limits of Neo-Liberalism: The Enterprise of the Future as a Place of Learning. *Work, Employment & Society*, 3(1), 89–104.

Streeck, W. (1992). *Social Institutions and Economic Performance: Studies of Industrial Relations in Advanced Capitalist Economies*. London, Newbury Park, CA, and New Delhi: Sage.

Streeck, W. (1994). Training and the New Industrial Relations: a Strategic Role for Unions? In M. Regini (ed.), *The Future of Labour Movements* (pp. 250–69). London, Newbury Park, CA, and New Delhi: Sage.

Streeck, W. (1996). Lean Production in the German Automobile Industry: A Test Case for Convergence Theory. In R. Dore & S. Berger (eds), *National Diversity and Global Capitalism* (pp. 138–70). Ithaca, NY and London: Cornell University Press.

Streeck, W. (2008). Flexible Markets, Stable Societies? MPIfG Working Paper 08/6.

Streeck, W. (2009). *Re-Forming Capitalism: Institutional Change in the German Political Economy*. Oxford and New York, NY: Oxford University Press.

Streeck, W. (2010). E Pluribus Unum? Varieties and Commonalities of Capitalsim. MPIfG Discussion Paper 10/12.

Streeck, W. (2012). Skills and Politics: General and Specific. In M. R. Busemeyer & C. Trampusch (eds), *The Political Economy of Collective Skill*

Formation (pp. 317–52). Oxford and New York, NY: Oxford University Press.

Streeck, W. & Schmitter, P. C. (1985). Community, Market, State – And Associations? The Prospective Contribution of Interest Governance to Social Order. In W. Streeck & P. C. Schmitter (eds), *Private Interest Government: Beyond Market and State* (pp. 1–29). London, Beverly Hills, CA, and New Delhi: Sage.

Streeck, W. & Thelen, K. (2005). Introduction: Institutional Change in Advanced Political Economies. In W. Streeck & K. Thelen (eds), *Beyond Continuity: Institutional Change in Advanced Political Economies* (pp. 1–39). Oxford and New York, NY: Oxford University Press.

Streeck, W., Hilbert, J., Van Kevelaer, K.-H., Maier, F., & Weber, H. (1987). *Steuerung und Regulierung der beruflichen Bildung: Die Rolle der Sozialpartner in der Ausbildung und beruflichen Weiterbildung in der Bundesrepublik Deutschland*. Berlin: edition sigma.

Svallfors, S. (1997). Worlds of Welfare and Attitudes to Redistribution: A Comparison of Eight Western Nations. *European Sociological Review*, 13(3), 283–304.

Svallfors, S. (2004). Class, Attitudes and the Welfare State: Sweden in Comparative Perspective. *Social Policy & Administration*, 38(2), 119–38.

Svallfors, S. (2010). Policy Feedback, Generational Replacement, and Attitudes to State Intervention: Eastern and Western Germany, 1990–2006. *European Political Science Review*, 2(1), 119–35.

Swenson, P. A. (2002). *Capitalists against Markets: The Making of Labor Markets and Welfare States in the United States and Sweden*. Oxford and New York, NY: Oxford University Press.

Taylor-Gooby, P. (2008). The New Welfare State Settlement in Europe. *European Societies*, 10(1), 3–24.

Taylor-Gooby, P. & Stoker, G. (2011). The Coalition Programme: A New Vision for Britain or Politics as Usual? *The Political Quarterly*, 82(1), 4–15.

Thelen, K. (1999). Historical Institutionalism in Comparative Politics. *Annual Review of Political Science*, 2, 369–404.

Thelen, K. (2003). How Institutions Evolve. In J. Mahoney & D. Rueschemeyer (eds), *Comparative Historical Analysis in the Social Sciences* (pp. 208–40). Cambridge: Cambridge University Press.

Thelen, K. (2004). *How Institutions Evolve: The Political Economy of Skills in Germany, Britain, the United States and Japan*. Cambridge, New York, NY, and Melbourne: Cambridge University Press.

Thelen, K. (2012). Varieties of Capitalism: Trajectories of Liberalization and the New Politics of Social Solidarity. *Annual Review of Political Science*, 15, 137–59.

Thelen, K. & Busemeyer, M. R. (2008). From Collectivism towards Segmentalism: Institutional Change in German Vocational Training. MPIfG Discussion Paper 08/13.

Thelen, K. & Busemeyer, M. R. (2012). Institutional Change in German Vocational Training: From Collectivism toward Segmentalism. In M. R. Busemeyer & C. Trampusch (eds), *The Comparative Political Economy of Collective Skill Formation Systems* (pp. 68–100). Oxford and New York, NY: Oxford University Press.

Thränhardt, D. (1990). Bildungspolitik. In K. Von Beyme & M. G. Schmidt (eds), *Politik in der Bundesrepublik Deutschland* (pp. 177–202). Opladen: Westdeutscher Verlag.

Toner, P. (2008). Survival and Decline of the Apprenticeship System in the Australian and UK Construction Industries. *British Journal of Industrial Relations*, 46(3), 413–38.

Trampusch, C. (2009). *Der erschöpfte Sozialstaat: Transformation eines Politikfeldes*. Frankfurt: Campus.

Trampusch, C. (2010). Employers, the State and the Politics of Institutional Change: Vocational Education and Training in Austria, Germany and Switzerland. *European Journal of Political Research*, 49, 545–73.

Unwin, L. (1996). Employer-Led Realities: Apprenticeship Past and Present. *Journal of Vocational Education and Training*, 48(1), 57–68.

Vail, M. I. (2007). The Evolution of Bargaining under Austerity: Political Change in Contemporary French and German Labor-Market Reform. MPIfG Discussion Paper 07/10.

Vandenbroucke, F. & Vleminckx, K. (2011). Disappointing Poverty Trends: Is the Social Investment State to Blame? *Journal of European Social Policy*, 21(5), 450–71.

Van Kersbergen, K. (1994). The Distinctiveness of Christian Democracy. In D. Hanley (ed.), *Christian Democracy in Europe: A Comparative Perspective* (pp. 31–47). London and New York, NY: Pinter Publishers.

Van Kersbergen, K. (1995). *Social Capitalism: A Study of Christian Democracy and the Welfare State*. London and New York, NY: Routledge.

Van Kersbergen, K. (1999). Contemporary Christian Democracy and the Demise oft he Politics of Mediation. In H. Kitschelt, P. Lange, G. Marks, & J. D. Stephens (eds), *Continuity and Change in Contemporary Capitalism* (pp. 346–70). Cambridge and New York, NY: Cambridge University Press.

Van Oorschot, W. (2006). Making the Difference in Europe: Deservingness Perceptions among Citizens of European Welfare States. *Journal of European Social Policy*, 16(1), 23–42.

Van Oorschot, W., Opielka, M., & Pfau-Effinger, B. (eds). (2008). *Culture and Welfare State: Values and Social Policy in Comparative Perspective*. Cheltenham: Edward Elgar.

Visser, J. (2011). ICTWSS: Database on Institutional Characteristics of Trade Unions, Wage Setting, State Intervention and Social Pacts in 34 Countries between 1960 and 2007, www.uva-aias.net/208 (last accessed April 30, 2014).

Voegtle, E. M., Knill, C., & Dobbins, M. (2011). To What Extent Does Transnational Communication Drive Cross-National Policy Convergence? The Impact of the Bologna-Process on Domestic Higher Education Policies. *Higher Education*, 61, 77–94.

Von Below, S. (2002). *Bildungssysteme und soziale Ungleichheit: Das Beispiel der neuen Bundesländer*. Opladen: Leske + Budrich.

Walkenhorst, H. (2008). Explaining Change in EU Education Policy. *Journal of European Public Policy*, 15(4), 567–87.

Wallerstein, M. (1999). Wage-Setting Institutions and Pay Inequality in Advanced Industrial Societies. *American Journal of Political Science*, 43(3), 649–80.

Weaver, R. K. (2010). Paths and Forks or Chutes and Ladders?: Negative Feedbacks and Policy Regime Change. *Journal of Public Policy*, 30(2), 137–62.

Wiborg, S. (2010). Why Is There No Comprehensive Education in Germany? A Historical Explanation. *History of Education*, 39(4), 539–56.

Wilensky, H. L. (1975). *The Welfare State and Equality: Structural and Ideological Roots of Public Expenditures*. Berkeley, CA, Los Angeles, CA, and London: University of California Press.

Wilensky, H. L. (1981). Leftism, Catholicism, and Democratic Corporatism: The Role of Political Parties in Recent Welfare State Development. In P. Flora & A. J. Heidenheimer (eds), *The Development of Welfare States in Europe and America* (pp. 345–82). New Brunswick, NJ and London: Transaction Books.

Wilensky, H. L. (2002). *Rich Democracies: Political Economy, Public Policy, and Performance*. Berkeley, CA and Los Angeles, CA: University of California Press.

Willemse, N. & de Beer, P. (2012). Three Worlds of Educational Welfare States? A Comparative Study of Higher Education Systems across Welfare States. *Journal of European Social Policy*, 22(2), 105–17.

Williams, G. (2004). The Higher Education Market in the United Kingdom. In P. Teixeira, B. Jongbloed, D. Dill, & A. Amaral (eds), *Markets*

in Higher Education: Rhetoric or Reality? (pp. 241–69). Dordrecht, Boston, MA, and London: Kluwer Academic Publishers.
Wilms, D. (1983). CDU-Berufsbildungspolitik – Erbe und Perspektiven. In A. Lipsmeier (ed.), *Berufsbildungspolitik in den 70er Jahren: Eine kritische Bestandsaufnahme für die 80er Jahre* (pp. 59–68). Wiesbaden: Franz Steiner Verlag.
Wilms, D. (1986). Bildungspolitik im Umbruch. In H.-J. Demuth (ed.), *Berufsbildung 2000, DIHT-Jubiläum in Ludwigshafen, 30. September 1986* (pp. 9–24). Bonn: Deutscher Industrie- und Handelstag.
Wlezien, C. (1995). The Public as Thermostat: Dynamics of Preferences for Spending. *American Journal of Political Science*, 39(4), 981–1000.
Wlezien, C. & Soroka, S. N. (2012). Political Institutions and the Opinion-Policy Link. *West European Politics*, 35(6), 1407–32.
Wolbers, M. H. J. (2007). Patterns of Labour Market Entry: A Comparative Perspective on School-to-Work Transitions in 11 European Countries. *Acta Sociologica*, 50(3), 189–210.
Wolf, A. (1998). Politicians and Economic Panic. *History of Education*, 27(3), 219–34.
Wolf, F. (2006). *Die Bildungsausgaben der Bundesländer im Vergleich: Welche Faktoren erklären ihre beträchtliche Variation?* Münster: LIT Verlag.
Wolf, F. (2009). The Division of Labour in Education Funding: A Cross-National Comparison of Public and Private Education Expenditure in 28 OECD Countries. *Acta Politica*, 44, 50–73.
Wolf, F. & Zohlnhöfer, R. (2009). Investing in Human Capital? The Determinants of Private Education Expenditure in 26 OECD Countries. *Journal of European Social Policy*, 19(3), 230–44.
Wren, A. (2013). Introduction: The Political Economy of Post-Industrial Societies. In A. Wren (ed.), *The Political Economy of the Service Transition* (pp. 1–70). Oxford and New York, NY: Oxford University Press.

Index

Abitur, 93
academies, 76
Academies Act (2010), 76
actor-centered institutionalism, 39
actors, 38–9
Agrarian Party, 79, 80
Anglo-Saxon countries, educational and socioeconomic inequality in, 184
apprenticeship training, 62. *See also* vocational education and training (VET)
   Christian democratic government and, 169
   coalition government's policy on, 76–7
   decline in 1970–85, 67–8
   economic coordination and, 169
   in Germany, 102, 105–6
   John Major government's policy on, 74
   partisan politics and, 169
   rightist government and, 169
   socioeconomic inequality and, 197–9
   staged apprenticeship, 105
   in Sweden, 86–7
   Swedish Conservative party's support for, 87
   upper-secondary students in, 168–9
Apprenticeships, Skills, Children and Learning Act, 75
Arbeitsausschuß für Berufsbildung, 94
Arbeitsstelle für Betriebliche Berufsausbildung (ABB), 97
Area Manpower Boards (AMBs), 72
asset theory of social policy preferences, 34
Assisted Places Scheme, 73
Atlee, Clement, 60–1

attitudes, 2
   education policy and, 17–18
   educational choices and, 221–2
   educational institutions and, 22–4
   feedback effects and, 216
   impact of educational institutions on, 215–52
   institutional factors and, 218
   self-interest and, 218–19
Ausbildungsberufe, 98
Australia, 33
   Gini index, 199
   skills formation in, 129
   vocational education and training in, 128
Austria, 33

balance of power
   cross-country differences in, 6–7
   long-term, 51–3
   partisan, 58–9
   partisan theory and, 51–3
battle of the sexes game, 12
Beck–Katz standard, 156
Belgium, 33
   educational and socioeconomic inequality in, 184
   political/institutional determinants of educational institutions in, 153
   skills formation in, 131–2
Berufsbildungsförderungsgesetz (BerBiFG), 103
Berufsbildungsgesetz (BBiG), 102, 120
Berufsgrundbildungsjahr (Vocational Foundation Year), 104
Berufsprinzip, 73
Bildungsgesamtplan, 101
Bildungsrat, 101, 102
bivariate analyses, 136–55

Index

Black Papers, 65, 85
Blair, Tony, 177, 259
Bologna Process, 108
Boyle, Edward, 65
British Employers' Confederation, 62
Bundesausbildungsförderungsgesetz (BAFöG), 100
Bundesinstitut für Berufsbildung (BIBB), 103
Bundesrat, 91
Bundestag, 98
Bundesverband der Deutschen Industrie (BDI), 97
Bund-Länder Kommission (BLK), 100–1
Butler Education Act (1944), 60

cabinet share, public spending and, 141–3
Callaghan, James, 65
Canada, 33
  Gini index, 199
  VET and inequality in, 192
capitalism, varieties of, 38
Carr Committee, 63
centralized wage bargaining, 209–11
child-centered social investment, 259–60
China, 257
Christlich Demokratische Union Deutschlands (CDU), 91
  corporatist policy approach of, 116
  education policy, 96
  employers' associations and, 98
  as formateur of cross-class coalition, 120
Christian democrats, 10
  apprenticeship training and, 169
  versus conservatives, 54–5
  cooperation between unions and employers, 46–7
  cross-class compromise and, 54–5
  as Germany's dominant political force in 1949–69, 14–15
  ideology, 46
  influence of business interests, 46
  politics of mediation, 46, 116–17
  private spending and, 137–8
  spending on VET, 143, 150–1
  subsidiarity, 46

tertiary enrollment and, 165
upper-secondary students in VET and, 151–2
welfare state and, 45–7
cluster analysis, 132–3
coalition government
  apprenticeship training and, 76–7
  education policy, 113–14
coalition of actors, 38–9
coalitional approach, 40, 41
collective skill-formation regime, 14
  descriptive statistics, 130–1
  promotion of education in, 134–5
  socioeconomic inequality in, 189
collective wage bargaining, vocational education and training and, 168
commodification
  in higher education, 32
  of labor, 29–33
  in VET, 32
Comparative Political Data Set, 201
comparative public policy analysis, 17
Confederation of British Industry (CBI), 67
conservatives
  apprenticeship training and, 116
  versus Christian democratic ideology, 54–5
  cross-class consensus, 117
  decentralized education system and, 60–1
  higher education and, 69–70
  political process preferences, 47
  private education spending and, 159
  vocation education and, 70
continental Europe
  collective skill systems in, 134–5
  educational and socioeconomic inequality in, 184
  social spending in, 136
  statist skill-formation regime in, 33
coordinated market economies (CMEs)
  cross-class coalitions in, 54–5, 118, 119
  partisan politics in, 54–5
Crosland, Anthony, 64
cross-class coalitions
  Christian democrats and, 54–5
  in coordinated market economies, 54–5

cross-class coalitions (*cont.*)
  in design of vocational education and training, 54–5
  social democrats and, 55
Crowther Report, 61

de-commodification, 29–33, 262–3
  educational stratification and, 31–2
  social investment and, 262–3
  welfare state and, 263
deindustrialization, 164–5
Denmark
  apprenticeships in, 77
  Gini index, 199
  political/institutional determinants of educational institutions in, 152–3
  skills formation in, 131
  vocational education and training in, 128, 131
Deutsche Bildungsrat (German Education Council), 100
Deutscher Ausschuß für Technisches Schulwesen (DATSCH), 94, 100
Deutscher Gewerkschaftsbund, 98
devolution, 59

economic coordination
  apprenticeship training and, 169
  private education spending and, 159
  vocational education and training and, 168
education
  difference from other social policies, 253
  in social investment state, 259–64
Education Act (1988), 113
Education Act (2011), 77
education and training reforms, 58–122
  case studies, 58–122
  Germany, 90–109
    consolidation and incremental adaption of education system after 1982, 104–9
    expansion and reform in 1965–82, 99–104
    reconstruction and restoration in 1945–65, 92–9
  partisan politics and, 114–20
  postwar development of upper/post-secondary education, 109–14
  Sweden, 78–90
    comprehensive education system (1945–75), 79–84
    consolidation and conflict (1975–90), 84–7
  United Kingdom, 58–78
    consolidation of liberal skill regime (after 1997), 74–8
    neoliberal transformation of education and training policy (1979–97), 68–74
    partisan conflict and crisis in 1964–79, 64–8
    postwar consensus/institutional consolidation in 1945–64, 60–4
education policy
  application of partisan theory in, 40–1
  attitudes and, 17–18
  de-commodification in, 158
  institutions and, 231–48
  in OECD countries, 220–3
  versus other social policies, 224–31, 253
  preferences for different kids of education, 222–3
  voters' preference and, 40–1
Education Reform Act (1988), 68–9
education systems, 3–5
  de-commodification in, 29–33
  in Germany, 3
  partisan politics and, 6–7, 41
  stratification in, 29–33
  in Sweden, 4
  in United Kingdom, 3
educational background
  educational stratification and, 233
  public support for educational spending and, 228
  recommendation for education and, 242–5
  support for private education spending and, 241
  support for public education spending and, 228

Index

educational choices, 242
educational inequality
  in Anglo-Saxon countries, 184
  in Belgium, 184
  in continental Europe, 184
  in France, 183–4
  in Netherlands, 183–4
  in OECD countries, 181–3
  in Scandinavian countries, 183–4
  skills and, 185–90
  socioeconomic inequality and, 181–5
  in southern European countries, 184–5
  vocational education and training and, 195–7
educational institutions
  attitudes and, 22–4
  education policy preferences and, 231–48
  impact on attitudes and preferences, 22–4, 215–52
  impact on popular attitudes and preferences, 215–52
  investing in human capital and, 177
  political and institutional determinants of, 136–55
    cabinet share of party families, 137
    educational stratification, 143–5
    enrollment patterns, 145–6
    labor-market institutions, 154–5
    partisan legacies, 137–8
    private versus public share of education financing, 137
    social spending, 138–41
    socioeconomic institutions, 152
  redistributive preferences and, 248–51
  socioeconomic inequality and, 20–2, 177–214
educational investments. *See* educational spending
educational spending, 138–41
  age of population and, 164–5
  cabinet share and, 141–3
  conservatives and, 159
  de-commodification in education policy and, 158

division of labor between private sources and, 186
division of labor between public and private sources of, 30–1
division of labor between public sources and, 186
economic coordination and, 159
educational background and, 241
enrollment patterns and, 157, 207
GDP and, 164–5
individual income and, 241
individual-level support for, 224–5
public spending on education, 221
public support for, 229–31
  age and, 228
  educational background and, 228
  gender and, 228
  increased spending, 231
  labor market and, 228
  partisanship and, 228
  public as thermostat model, 239
recommendation for academic education and, 245
redistributive implications of, 224, 231–2
redistributive preferences and, 250
right-wing parties and, 150
social democrats and, 159
socioeconomic inequality and, 177–8, 199
supply of high-skilled workers and, 256–7
support for increased public spending and, 233, 241
VET enrollment and, 207–9
educational stratification
  employer involvement and, 188
  enrollment patterns and, 143–5
  individual income/educational background and, 233
  redistributive preferences and, 251
  socioeconomic inequality and, 187
  support for educational spending and, 232, 239–41
  welfare state and, 31
employers
  educational stratification and, 50
  involvement of, 187–8
  VET design and, 50

Employment and Training Act (1973), 67
enrollment patterns
 cross-country differences in, 145–6
 partisan legacies and, 146–50
 private education spending and, 207
 spending and, 157
 vocational education and training, 203–4
Entschließungsantrag, 98
EPL index, 211
Erhard, Ludwig, 99
Eurobarometer, 222, 242
European Union, education policy, 263
Expert School of Committee, 80

Fachhochschulen, 100
Federal Constitutional Court (Germany), 103
federalist countries, 134–5
feedback effects, 18–19
 attitudes and, 216
 weakness of, 217–18
Finland, public spending on education, 221
Foundation Apprenticeships, 75
foundation schools, 76
Framework for the Reform and Unification of the General School System, 97
France, 33
 educational and socioeconomic inequality in, 183–4
 skills formation in, 131–2
free schools, 89
Further and Higher Education Act, 69
future research, 264–5

Gemeinschaftsaufgaben, 99
gender, public education spending and, 228
General National Vocational Qualifications (GNVQs), 73
German Association of the Industry and Commerce Chambers, 98
German Committee for the Education System, 97
Germany, 33, 90–109
 apprenticeship training in, 77, 102, 105–6
 Christian democrats, 14–15
 collective skill-formation regime in, 14
 consolidation and incremental adaption of education system after 1982, 104–9
 critical juncture in, 112
 cross-class consensus in, 117–18, 120
 education policy preferences in, 223
 education system in, 3, 4
 education system in postwar period, 94–5
 educational system in the 19th and early 20th centuries, 93
 expansion and reform in 1965–82, 99–104
 Gini index, 199
 PISA debate, 107
 postwar development of upper/post-secondary education, 112
 reconstruction and restoration in 1945–65, 92–9
 trade unions, 98
 unions and apprenticeship training in, 216
 vocational education and training in, 97–9, 101–3, 104–5, 108–9, 112, 114
 Weimar period, 93–4
Gini index, 199, 201
globalization, 257–8, 259
Gove, Michael, 77
Greece, 33
Green Paper, 67
green party, 91
gross domestic product (GDP), 135
 education spending and, 199
 educational spending and, 164–5, 205
 public education spending and, 164–5
grundskola, 81
Gymnasien, 93, 94, 106, 108
Gymnasieskola, 81
Gymnasium, 81, 94, 101

Habilitation, 108
Handwerkerschutzgesetz, 93
Handwerksordnung (Crafts Ordinance), 97
Hauptschule, 106, 107
higher education
  commodification in, 32
  Conservative government's policy on, 69–70
  enrollment patterns, 145–6
  Labour government's policy on, 76
  political parties and, 44
  right-wing parties and, 150
  social investment state and, 261
  socioeconomic inequality and, 193–5
  state involvement in, 188
Higher Education Act (1993), 90
high-skilled workers
  private education spending and, 256–7
  supply and demand for, 255
historical institutionalism
  criticism of, 37–8
  inconsistencies in, 38
  path dependency and, 37
Hochschulrahmengesetz, 100
Högskola, 84
human capital
  investing in, 177
  redistributive preferences and, 250
  social investment state and, 259–60
human capital theory, 30

income
  educational stratification and, 233
  support for private education spending and, 241
India, 257
Individual Learning Accounts (ILAs), 74
Industrial Training Act (1964), 64
  Conservative government and, 113
  Industrial Training Boards, 13, 63
  Labour government and, 67
Industrial Training Boards (ITBs), 13, 63–4
industrial training organizations (ITOs), 72
inequality, 177–214

  apprenticeship training and, 197–9
  in collective skill-formation regimes, 189
  cross-section time-series analyses, 199–213
  cross-sectional evidence for, 190–9
  degree of state involvement and, 187
  education spending and, 205
  educational inequality and, 181–5
  educational institutions and, 20–2, 177–214
  educational investment and, 177–8
  educational stratification and, 187
  higher education and, 193–5
  in liberal skill-formation regimes, 189–90
  limiting of, with VET investments, 178–9
  partisan politics and, 18
  political economies and, 179–80
  private education spending and, 199
  public education spending and, 199
  redistributive preferences and, 249
  skills and, 185–90, 255–6, 258
  social transfer spending and, 205–7
  support for redistribution and, 249–50
  VET enrollment and, 203–4
  vocational education and training's role in, 179, 190–3
institutional context, 48–50
institutional gardeners, 54
institutionalism, actor-centered, 39
Ireland, 33
  skills formation in, 129
  VET and inequality in, 192
ISSP Role of Government IV survey, 248
Italy, political/institutional determinants of educational institutions in, 153–4
Iversen, Torben, 34

Japan, 33
  public spending on education, 221
  skills formation in, 129–30

Keynesianism, 259, 263
Kohl, Helmut, 104

Kultusministerkonferenz (KMK), 96, 104

labor, commodification of, 29–33
labor market
  economic globalization and, 257–8
  public education spending and, 228
  VET and, 49, 154–5
labor unions
  apprenticeship training and, 62
  employer cooperation in VET design, 48–50
Labour government
  cross-class consensus, 117
  general schooling policioes, 75–6
  higher education and, 76
  industrial training boards and, 67
  vocational education at tertiary level, 66
Labour Party
  access to grammar school in 1950s and, 61
  education policy in 1974–79, 65–6
  skill regime and, 74–5
Länder, 91–2, 95, 99–101, 106–7
Landsorganisationen, 79, 90
Learning and Skills Council (LSC), 75
left-wing parties, 40
  educational expansion and, 43–4
  political process preferences, 47–8
  public education spending and, 157
  tertiary enrollment and, 165–6
liberal market economies (LMEs), 34, 118–19
  interest mediation in, 117
  partisan politics in, 53–4
liberal skill-formation regime, 12–13, 33, 129
  consolidation after 1997, 74–8
  promotion of education in, 134
  socioeconomic inequality in, 189–90
  in United Kingdom, 12–13
Local Education Authorities, 64–5, 68–9, 76
Local Enterprise Councils, 72
Local Learning and Skills Councils (LLSCs), 75

macro-corporatism, 55
Major, John, 73
Manpower Services Commission (MSC), 13, 67, 70–1
Marshall, T.H., 30
Mecklenburg-Vorpommern, 106
Mittelstandspolitik, 98
Modern Apprenticeships, 74
modernization theory, 36
multivariate regression analyses, 155–69

National Council for Vocational Qualifications (NCVQ), 73
national curriculum (Sweden), 89
National Health Service, 60
National Joint Apprenticeship Councils, 62
National School Board, 84
National Vocational Qualifications (NVQs), 72–3, 78–90, 192
neoinstitutionalism. *See* historical institutionalism
Netherlands, 33
  educational and socioeconomic inequality in, 183–4
  political/institutional determinants of educational institutions in, 153
  skills formation in, 131
  VET in, 131
New Deal for Young People program, 75
New Labour government, 74, 113–14
New Training Initiative (NTI), 70
new vocationalism, 73, 90
New Zealand, 33
Nordic model of education, 79, 112
Nordic welfare state, 79

OECD countries
  cross-country differences in financing/provision in, 264
  education policy, 263
  educational and socioeconomic inequality in, 181–3
  educational stratification in, 143–5
  public/private division of labor in education financing, 156
  skills formation in, 123–8

Index

variation of education policy preferences in, 220–3
vocational education and training in, 124–8
OECD Education Statistics Database, 124, 190
outcomes, 2
outsourcing, 257

Palme, Olof, 84
partisan actors, 39–40, 189
partisan politics, 8–17, 29–57
  analysis of, 157–8
  apprenticeship training and, 169
  balance of power and, 11
  blind spot of, 9–10
  in coordinated market economies, 54–5
  education and, 6–7
  education systems and, 41
  educational reforms and, 114–20
  enrollment patterns and, 146–50
  inequality and, 18
  in LMEs, 53–4
  public education spending and, 157, 228
  public spending and, 138–41
  social spending and, 138–41
  socioeconomic institutional context, 10–11
  standard model of, 9
  theoretical framework, 41–55
partisan theory, 40–1, 42
  education policy and, 40–1
  institutional context and, 48–50
  long-term balance of power and, 51–3
  modifications to, 42–3
  political process preferences and, 45–8
  standard model of, 43–5, 116–17
path consolidation, 51–2, 113
path dependency, 36
  historical institutionalism and, 37
  periods of stasis versus period of institiutional breakdown, 38
  public opinion and, 38
path formation, 51–2, 111
path initialization, 110–11
pensions, 228–9

petite bourgeoisie, 93
PISA debate, 107
policies
  popular attitudes and, 18–19
  self-interest and, 18–19
policy analysis, 17
policy-making, 17–18
political economies
  institutional spheres of, 34
  socioeconomic inequality and, 179–80
political parties, 40–1
  cabinet share of, 137
  educational expansion and, 43–4
  preferences regarding political process, 45–8
political process, 45–8
Political School Commission, 80
political science, 17
politics, 2
politics of mediation, 10, 46, 54
polytechnische Oberschule (POS), 106
Portugal, public spending on education, 221
positive feedback, 215, 245–8
post-secondary education, 143–5
  future research, 264–5
  partisan legacies and, 146–50
  postwar development of, 109
  public/private division of labor in financing, 265
  socioeconomic inequality and, 186
power resources, 38, 42
preferences, 2
  educational investments and, 221–2
  education/welfare institutions and, 231–48
  feedback effects, 216
  impact of educational institutions on, 22–4, 215–52
  material self-interests and, 218–19
  political process, 45–8
  redistributive, 248–51
private education spending. *See also* private education spending
  conservatives and, 159
  de-commodification in education policy and, 158
  division of labor between public sources and, 186

private education spending (*cont.*)
  economic coordination and, 159
  educational background and, 241
  enrollment patterns and, 207
  individual income and, 241
  recommendation for academic education and, 245
  redistributive preferences and, 250
  social democrats and, 159
  socioeconomic inequality and, 199
  supply of high-skilled workers and, 256–7
  support for increased public spending and, 233, 241
  VET enrollment and, 207–9
private schools, subsidies to, 88
Prussia, 93
public as thermostat model, 217, 239
public education spending, 138–41. *See also* private education spending
  age of population and, 164–5
  cabinet share and, 141–3
  division of labor between private sources and, 186
  enrollment patterns and, 157
  individual-level support for, 224–5
  public spending on education, 221
  public support for, 229–31, 239
    age and, 228
    educational background and, 228
    gender and, 228
    increased spending, 231
    labor market and, 228
    partisanship and, 228
  redistributive implications of, 224
  right-wing parties and, 150
  socioeconomic inequality and, 199
public opinion
  path dependency and, 38
  welfare state and, 217
public policy analysis, 17

Qualifications and Curriculum Authority (QCA), 73

Realschule, 93, 94, 106, 107
redistributive preferences
  educational stratification and, 251
  human capital and, 250
  private education spending and, 250
  socioeconomic inequality and, 249
Reichsgrundschulgesetz, 93
Richard Review of Apprenticeships, 77
rightist parties, 40
right-wing parties
  apprenticeship training and, 169
  educational expansion and, 43–4
  public spending on higher education and, 150
  tertiary enrollment and, 165

Saltsjöbaden Agreement of 1938, 11, 79, 119
Scandinavian countries, 33
  education spending in, 136
  education systems in, 134
  educational and socioeconomic inequality in, 183–4
  support for increased public spending in, 239
  welfare state benefits, 263–4
scatterplots, 136–55, 190
Schröeder, Gerhard, 259
segmentalist skill regime, 129–30
self-interest, 218–19, 250
service economy, 257
skill formation, 123–74
  bivariate analyses, 136–55
  cluster analysis, 132–3
  collective skill regime, 14, 130–1, 134–5, 189
  cross-national quantitative analysis, 123–74
  liberal regime, 11–13, 33, 74–8, 129, 130, 134, 189–90
  multivariate regression analyses, 155–69
  in OECD countries, 123–8
  political and institutional determinants of educational institutions and, 136–55
  scatterplots, 136–55
  segmentalist skill regime, 129–30
  statist skill regime, 11–12, 130
  unimodal distribution of, 185–6
  vocational education/training and, 257
skills
  educational inequality and, 185–90

inequality and, 185–90, 255–6
socioeconomic inequality and, 185–90, 258
specificity, 248–9
technological changes and, 255–8
welfare state and, 34–5
Social Democratic Party (SDP), 91, 100
comprehensive school model, 96–7
cross-class coalitions and, 120
social democrats
cross-class alliances, 55
cross-class consensus, 117
lower level of private spending and, 137–8
political process preferences, 47–8
private education spending and, 159
public spending and, 141–3
statist skill-formation regime, 11–12
social investment state
child-centered social investment, 260
de-commodification and, 262–3
education in, 259–64
human capital investments in, 259–60
policy paradigm, 262
political driving force in, 260
social policies
education policy, 224–31
asset theory of social policy preferences, 34
support for, 228–9
social rights, 30
social spending, 138–41
social transfer spending, 205–7
socioeconomic inequality, 177–214
in Anglo-Saxon countries, 184
apprenticeship training and, 197–9
in Belgium, 184
in collective skill-formation regime, 189
in continental Europe, 184
cross-section time-series analyses, 199–213
cross-sectional evidence for, 190–9
degree of state involvement and, 187
education spending and, 205

educational inequality and, 181–5
educational institutions and, 20–2, 177–214
educational investment and, 177–8
educational stratification and, 187
in France, 183–4
higher education and, 193–5
in liberal skill-formation regimes, 189–90
limiting of, with VET investments, 178–9
in the Netherlands, 183–4
in OECD countries, 181–3
political economies and, 179–80
private education spending and, 199
public education spending and, 199
redistributive preferences and, 249
in Scandinavian countries, 183–4
skills and, 185–90, 255–6, 258
social-transfer spending and, 205–7
in southern European countries, 184–5
support for redistribution and, 249–50
VET enrollment and, 203–4
VET's role in, 179, 190–3
socioeconomic institutions, 118, 152
Soskice, David, 34
southern European countries
Arendt, Hannah, 132
educational and socioeconomic inequality in, 184–5
statist skill-formation regimes in, 33
Spain, public spending on education, 221
staged apprenticeship, 105
state actors, 39–40
statist skill-formation regimes, 11–12
decommodification and stratification in, 33
descriptive statistics, 130
promotion of education in, 134
in Sweden, 11–12
stratification, 29–33
de-commodification and, 31–2
employer involvement and, 188
enrollment patterns and, 143–5
individual income/educational background and, 233
redistributive preferences and, 251

stratification (*cont.*)
  socioeconomic inequality and, 187
  support for educational spending and, 232, 239–41
  welfare state and, 31
Studentexamen, 79–84
subsidiarity, 46
Svenska Arbetsgivareföreningen (SAF), 79, 90, 119–20
Sweden, 78–90
  apprenticeship training in, 86–7
  comprehensive education system (1945–1975), 79–84
  consolidation and conflict (1975–1990), 84–7
  critical juncture in, 112
  cross-class consensus in, 117–18, 119–20
  decentralization and reform after 1991, 87–90
  decentralized education system in, 85–6
  education policy preferences in, 223
  education system in, 4
  free schools, 89
  general schooling policies, 85–6
  postwar development of upper/post-secondary education, 112, 114
  statist skill-formation regime in, 11–12
  subsidies to private schools in, 88
  VET in, 82–3, 86–7, 89–90
  welfare state in, 5, 78, 216, 263
Swedish Social Democrats (SAP), 79, 80, 84, 87
Switzerland, 33
  apprenticeships in, 77
  education policy preferences in, 222

Technical and Vocational Education Initiative (TVEI), 73
technological changes, skill-biased, 255–8
tertiary enrollment
  analysis of, 159–64
  Christian democrats and, 165
  left-wing parties and, 165–6
  nonstationarity and, 164
  right-wing parties and, 165
  VET enrollment and, 145–6
Thatcher, Margaret, 58–9, 65
Thelen, Kathleen, 38–9
time and timing, 51, 52
trade unions, 98
Training and Enterprise Councils (TECs), 72
trajectories of liberalization, 258
transition system, 109

unemployment, 197, 211–13
United Kingdom, 33
  consolidation of liberal skill regime (after 1997), 74–8
  critical juncture in, 108
  devolution in, 59
  education and training reforms in, 58–78
  education system in, 3, 4
  LME in, 118–19
  liberal skill-formation regime in, 12–13
  neoliberal economic policies in, 59
  neoliberal transformation of education and training policy (1979–97), 68–74
  partisan balance of power in, 58–9
  partisan conflict and crisis in 1964–79, 64–8
    comprehensive schools, 65
    decline of apprenticeship training, 67–8
    local education authorities, 64–5
  postwar consensus/institutional consolidation in 1945–64, 60–4
    apprenticeship training, 62
    expansion of secondary and higher education in, 61
    industrial training boards, 63–4
    VET, 61
  skills formation in, 129
  VET and inequality in, 192
  welfare state in, 4
United States, 33
  collective skill-formation regime in, 64
  post-secondary education in, 56
  VET and inequality in, 192

upper education
  educational stratification and, 143–5
  postwar development of, 109–14
    path consolidation, 113
    path formation, 111
    path initialization, 110–11
upper-secondary education
  apprenticeship training and, 168–9
  Christian democratic approach to, 151–2
  partisan legacies and, 146–50

varieties of capitalism (VoC), 8–9, 34–6
venture capital, 31–2
vocational education and training (VET). *See also* apprenticeship training
  Christian democratic approach to, 143, 150–2
  collective skill-formation regimes and, 131
  collective wage bargaining and, 168
  commodification in, 32
  Conservative government's policy on, 70
  conservative versus Christian democrats in, 54–5
  cross-class compromise in, 54–5
  economic coordination and, 168
  educational inequality and, 195–7
  employer involvement in, 187–8
  employer-designed, 50
  enrollment patterns, 145–6, 166–8
  enrollment versus socioeconomic inequality, 203–4
  in Germany, 97–9, 101–3, 104–5, 108–9, 112, 114
  labor market and, 154–5
  labor union–employer cooperation in design of, 48–50
  Labour government and, 66
  left-right difference in spending for, 143
  in OECD countries, 124–8
  partisan politics and, 6–7, 54
  positive feedback effects, 245–8
  private education spending and, 207–9
  right-wing parties and, 44
  role in social inequality, 179
  skill formation and, 257
  skills demand on labor market and, 49
  social investment state and, 261
  socioeconomic inequality and, 178–9, 190–3
  state involvement in, 187, 188
  statist skill-formation regime and, 12, 130
  support for educational spending and, 240
  survival of, 7, 253–4
  in Sweden, 82–3, 86–7, 89–90
  youth unemployment and, 197, 211
Volksschule, 93, 94

wage bargaining, 209–11
Weimar period, 93–4
welfare capitalism, 33, 129, 216–17
welfare state, 18–19, 33
  attitudes and, 216–17
  Christian democrats and, 45–7
  de-commodification and, 263
  education and, 4–5
  feedback effects, 215–16
  public opinion and, 217
  skills and, 34–5
  social investment paradigm and, 262–3
  social investment pillar, 261–2
  social protection pillar, 261–2
  southern European countries, 132
  stratification and, 31
Wilensky, Harold, 1
Wilms, Dorothee, 104–5
Winter of Discontent (1978–79), 118
Workers' Educational Association (ABF), 81

Youth Opportunities Programme (YOP), 68, 70
Youth Training (YT), 73
Youth Training Scheme (YTS), 70–2
youth unemployment, 197, 211–13

For EU product safety concerns, contact us at Calle de José Abascal, 56–1°,
28003 Madrid, Spain or eugpsr@cambridge.org.

www.ingramcontent.com/pod-product-compliance
Ingram Content Group UK Ltd.
Pitfield, Milton Keynes, MK11 3LW, UK
UKHW020354060825
461487UK00008B/646